Broken Mirrors/
Broken Minds
the dark dreams of
Dario Argento

Broken Mirrors/ Broken Minds

the dark dreams of Dario Argento

Maitland McDonagh

A CITADEL PRESS BOOK
Published by Carol Publishing Group

First Carol Publishing Group edition 1994

Copyright © 1991, 1994 by Maitland McDonagh

A Citadel Press Book
Published by Carol Publishing Group
Citadel Press is a registered trademark of Carol Communications Group
Editorial Offices: 600 Madison Avenue, New York, N.Y. 10022
Sales and Distribution Offices: 120 Enterprise Avenue, Secaucus, N.J. 07094
In Canada: Canadian Manda Group, P.O. Box 920, Station U, Toronto,
    Ontario M8Z 5P9
Queries regarding rights and permissions should be addressed to
Carol Publishing Group, 600 Madison Avenue, New York, N.Y. 10022

First published in England by sun taven fields, London, 1991

Carol Publishing books are available at special
discounts for bulk purchases, for sales promotions, fund-raising,
or educational purposes. Special editions can be created to
specifications. For details, contact Special Sales Department,
Carol Publishing Group, 120 Enterprise Avenue, Secaucus, N.J.
07094

Manufactured in the United States of America
10 9 8 7 6 5 4 3 2 1

Library of Congress Cataloging-in Publication Data

McDonagh, Maitland.
        Broken mirrors / broken minds : the dark dreams of Dario Argento /
    by Maitland McDonagh.
        p. cm.
        Originally presented as the author's thesis (M.F.A—Columbia
    University, 1986).
        Includes bibliographical references (p.   ), filmography (p.   )
    and index.
        ISBN 0-8065-1514-7
        1. Argento, Dario—Criticism and interpretation. 2. Horror films—
    Italy—History and criticism. I. Title.
    PN1998.3A74M37   1994
    791.43'0233'092—dc 20   93-45770
                                                                   CIP

ACKNOWLEDGEMENTS

This book is adapted from my master's thesis, submitted to Columbia University in 1986. Many people helped in its preparation and without their contributions it could never have been completed. First and foremost, I extend my thanks to Gary Hertz, who provided invaluable help and encouragement during every stage of the project. In addition, my thesis advisor, Professor John Belton, provided me with constructive criticism and suggestions that helped me refine and explicate my original notion to book length.

I also extend my sincerest thanks to everyone who has directly or indirectly helped me through either incarnation of this project. Among those who helped with the research, development and preparation of my original thesis or who contributed ideas, research or other material that has been incorporated into this revised version are: Tom Allen, Everett Burrell, Ernest Callenbach, Aldo de Cecco, Greg Day, Michael Halsband, Marvin Hoshino, Barbara Glazer, Robert Lang, Yves-Marie Lavendier, Rebecca Lieb, Tim Lucas, Bill Lustig, John Martin, Bill Murray, Alain Schlockoff, Greg Snead, Tony Timpone, John Vulich and Michael Weldon. *Broken Mirrors/Broken Minds: The Dark Dreams of Dario Argento* could never have been written without their assistance, and I'm truly grateful. In the editing phase, Tom Phillips, Anthony Blampied and John Gingrich provided invaluable assistance, and I appreciate their care and generosity.

Finally, a special word of thanks to Alan Jones, whose enthusiasm for Dario Argento's films is at least equal to my own. His knowledge of Argento's work is both daunting and inspiring, and he helped me see many things I would otherwise have missed.

Stills by courtesy of A.D.C. srl Films, Avatar, Castle Premiere, Columbia, DACFilm, Gala, Glenbuck, Medusa, New Line, Palace, Paramount, Rank, Seda Spettacoli, Target International, Thorn EMI, Twentieth Century-Fox, Universal.

3

CONTENTS

AN INTRODUCTION TO
THE DARK DREAMS OF DARIO ARGENTO

A man named Flitcraft had left his real-estate office, in Tacoma, to go to luncheon one day and had never returned... here's what happened to him. Going to lunch he passed an office building that was being put up - just the skeleton. A beam or something fell eight or ten stories down and smacked the sidewalk alongside him. It brushed pretty close to him, but didn't touch him, though a piece of the sidewalk was chipped off and flew up and hit his cheek. It only took a piece of skin off, but he still had the scar when I saw him. He rubbed it with his finger - well, affectionately - when he told me about it. He was scared stiff of course, he said, but he was more shocked than really frightened. He felt like somebody had taken the lid off life and let him look at the works.Flitcraft had been a good citizen and a good husband and father, not by any outer compulsion, but simply because he was a man who was most comfortable in step with his surroundings... The life he knew was a clean, orderly, sane, responsible affair. Now a falling beam had shown him that life was fundamentally none of these things. He, the good citizen-husband-father, could be wiped out between office and restaurant by the accident of a falling beam. He knew then that men died at haphazard like that, and lived only while blind chance spared them. It was not, primarily, the injustice of it that disturbed him: he accepted that after the first shock. What disturbed him was the discovery that in sensibly ordering his affairs he had got out of step, and not into step, with life.
  - Dashiell Hammett, *The Maltese Falcon*

You understand Flitcraft's feeling of dislocation when you watch Dario Argento's *Deep Red* or *Tenebrae*; it's as though somebody has indeed taken off the lid and exposed the works. Horror movie fans are well aware of Argento's work, though more mainstream movie-goers aren't. Since 1970 he's written (or co-written) and directed 11 films that constitute a dense, extended meditation on certain conventions of the horror film and, by extension, the nature of the cinematic text. And those

7

films are supremely weird: mannered, violent and quirky enough to catch the attention of hardened horror movie-goers at the same time they pique the curiosity of the critical viewer.

Argento's colour schemes are aggressively unnatural: like stained glass - saturated yellow and deep cobalt blue - or artificially limpid, glittering pale turquoise and green. And always red, rich and clear. His camera is nervous, restless... it swoops and glides, slinking along corridors, crouching at the bottom of staircases, perching on rooftops. It cranes up for dizzying high-angle panoramas, hunkers down to admire the tippy-tops of buildings against the blue, blue sky. Unrestrained by strictly narrative concerns, the camera reflects no point-of-view save its own as it creeps across the façade of a sharply angled building for a startling two-and-a-half minutes or hovers over two girls in a baroque swimming pool, their pale legs floating like seaweed beneath the water's rippling surface.

Argento's imagery is bizarre, almost surreal; he thrives on aggressively inappropriate juxtapositions. A lightbulb glows until its glass skin is shattered by a straight razor; a puff of smoke and then the darkness. A man's drawn face is reflected in a pool of blood; a black gloved hand manipulates a curious collection of fetishized objects - children's toys, knives, bits of braided yarn - in disorienting close-up; a young woman reaches into the shallow puddle where her keys have fallen only to see her arm vanish into water up to the elbow. A woman's shiny red high heel in a boy's screaming mouth, the blue sky above, the white sand below.

The world of Dario Argento is one of twisted logic, rhapsodic violence, stylized excess; it's true 20th Century Gothic with all the inversion, formal imbalance and riotous grotesquerie the term can encompass. His is a romantic vision, informed by an instinctive appreciation of the contradictory nature of erotic appeal: Argento's camera is alternately enthralled and repelled by ripe flesh and blood-drenched fantasy. Some viewers find it all too off-putting, and indifference is rare - it seems you either pull back from Argento's films or dive in head first.

First and foremost, of course, this is an *auteur* study: it examines the dark dreams of *Dario Argento*, and proceeds from

8

the notion that Argento is the author of his films. Critic André Bazin warned against the "aesthetic cult of personality," pointing out quite rightly that there's nothing interesting or enlightening about simply demonstrating repeated elements in a filmmaker's work. I intend to do better than that, isolating the elements that distinguish Argento's work and then examining the reason they're interesting.

It's been fashionable for years to deride the *politique des auteurs*, to dismiss it as unsophisticated and so hopelessly compromised that it doesn't mean anything at all. There's some truth in just about every criticism of the *politique*, and its second and third generation advocates have sometimes found themselves struggling to construct complex defences that try too hard for their own good. Nevertheless, it's a useful and practical starting point from which to examine a body of work, particularly one so distinctive as Argento's. Yes, film is a collaborative medium, and it's ignorant to try to speak of a director's vision as though it existed in some vacuum. Argento, like many filmmakers, works repeatedly with the same cinematographers, assistant directors, co-writers, designers, producers and actors; the choice of collaborators is in and of itself an aesthetic one, particularly when the same individuals return again and again. It stands to reason that their sensibilities have inflected Argento's, and it's possible that an enterprising viewer could identify traits distinguishing films on which the second unit director was Lamberto Bava from those on which Michele Soavi took over the task.

Argento's first producer was his late father, Salvatore (he died during the shooting of *Opera*), who produced *The Bird With the Crystal Plumage*, *The Cat O'Nine Tails*, *Four Flies on Grey Velvet* and *Le cinque giornate*. Despite an often volatile sibling relationship, Argento's younger brother Claudio took over the task with *Deep Red* and continued through *Tenebrae*, returning after several years for *Two Evil Eyes*. Claudio both produced and co-wrote Alejandro Jodorowsky's (*El Topo*) grotesque *Santa Sangre* that same year, and you couldn't help but notice that the soundtrack (by Simon Boswell, formerly a member of Goblin - more on them below) and murderously

Dario Argento on the set of *Creepers*.

inventive *mise en scène* recalled Dario Argento's work as much as - if not more than - Jodorowsky's earlier films. In addition to his own pictures, Argento has produced for George Romero (*Dawn of the Dead*), and for his protégés Lamberto Bava (son of director Mario Bava, whose stylistic influence on Argento was tremendous), Luigi Cozzi and Michele Soavi. *Demons* (Bava) and *Bloody Bird*, *The Church* and *The Sect* (Soavi) mimic Argento's hyper-stylized aesthetics, while Cozzi's *The Black Cat* alludes to the "Three Mothers" trilogy of which *Suspiria* and *Inferno* form two thirds, dipping into the same obscure source material and shot through with intertextual allusions. All three have served as Argento's assistant directors and comprise part of his personal entourage as well. The same is true of the musicians who make up Goblin, who scored *Deep Red* and *Suspiria*; former Goblins Claudio Simonetti and Simon Boswell went on to work on *Tenebrae*, *Creepers*, *Opera* and *Two Evil Eyes*, sometimes with Argento's collaboration. Argento is surrounded by an extended filmmaking family[1] whose aesthetics constitute significant parts of the larger system of influences, reflecting and inflecting his own.

The importance of generic conventions and the production practices of the Italian film industry can't be discounted either; all these factors contribute significantly to making Argento's films the films they are. So then, what are they?

In Argento's three supernatural horror films and seven *gialli*[2] the intricate story lines, improbably constructed and

[1]And literal family as well. In addition to working with his father and brother, Argento collaborated with longtime companion Daria Nicolodi (often referred to as his wife, though they were in fact never married) on the screenplay of *Suspiria*, and she has had major roles in *Deep Red*, *Tenebrae*, *Creepers* and *Opera*. Nicolodi also acted in Mario Bava's *Shock* and co-wrote Luigi Cozzi's *Paganini Horror*. Argento's daughter Fiore appears in *Creepers*, as well as Lamberto Bava's *Demons*; her sister Asia is featured in Bava's *Demons 2* and Soavi's *The Church*.
[2]As discussed later in the text, the eleventh film, *Le cinque giornate* is an exception in Argento's career and doesn't fit into the overall pattern of his work.

Argento with protégé Lamberto Bava on the set of *Demons*.

Argento protégé Luigi Cozzi on the set.

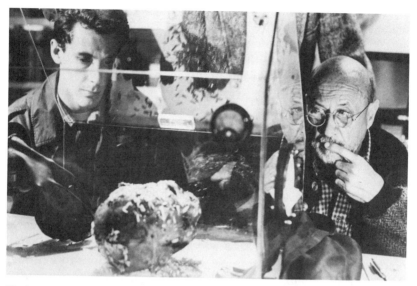

The insects are our friends: Dr. MacGregor (Donald Pleasence) explains some fine points of forensic science to actor-turned-Argento protégé Michele Soavi in *Creepers*.

Argento with Stefania Casini on the set of *Suspiria*.

deceptive in intent, are only the beginning. Argento's films systematically sublimate their narratives to *mise en scènes* whose escalating complexity is characterized (though only partially defined) by a series of baroque stylistic devices. They include bizarre camera angles, convoluted pans and tracks whose narrative motivation is woefully inadequate to their extravagance, unbalanced framing, grotesque close-ups, jarring shot transitions and obtrusively off-kilter composition within the frame, all of which conspire to delineate a world gone mad.

The term *giallo*, unfamiliar to most non-Italians, needs some explanation. Literally "yellow" in Italian, its derivation is literary, alluding to the yellow covers associated there with mystery novels, in the same way the black covers of the *Série Noire* and *Fleuve Noir* connote hardboiled thrillers in France. Applied to film, *giallo*, like *noir*, designates more than a genre: all mysteries are no more *gialli* than all detective thrillers are *films noirs*.

In his essay *The Typology of Detective Fiction*, literary theorist Tzvetan Todorov divides the genre into two distinct types, defined by the relationship of the two stories he claims are present in every mystery: the story of the crime and the story of the investigation. In the first type of detective fiction, the 'whodunit,' the story of the crime, is over before the story of the investigation begins: a body is found in the summerhouse. The second story, which uncovers the first - who was this man, who killed him, how, when and why? - takes up the "hundred and fifty pages which separate the discovery of the crime from the revelation of the killer," and constitutes the narrative proper. A detective, amateur or professional, asks questions, finds clues, makes deductions and brings it all together in a stunning *dénouement*. Everything from the drawing-room puzzles of Agatha Christie to the courtroom dramas of *Perry Mason* play by these rules. The second type Todorov calls the *série noire*, which "fuses the two stories or, in other words, suppresses the first and vitalizes the second. We are no longer told about a crime anterior to the moment of the narrative; the narrative coincides with the action... Prospection takes the place of

14

retrospection." This is the model for the two-fisted thriller made famous by Raymond Chandler and Dashiell Hammett. A crime committed before the story starts may get the narrative ball rolling, but once it's underway the investigation and new acts of mayhem unfold together, inextricably intertwined.

Again like the *film noir*, the *giallo*'s distinctive visual vocabulary is the principal way in which it is defined and recognized. The *giallo* film also has its recurring characters: haunted protagonists touched by madness and irrational violence, psychopaths whose depredations are as bizarre as they are brutal and petty criminals, perverts and eccentrics who emerge from around every corner and beneath every metaphorical rock. Dashiell Hammett looms large in the hierarchy of *noir* writers, and the story of Flitcraft-gone-missing contains the essential notion that also nourishes the *giallo*: rudely shocked by the falling beam whose message is engraved into his very flesh, Flitcraft is briefly blinded by a glimpse of the chaos that is always beneath the surface of the apparently rational world. That chip of cement produces a hairline crack in his world view, making Flitcraft aware of the intervening presence of some great glass wall that keeps out the tempest. And he can only wonder how long the window will hold. Flitcraft doesn't gaze overlong into the abyss, and after a while he's able to shake the shadow of chaos and recreate his contented life, one in which no beams fall. The protagonists of Argento's films are seldom so fortunate.

Sam Dalmas of *The Bird With the Crystal Plumage* emerges unscathed from his encounter with that which lies beneath the surface of his ordered existence (and which he first glimpses as he stands trapped between a pair of double glass doors, which literalize the notion of the window onto chaos), but the abyss gazes back at Roberto Tobias, Marcus Daly and Peter Neal (in *Four Flies on Grey Velvet*, *Deep Red* and *Tenebrae*, respectively), and they are irrevocably altered by the experience.

Argento's films consist of the following titles: *The Bird With the Crystal Plumage/L'uccello dalle piume di cristallo* (1970), *The Cat O'Nine Tails/Il gatto a nove code* (1971), *Four Flies on Grey Velvet/Quattro mosche di velluto grigio* (1972), *Le cinque giornate* (1973), *Deep Red/Profondo rosso* (1976), *Suspiria* (1977), *Inferno* (1980), *Tenebrae/Tenebre* (1982), *Creepers/Phenomena* (1985), *Opera* (1987) and *Two Evil Eyes/Due occhi malocchio* (1990). The body of work they constitute is uneven in many respects and can't be said to embody the clear development of a discrete thematic or stylistic theory. What Argento's films are, consistently, is fascinating, even if the precise nature of their fascination is sometimes difficult to isolate.

Certainly, part of their appeal lies in the fact that they're so self-aware, flagrant in their manipulation of commercial narrative cinema's conventions. When theorist Stephen Heath chose to subject Orson Welles' *Touch of Evil* to extended formal analysis, he was selecting a film widely damned with faint praise or "excused" in light of the turbulent production history which pitted the aggressively individualistic Welles against the commercial expectations of Universal Pictures and the apparent limitations of the B-picture police thriller. Heath's explanation of the selection (in his inimitable clotted style) could apply equally to Argento's work as a whole:

... several reasons led to the choice of this film; most notably the original... feeling of an extremely openly coded film - an obviousness of systems: from, say, the straightforward adoption of stock modes of continuity transition or the simple coding of shot angles into one or two dramatically available systems to the easy 'difficulty' of the various elements that go up to make the signature of "Welles" ("baroque," "expressionism," "chiaroscuro" - the usual terms for that mixture of effects of depth of focus, 18.5 distortion, lighting, composition in frame, etc.) - constantly rendered oblique, overturned; the impression of a filmic system in which the narrative was constantly deflected, out of true.[3]

The terms may differ from film to film, but Argento's work is suffused with evidence of a variety of systems in operation, and

[3]"Film and System: Terms of Analysis" (Part 1), *Screen* Volume 16, Number 1 (Spring, 1975), p.11

Sam Dalmas (Tony Musante) confronts the demons of his mind in *The Bird With the Crystal Plumage.*

it entices - even dares - the viewer to enter into a dialogue with the filmic text[4].

The range of allusion in Argento's films extends from visionary writer Thomas De Quincey to filmmaker Alfred Hitchcock; a web of intertextual references links his films on images of perverse sexuality and extreme violence, water, curtains and vast quivering eyes. Flashbacks and dreams interrupt the flow of narrative, disorienting close-ups and high-angle extreme long shots disrupt any sense of continuous internal space established by Argento's ever-restless camera eye. Yet he's a commercial filmmaker, not an avant-garde experimenter, and his films are phenomenally successful in European markets. Even in the United States, which has embraced his work less warmly, several of Argento's films have proved commercially profitable, notably *Deep Red* and *Suspiria*. The durability of *The Bird With the Crystal Plumage* is such that it sustained a limited theatrical re-release as recently as 1982 (*12 years* after its initial release) under the title *The Phantom of Terror*, even though it's been widely seen on television. Argento's films are always informed by a tension between the demands of the popular market-place and his own interest in cinematic techniques which - however much they may intrigue the sophisticated viewer and delight the fan - run the risk of alienating the broad-based movie-going audience needed to make a movie into a box office success.

It's been suggested that the radical difference between the American box office performance of *The Bird With the Crystal Plumage* (which was enormously successful) and *The Cat O'Nine Tails* (which wasn't) lay in Argento's decreasing interest in even rudimentary mystery/suspense plotting, and ever greater concern with dramatically foregrounded cinematic technique. Many things it may be, but *The Cat O'Nine Tails* is not "Nine times more suspenseful than *The Bird With the Crystal Plumage*," as its theatrical trailers claimed. Of all

[4]This is the term Heath uses to differentiate between that which one views, "the text engaging the action of reception," and "the physical object that is produced over a period of time under a given set of circumstances;" this he designates the "filmic system." *Ibid*, p.9

Introduction

Argento's films, *The Bird With the Crystal Plumage* plays most closely by the rules of the classical thriller, a form that is, to enter the realm of Barthesian terminology, the embodiment of the "readerly" text. *The Bird With the Crystal Plumage* comes closest to inviting the reader to sit back and enjoy the passive titillation of a well-crafted mystery whose transgressions - against the law, against religion, against conventional morality - are confined to matters of plot and swiftly resolved. Consumers of readerly texts "purchase at the cost of a minor and passing disturbance the comfort of knowing that the disturbance [is] *contained*, and that at the end of the story the world they [imagine will] be continued in its innocence and familiarity," as critic David I. Grossvogel observed in reference to the well-mannered world of Agatha Christie. By virtue of the tyranny of all-important plot (the need to hide the identity of the criminal, to efface the evidence that would reveal his or her face too early, to plant clues where the astute reader can find and make use of them), the reader/viewer of the conventional mystery is, in Roland Barthes' words, "plunged into a kind of idleness - he is intransitive; he is, in short, serious: instead of functioning himself, instead of gaining access to the magic of the signifier, to the pleasure of writing, he is left with the poor freedom either to accept or reject the text: reading is nothing more than a *referendum*." The reader who enters wholeheartedly into the game of solving the mystery before the fictional sleuth does may seem to be casting off the chains of passive consumption, but his or her liberation is an illusion; no true "writerly" enterprise can take place when there is only one correct solution contained within the text, a single solution to which all roads lead.

Argento's *gialli*, their stories reduced to skeletal frameworks, their diegeses encrusted with signifiers, belong to the class of the writerly text as surely as do more conventionally "difficult" works as Alain Resnais' *Last Year at Marienbad*, Bernardo Bertolucci's *The Spider's Stratagem* or Michelangelo Antonioni's *Blow-Up*.[5] Their complex internal logic is connota-

[5]The terms "story" (*histoire*) and "discourse" (*discours*), appropriated

19

The first tail is . . .

The second tail is . . .

The third tail is . . .

The fourth tail is . . .

The fifth tail is . . .

MR. EXHIBITOR:

These teasers can be used individually or in any combination in advance of your opening.

20

The sixth tail is . . .

The seventh tail is . . .

The eighth tail is . . .

The ninth tail is . . .

American ad slicks for *The Cat O'Nine Tails* create a deceptive linear chronology of mayhem.

tive rather than denotative, metaphoric rather than met-
anymic (to use the terms proposed by Russian formalist Victor
Shklovsky in the essay *Art as Technique*); images proceed from
one to another not in the service of advancement of linear
narrative, but by way of poetic connections, a kind of alchemical
reasoning.

If Pauline Kael's iconoclastic criticism of Sergei Eisenstein's
Ivan the Terrible - "a brilliant collection of stills," she writes, but
"static, grandiose and frequently ludicrous" - contains some
grain of truth, it is still as misguided as similar criticisms of,
say, *Deep Red*. Both are films whose sheer *excess* arouses an
almost puritanical distaste in many (re)viewers. The excess in
question here is not mere excessiveness; that's what you get
from a filmmaker who's bought into the notion that "more is
more": more elephants, more extras, more lavish costumes,
more stuff blowing up = more entertainment value for the box
office dollar. This excess is what Barthes identifies as the realm
of obtuse meaning, when he discusses *Ivan* in *The Third
Meaning*.

On the one hand, it cannot be conflated with the simple *existence*
of the scene, it exceeds the copy of the referential motif, it compels an
interrogative reading... on the other, neither can it be conflated with
the dramatic meaning of the rest of the episode... By contrast with the
first two levels, communication and signification, this third level -
even if the reading of it is still hazardous - is that of *significance*, a
word which has the advantage of referring to the field of the signifier
(and not of signification) and of linking up with... a semiotics of the
text.

---

by film theorists from the language of structural linguistics make the
same distinction. The story film - which is to say, virtually all
mainstream films - constitutes a closed system whose glossy surface
is designed to keep the viewer resolutely on the outside, looking in.
The discourse, by contrast, is an open text, one which explicitly -
through a variety of structural devices - invites the viewer (or reader)
to participate in the construction of a text.

Introduction

It's tough to get a handle on the concept of obtuse meaning; it wouldn't be obtuse if it weren't. Obtuse meaning is obtuse precisely because it lies outside of whatever system the reader has adopted in order to make sense of a particular work; it seems unnecessary, excessive. Your mind rebels because the material doesn't fit, doesn't make sense. If the reader adopts the scientific method to the task of reading a work of art (and many readers, especially critics, do), one theory must be found that can incorporate every diegetic element within its boundaries. If no single theory can be proposed, the work may well be labelled "incoherent." Barthes' radical proposal is that the excess, all the meaning that falls outside the system or systems that determine the work's overall structure, forms its *own* system, one which may exist parallel or tangentially to the others. The parameters of the system of the excess are shifting and elusive but none the less there, persistent, allusive and tantalizing.

Argento's insistent foregrounding of stylistic elements whose narrative function is minimal or non-existent is one sort of

well have something to do with the fact that it's often linked to the spectacle of violent death, but it's also important to remember that visual excess in and of itself often offends sensibilities formed by classical Hollywood cinema, which strives above all for expediency: the perfect match of signifying device and (usually narrative) signified. Even the glorious excessiveness of, say, Busby Berkeley's musical numbers isn't misaligned with their diegetic function: they're designed to be pure spectacle, and so they are spectacular. The voluptuousness of the murderous tableaux that are the centrepieces of Argento's works damns them doubly: they're distasteful both by virtue of their subject matter and in light of their technical prodigality.

Clearly much of the appeal of Argento's work lies in the way his films lend themselves to reading through readily apparent critical systems: there's something satisfying about being able to put an object in its place, locate it within a familiar system of meaning.

To see the oneiric phallocentricity - visually apparent in the

Mater Tenebrarum (Veronica Lazar) as the walls come tumbling down in *Inferno*.

Rose Elliott (Irene Miracle) in *Inferno*'s underwater ballroom sequence, featuring effects by Mario Bava.

omnipresent knives, razors, sword canes, axes and sundry sharp objects too numerous to mention - of *The Cat O'Nine Tails* or *Tenebrae* is to scurry to the Freudian notion of dreamwork (the activity by which, through the processes of displacement and condensation, disturbing thoughts are transformed into the fantastic material of dreams) is to make perfect sense of these child's gardens of perversity. *Suspiria* and *Inferno*, with their pervasive images of fire and water conflated into an apocalyptic mandala, beg discussion in terms of Jungian archetypes. The insistent defamiliarizing effect of Argento's visual trademarks indicate a formalist and/or structural approach to the text. But the seductiveness of these films lies ultimately in the realm of their excess: the spatial and temporal warping, the curious disjunction between soundtrack and image (principally a matter of music so far out of line with the imagery as to be bizarre; Italian Westerns are justly famous as showcases for this device), the violently saturated colour palette, the obsessive examination of surfaces (particularly apparent post-*Four Flies*), the full panoply of non-narrative detail that generates the overwhelming sense of *weirdness* evoked by Argento's work. This weirdness is compelling, enticing and purely cinematic; it makes Argento's work stand out in sharp relief from the ranks of hundreds of films whose subject matter is the same, and even from those whose cinematic technique is superficially similar.

Closest to Argento's concerns and historically indispensable to any consideration of his films is Mario Bava, whose long and wide-ranging career includes five thrillers made in the wake of Alfred Hitchcock's *Psycho*. *The Girl Who Knew Too Much/The Evil Eye/La ragazza che sapeva troppo* (1963), *Blood and Black Lace/Sei donne per l'assassino* (1964), *Hatchet for the Honeymoon/Il rosso segno della follia* (1969), *Five* (or *Four*) *Dolls for an August Moon/Cinque bambole per la luna d'agosto* (1970) and *Twitch of the Death Nerve/A Bay of Blood/Last House on the Left Part II/ L'Antefatto/Ecologia del delitto* (1972) are all *gialli* proper, but they lack something - some peculiarity present in Argento's mature work. If *The Bird With the Crystal Plumage* could be a late Bava film, *Deep Red* and *Tenebrae* could have

Inner darkness made visible: Massimo Morlacchi (Cameron Mitchell) and Countess Christina (Eva Bartok) in Mario Bava's seminal *Blood and Black Lace*.

Nora Davis (Leticia Roman) is Mario Bava's *Girl Who Knew Too Much*.

26

Stalwart men in suits and ties (Cameron Mitchell and Thomas Reiner) are no match for the whirlpool of madness that engulfs everyday life in *Blood and Black Lace.*

When *Black Sunday* Comes: Katia (Barbara Steele), Javotich (Arturo Dominici) and Dr. Gorobek (John Richardson) in Mario Bava's first film.

been made only by Argento. What Bava's work provides, however, is a clear link, a transition, between Argento's films and those of Hitchcock. More to the point, it indicates the road Argento took to get from *Psycho* to *Tenebrae*. You can't speak of thrillers made after 1960 without alluding to *Psycho*, but in this case the allusion must be fairly specific. In *Psycho* the roots of the *giallo* are laid bare. *Psycho*'s conventional elements, derived from the longstanding thriller tradition, are undermined constantly on a number of levels. On the narrative level one need only cite the most obvious example to make the point: it's still a shock when Marion Crane - both the apparent protagonist and the character played by star Janet Leigh - is butchered before the film is one third over.

As to the style, as little as five years earlier (and certainly ten) *Psycho*'s *noir*-ish expressionism would have been perfectly ordinary, but by 1960 - and particularly in light of Hitchcock's enthusiastic conversion to colour filmmaking in 1954 with *Dial M for Murder*[6] - it read as unusual, *stylized*, and that stylization is further evident in shots like those of Norman Bates poised beneath the silent stuffed birds perched on his walls, staring sightlessly into the camera eye. Most conspicuously odd is *Psycho*'s overall dramatic emphasis: it's Norman Bates, homicidal maniac, who provides the film's point of view, his warped perceptions overwhelming the fictive space with bizarre camera angles and insanely dramatic lighting that seems as much a product of the landscape of his twisted mind's eye as of practical filmmaking decisions. *Psycho*'s reputation doesn't rest on its story, and Hitchcock himself told François Truffaut: "I don't care about the subject matter, I don't care about the acting; but I do care about the pieces of film and the photography and the soundtrack and all of the technical ingredients." Elsewhere, Hitchcock declared his commitment to narrative

[6]*The Wrong Man*, made in 1957, is in black and white, but this is clearly part of a self-contained system of reference. Hitchcock speaks of the film in terms of his attempts to generate a sense of documentary authenticity because it was based on a true story; in the 1950s "documentary realism" demanded black and white film.

control over technological display, to conventional economy of means. But in *Psycho* style is, if not all, then certainly conspicuous.

It's tempting to single out certain elements of *Psycho* and identify them as direct antecedents of Argento's chaotic cinematic vocabulary, but it pays to be careful. There is, for example, a tracking shot in *Psycho* that seems ostentatious to no narrative end. When Norman climbs the stairs to his mother's room in order to fetch her to the fruit cellar, safe from the prying eyes of those who would uncover the secret of Marion Crane's disappearance, the camera follows him as he goes. When he reaches the landing it does not - as one would expect - follow him, but rather turns and continues up the *next* flight of stairs while Norman enters the room and closes the door behind him. The camera then turns around and gazes downward as Norman, mother cradled in his arms, re-emerges and descends the stairs. This conspicuous, curious camera movement is not, however, the unmotivated *tour de force* it at first appears. Hitchcock's own account clears up the mystery. "I didn't want to cut, when he carried her down, to a high [angle] shot, because the audience would have been suspicious as to why the camera has suddenly jumped away. So I had a hanging camera follow Perkins [Norman] up the stairs, and when he went into the room I continued going up without a cut... Meanwhile, I had an argument take place between the son and his mother to distract the audience and take their minds off what the camera was doing. In this way the camera was above Perkins again as he carried his mother down and the public hadn't noticed a thing. It was rather exciting to use the camera to deceive the audience." Rooted in a solid understanding of audience psychology, this is a statement of controlled manipulation, and it's a far cry from the wholesale embrace of spectacular technique for its own sake evident in Argento's work.

It seems inevitable that Argento - the son of a Brazilian fashion photographer and an Italian movie producer - adopted the relentless visual orientation that distinguishes his work. But he also belongs to the small but influential group of directors - which includes Bertolucci, Pier Paolo Pasolini, Truf-

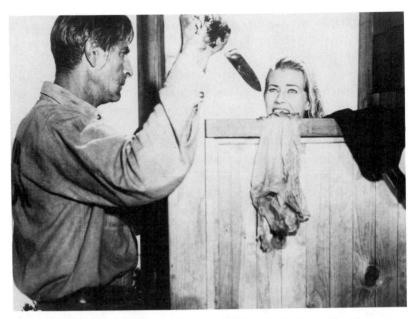

The primal trauma in Gerd Oswald's film of Fredric Brown's *The Screaming Mimi*.

Victims-to-be Gerry (William Berger), Peggy (Helena Ronee) and Trudy (Ira Furstenberg) discover Nick (Maurice Poli) on the beach covered with sand crabs, in Mario Bava's *Five Dolls for an August Moon*.

faut, Paul Schrader and Jean-Luc Godard - who began their careers as critics. As a screenwriter, Argento wrote (or co-wrote) numerous scripts in the popular genres of the hour - including war pictures and Westerns - before gravitating towards the thriller for his first directorial effort. You can't reasonably look at Argento's work without bearing in mind the contradictory context from which he springs: on the one hand, the practical Italian film industry, with its relentless emphasis on genre and its quick and dirty production practices; on the other, the cerebral world of film criticism, with its inevitable emphasis on analysis and intellectual distance. Rather than propose a single critical methodology through which to examine Argento's films, I have brought to bear on the subject a number of different approaches.

The interest of *The Bird With the Crystal Plumage* lies mostly in its incidental elements; the story and structure are the most conventional of any with which Argento has worked, largely because it was adapted from a fairly conventional novel - Fredric Brown's 1949 *The Screaming Mimi*. In writing the screenplay, however, Argento incorporated into the story several important changes and the film's most memorable (and indicative) image - that of a man trapped between the panes of a set of glass doors, powerless to do anything about the assault he sees being committed - has no basis in the book. *The Bird With the Crystal Plumage*, whose lilting Ennio Morricone score provides a none-too-subtle counterpoint to its lurid story, closely resembles its predecessors (Mario Bava's films) while anticipating the direction taken by Argento in his more mature work.

The Cat O'Nine Tails and *Four Flies on Grey Velvet* were both made from original screenplays, and their convoluted narratives take a hint from Hitchcock, who remarked that plausibility was the easiest part of plotting, so why bother with it, and carry it to a fabulous extreme. Each film is fashioned from a melange of weird science - the notion that the XYY chromosome indicates criminality in the former, a machine that captures the last image on a dead person's eye in the latter - and occluded exposition. But what really makes them cook is an atmosphere of extreme paranoid dislocation that springs equally from the plots, which posit worlds in which chaotic madness laps constantly at the shores of conventional "reality," and the bizarre *mise en scènes*, which give equal weight to important plot points and fetishistic detail.

Deep Red, whose evocative title signalled a departure from the quirky verbosity of Argento's first three films, is the first of his truly accomplished works. Lushly photographed and shot from a screenplay by Bernardino Zapponi (who co-wrote Fellini's *Satyricon* and *Roma*) based on a story by Argento, *Deep Red* is a systematic - no, *obsessive* - study in thematic doubling. Two pianists, one English and one Italian, function as one another's warped reflections in a mirror clouded by the sins of a past whose repression hasn't diminished its potency. *Deep Red*'s plot pivots on reflections of reality: photographs, drawings copied and recopied, events re-enacted like scenes from a play or parlour charades, frozen by time and neglect into ghastly dioramas. Further, *Deep Red* abounds in spatial dislocations. Conventionally photographed scenes are juxtaposed with extreme close-ups of bizarre and/or unidentifiable objects isolated in stygian blackness, over which the camera pans as though it were exploring some vast physical terrain rather than the icons that define some particularly dirty back road of the mind. Argento's audacious imagery is supported by a score that alternates between the tinkling eeriness of a child's song and the throbbing menace of bass-dominated rock. Unlike Morricone's score for the first three films, which are designed to act as straightforward (if ironic) counterpoint to the images, Goblin's compositions are an integral part of the unpredictable diegesis, as inherently contradictory as the deceptive imagery.

Shot in three-strip Technicolor and manipulated in the laboratory to produce a palette of saturated, almost cartoonlike primary colours, *Suspiria* introduces Argento's unfinished cycle of "Three Mothers" films. The inspiration for *Suspiria*, *Inferno* and a third film yet to be made comes not from authentic folklore, but rather from a passage in a short essay by Thomas De Quincey, best known as the author of the autobiographical *Confessions of an English Opium Eater*. In *Levana and Our Ladies of Sorrow*, he writes of a drug-induced hallucination in which three unearthly sisters burden him with the revelation of their supernatural aspects. "The eldest of the three is named *Mater Lachrymarum*, Our Lady of the Tears... the second sister is called *Mater Susperiorum*, Our Lady of the Sighs... but the third sister, who is also the youngest! Hush! Whisper whilst we talk of *her*!... *her* name is *Mater Tenebrarum* - Our Lady of Darkness." Mysterious, allusive and elliptical, De Quincey's prose careens between wilful obscurity and drug-induced ecstasy; it's no wonder Argento embraced him as a kindred soul. In Argento's reading, the three mothers generate/inhabit a cinematic world informed by Jungian archetypal imagery, each holding sway over a particular city. *Suspiria* takes place in Freiburg, Germany, where Mater Susperiorum inhabits a Gothic dance academy built for her by a Satanic architect. Mater Tenebrarum lives in *Inferno*'s phantasmagoric New York, while Mater Lachrymarum - who makes a brief appearance in *Inferno* - is based in Rome. Perhaps because of the supreme glossiness of their supernatural imagery, *Suspiria* and *Inferno* operate on a far shallower level than the films that flank them - *Deep Red* and *Tenebrae*. They are simply dark magical mystery tours couched in the iconographies of witchcraft and alchemy, informed by the notion that magic is all around us.

Despite its title, *Tenebrae* is not the third Three Mothers film. It abandons the mystical universe of the supernatural for that of a writer of best-selling thrillers plunged into nightmarish collusion with a psychopath who takes murderous inspiration from his books. It's tempting to cast *Tenebrae* in an autobiographical light, since it was written after Argento found himself persecuted by an unbalanced fan obsessed with *Suspiria*, but such a reading is one-dimensional. *Tenebrae*'s visual landscape is illuminated by a powerful, clear light that bleaches it to a dazzling whiteness accentuated by touches of shimmering blue and green and pure, intense red. The influence of the archetypal thriller is everywhere. The protagonist, novelist Peter Neal, is cast in the role of amateur detective; his foil is elegant Inspector Giermani of Rome's police force. The names of Agatha Christie and Sir Arthur Conan Doyle punctuate the

Jennifer Corvino (Jennifer Connelly) talks to the insects in *Creepers*.

Argento adjusts Jennifer Connelly's costume in *Creepers*.

dialogue, conjuring the demons of the classical detective story. But *Tenebrae* is no story of the harmonious universe briefly disrupted and then put to rights; Dashiell Hammett, Ed McBain and Mickey Spillane are also invoked, and their weary nihilism is the film's leitmotif.

"When you have eliminated the impossible whatever remains, however improbable, must be the truth," remarks Neal (echoed later, with heavy irony, by Giermani), but Sherlock Holmes' system of ratiocination can make neither head nor tail of the psychosexual maelstrom of *Tenebrae*'s fictive space. *Tenebrae* bristles with threatening titillation and violent eroticism: the relationships around which it revolves are all sexual in nature, and all are at least potentially dangerous. Informed by a series of dreamy flashbacks so visually assertive that they threaten to overwhelm the primary narrative every time they are introduced, *Tenebrae* expands on much of the material explored in *Deep Red*, taking it just one step further. In *Tenebrae*'s inverted logic it's always lightest just before the dark[7], the dark that is not mere chronological consequence, but rather an echo of the liturgical Tenebrae, a service during which the serial extinguishing of altar candles robs the church of light bit by precious bit until it's enveloped in a physical gloom that evokes the spiritual darkness of betrayal, desertion and death.

[7]Credit here to consummate pulp writer Jim Thompson, much beloved of *Série Noire* readers but, until relatively recently, conspicuously under-appreciated in the US. Glossy reprints of his novels and the scramble for movie rights, which produced the 1990 release of three films based on his work - James Foley's *After Dark, My Sweet*, Stephen Frears' *The Grifters* and Maggie Greenwald's *The Kill-Off* - have raised his profile substantially. From *The Killer Inside Me*:

"T-tell you somethin'," he said. "T-tell you somethin' I bet you never thought of."

"Yeah?"

"It's...it's always lightest just before the dark."

Tired as I was, I laughed. "You got it wrong Bob," I said. "You mean..."

"Huh-uh," he said, "You got it wrong."

Creepers, a singularly incoherent film, takes off from an idea mentioned briefly in *Deep Red*. Early on, we are witness to the European Conference on Parapsychology, where one Professor Giordani introduces a telepath with a lecture on telepathy in the animal kingdom, specifically among insects. *Creepers'* protagonist, young Jennifer Corvino, has the gift (or curse) of telepathy, and it plunges her into unwanted awareness of a world of deformity and madness, the world of a murderer whose mutilated victims include several of her fellow students at an eerie Swiss boarding school. But it also connects her to the world of insects, who light on her palm, swarm around her head and ultimately protect her.

Simultaneously outlandish and prosaic, *Creepers* demonstrates all the weaknesses of Argento's earlier works and few of the assets; its system of internal logic is weak and despite some showy interludes, *Creepers* is less than engaging. Though technically accomplished, it's shallow and repetitive, distinguished only by the spectacular meanness of certain images. The scene in which the Inspector breaks his own hand to escape from a set of handcuffs is squirm-inducing, as is the one in which pretty Jennifer Corvino is cast into a pool of maggots; the image of a chimpanzee running amok with a razor is deliriously apt. Released in the US with extensive cuts and retitled (*Phenomena*'s marquee appeal was apparently insufficient), the film was not particularly successful at the box office.

Opera fared still worse, never making it to US screens at all. The story begins in the star is born mould: a world famous diva, scheduled to appear in a lavish and avant-garde production of Giuseppe Verdi's *Macbeth*, has an accident and cannot go on. Her youthful understudy, Betty, must appear in her place. She is, of course, a sensation. So far, so good, until the point at which the story lurches into Argento-land. Among Betty's admirers is a psychopath, a killer who calls her, writes to her, and finally forces her to watch him commit his (naturally) gruesome crimes. Betty's complicity with the killer terrifies her, and the police - once she confides in them - seem unable to protect her from his attentions.

The lavish *Opera*'s genesis can be traced back to 1985, when

Introduction

Argento spoke of his plans to stage Verdi's *Rigoletto* at the Sferisterio di Macerath in Rome. Though that project never panned out, the opulence and ritualistic atmosphere of the opera stayed with Argento, who saw in it yet another opportunity to articulate his mannered vision of a world gone mad. *Macbeth* the opera shares the reputation of *Macbeth* the play - cursed - so it was a natural choice for the production around which the film revolves. And the film's most memorable image could serve as a metaphor for the experience of everyone who's ever watched a horror film through splayed fingers, simultaneously enthralled and repelled: Betty, her staring eyes held open wide by an ingenious and sadistic arrangement of tape and straight pins. Despite its impressive production values, *Opera* opened to less than enthusiastic reviews in Italy and was never picked up for US distribution.

Argento's most recent film to date, *Two Evil Eyes*, marks a number of firsts: his first film shot entirely in America, his first Poe film, and his first compendium movie - *Two Evil Eyes* is in fact *two* short films, one directed by Argento himself and the other by George Romero. It also suggests a return to the past, in that it's the first film produced by Claudio Argento since *Tenebrae*, and it reunited Argento and Romero. The two directors worked together for the first time a decade ago on Romero's *Dawn of the Dead*, which Argento helped produce.

A longtime admirer of Poe, Argento chose to do far more than simply adapt his *Black Cat* to the screen. Instead, the director envisioned his segment as a full scale homage to the writer whose tales of terror are still the standard against which others are measured. He incorporates allusions to more than a dozen of the author's works into a convoluted story that revolves around a photographer whose gruesome images of crime scenes reflect the chaos in his mind. The figure of the photographer, Rod Usher, was inspired by the American photojournalist Weegee, whose stark and uncompromising pictures of death and despair are still prized by connoisseurs of the sordid. But Argento imbues him with many of Poe's own characteristics as well, and the result is a very personal response to Poe's literary vision, which partakes "much of madness, and more of sin."

As is always the case with studies of filmmakers who are still making movies, and particularly given the chaotic melange of sources and influences that contribute to making Argento's films the complex artifacts they are, this one can't hope to be definitive. What it can do is single out certain tendencies in Argento's work and examine them, while providing an overview of his career to date.

THE BIRD WITH THE CRYSTAL PLUMAGE

"Right. Bring in the Perverts."
- Inspector Morrosini

"To reproach Hitchcock for specializing in suspense is to accuse him of being the least boring of filmmakers," wrote François Truffaut. His enthusiasm for the thriller in the hands of a skilful director, however, isn't universally shared. It may take a lot of nerve to deny Hitchcock's greatness, but the thriller is still a low-rent genre; everybody's surprised when one actually turns out to be *great*, not just entertaining or pretty good or even great for a thriller. For all that highbrow critics and scholars have their reservations, *auteur* thinking has filtered down to the mass-market writers and the movie-going public as though it were the most natural thing in the world - nobody today looks askance when you talk about the new Steven Spielberg movie.

Genre theory has proved a tougher nut to crack. Audiences recognize genres, of course, readily and with some sophistication. And they make hard ticket-buying decisions based on genre. Half the trick of marketing is making sure your potential audience has the right tag for your picture and doesn't think *Tie Me Up! Tie Me Down!* is a porno movie, hence the controversy about its MPAA X rating, which implied just that. Nor do you want them to think *Slam Dance* (an erotic thriller) is something on the order of *Flashdance* or *Dirty Dancing*, witness the tag line, "It's *Not* About Dancing." As to the notion that if your title gives you so much trouble you ought to think about changing it, well... who can fathom it? And it's not that popular writers don't get it either, but that the concept of genre has something dismissive built into it. Just a horror movie (or a Western or a tear-jerker or an action/adventure picture)... those are words that chill filmmakers' hearts. Pigeonholing a film is a way of not dealing with it, of saying, however subconsciously, 'if it's just a Western, what more can there be to it?' This problem has

39

produced the risible spectacle of all kinds of filmmakers claiming their movies aren't exactly what they are - "I don't consider this a horror movie..." being the odds on favourite for most frequently uttered. Argento, it must be said, has never denied the thriller or the horror film; where even Hitchcock treated his work with an ironic distance, Argento is a true believer.

The Bird With the Crystal Plumage is the least baroque and most conventional in its story structure of any film Argento has ever made. Though hardly simple, the plot is linear and straightforward in its development. Argento receives sole credit for the screenplay, which carries with it the implication that he is also the author of the original story, but this isn't quite the case: it derives in large part from a novel written in 1950 by yet another American pulp writer. Fredric Brown's *The Screaming Mimi* was passed along to Argento for an opinion by Bertolucci, who intended to buy the rights for himself. Captivated by the novel's central idea, Argento resolved to borrow it and spin off a new story. In fact, he borrowed quite a bit more.

The plot of *The Bird With the Crystal Plumage* begins with Sam Dalmas (Tony Musante), an American writer living in Rome with his girlfriend Julia (Suzy Kendall), walking past an art gallery late one night. Glancing in, he sees two figures struggling: a woman, and a man in black gloves and a raincoat. There is a knife, and Dalmas rushes in to help. The entrance to the gallery contains a double set of glass doors; Dalmas gets through the first set and they lock behind him. The inner set is locked as well, and he realizes he's trapped like an insect in amber; Dalmas can only watch in horror as the man in black escapes and the woman, stabbed, writhes on the floor.

The police arrive, the woman is saved, and Dalmas is held first as a suspect, then as a witness to the crime, which is the most recent of a series of attacks on young women. The wounded Monica Ranieri (Eva Renzi), whose husband owns the gallery, is the only one to have survived. His passport confiscated by the police, haunted by the feeling that he saw something important that night that he's now unable to remember, Dalmas decides to investigate the killings on his own.

His search leads him to an antique store where the first

Sam Dalmas (Tony Musante) watches helplessly as Monica Ranieri (Eva Renzi) writhes. *The Bird With the Crystal Plumage.*

Sam Dalmas (Tony Musante), trapped and despairing, in *The Bird With the Crystal Plumage.*

victim worked; there he obtains a photograph of the painting she sold the day she was killed: it depicts a woman being attacked by a man with a knife. It leads eventually to an eccentric artist, who tells Dalmas the inspiration was something that happened years earlier. Dalmas and his girlfriend, meanwhile, receive threatening calls from the killer. A sound in the background of one call leads to a zoo, directly across the street from the Ranieri's apartment. Dalmas and the police converge on the gallery owner; he tries to escape and falls from a window. He confesses to the crimes as he lies dying.

But Dalmas realizes something is wrong, and finally comes face to face with the true killer: Monica Ranieri, who was attacked as a young woman and went violently insane when the painting in the antique store triggered her repressed memories. Her husband lied to protect her, and Dalmas barely escapes becoming her last victim. The protagonist of Brown's novel, William Sweeney, is also a writer, a newspaperman. Walking the streets of nighttime Chicago in the grip of an alcoholic binge, Sweeney sees an amazing thing. Trapped by a giant dog between the double glass doors of her apartment building, a beautiful woman writhes; she has been stabbed by an unknown assailant. She appears to be the fourth victim of a ripper (as Sweeney's paper has dubbed the killer), and she is the only one to have survived. Bewitched by the beautiful near-victim Yolanda Lang - a stripper whose act includes the dog, Devil - Sweeney begins his own investigation of the crimes. His first lead is a mass-marketed statuette of a terrified woman, the screaming mimi, sold by the first victim the day she was murdered. Sweeney buys his own copy, convinced it has something to do with the case. He suspects Yolanda's manager Greene, whose relationship with her borders on obsessive. But he has no proof, and the police - who briefly suspected Sweeney himself - are skeptical. Sweeney tracks down Wilson, the sculptor of the screaming mimi, and learns that he based the statue on his sister Bessie, who was attacked as a young woman by a knife-wielding maniac. But the maniac is dead - Wilson killed him. Bessie was placed in an insane asylum and reportedly died there, mad.

Soon after Sweeney returns to Chicago, the police announce the solution to the ripper killings: Greene, fatally injured in a fall from Yolanda's window, has confessed. A shattered copy of the screaming mimi is found on the pavement beside him. But Sweeney is not convinced. He tracks down Yolanda, and discovers that she is really Bessie Wilson, the killer. Manipulated by Greene, a psychiatrist who loved her not wisely but too well, Yolanda lapsed back into madness after seeing the screaming mimi. Greene was unable to control her, and she began killing. He attacked her half-heartedly, hoping the shock would break the grotesque statue's hold on her mind, but she was too far gone. She tries to kill Sweeney, who is rescued by the police.[1]

In Argento's hands Yolanda Lang, exotic dancer, becomes Monica Ranieri, wife of an art dealer, the screaming mimi mutates into a painting, Chicago becomes Rome and the murders are multiplied. Argento makes some subtle shifts in emphasis, diminishing the relationships between the protagonist and the killer, and the artist and his model. Bessie's brother sculpted the screaming mimi; the statuette in some way replaces the sister he lost (he thinks) to a maniac, at the same time turning an ordinary girl (what could be more down to earth than a girl named Bessie?) into a grotesque fetish. Berto Consaldi, Argento's cat-eating painter, thought little of Monica - she was just "a girl I knew" - but was inspired by the

---

[1]An authorized version of *The Screaming Mimi* was made in 1958, written by Robert Blees and directed by Gerd Oswald; the cast included Anita Ekberg as Yolanda, Phil Carey as Sweeney and Gypsy Rose Lee as the owner of the strip club where Yolanda works. Some fabulously tacky strip numbers aside, it isn't a tremendously interesting piece of work. Though the film doesn't tamper significantly with the subject matter, it alters the form considerably. *Screaming Mimi* opens with the attack on Virginia (as Bessie has been renamed), then follows her as she is committed to an asylum, becomes involved in an affair with her psychiatrist and resumes her interrupted career as an exotic dancer. Despite the superficial fidelity to Brown's book, this strategy renders the entire film dull and ordinary. Attempts to generate a sleazy and perverse atmosphere, mostly at the strip club El Madhouse, are largely unsuccessful.

fact of her victimization. At the same time, Argento intensifies the relationship between his protagonist and the killer, and tips the balance of power in the killer's favour. Yolanda doesn't know she's a murderer, so she doesn't care about Sweeney's investigation; he lusts after her, but she scarcely knows he's alive. When she finally tries to kill him, it's only because he's tracked her down and confronted her. Monica, by contrast, is totally aware of Dalmas and takes every opportunity to get closer to him. She calls his home, kills his friend Carlo, tries to kill Julia and lures him into her clutches, where he is trapped at the point of a knife. "You're going to *die*," she croons, her voice ragged; she cuts his palm and the wound recalls hers.

Sweeney and Yolanda play out their drama in an ingenious, Lacanian scenario: Yolanda has a knife (the phallus that should give her access to the power of language), but Sweeney is first and foremost a newspaper*man* and keeps her immobilized through the sheer power of language. As long as he talks, she's frozen in space, and he talks - for endless hours - until the police come to his rescue.

For Dalmas and Monica, the confrontation takes a different twist. Played out in the gallery, it begins with Dalmas trapped physically beneath a spiky piece of modern art (whose lethal spines foreshadow those of another *objet d'art* in *Tenebrae*) and ends when the police break in; all the emasculated Dalmas can do is wiggle silently like a worm on a hook.

Brown makes clear that there is a fundamental difference between Sweeney and Yolanda. He's a drunk, to be sure, but he finds solace in the consummate order of Mozart; she's a madwoman, pure and simple - she even works at El Madhouse. Sweeney knows the screaming mimi is a nasty thing, something that could "appeal only to a sadist, or someone who had some abnormality in him." He's attracted to Yolanda because she's beautiful and sexy; he doesn't know she's crazy, and starts investigating the crime because he wants to spend the night with her (as he eventually does, though not the way he had in mind) and it's a way of getting close.

Argento, by contrast, does nothing but stress the connection between Dalmas and Monica. Julia finds Consaldi's bloody painting "a bit perverted" and shudders when she looks at it; the only thing that bothers Dalmas is that he can't figure out what it *means*, where it fits into the puzzle. It grips his imagination to such a degree that he'd rather look at it than make love to his girlfriend, and the thrill of his brush with bloody death is enough to jar him free from the writer's block with which he's been afflicted for years. Dalmas is in thrall to the aura of madness; "Forty pages - all written in the last few days," he gloats soon after the phone call threatening Julia if he doesn't stop the investigation. "If nothing else, this little adventure has started me writing again. Broken me loose."

Argento changed many details in the process of turning *The Screaming Mimi* into *The Bird With the Crystal Plumage*, but the most important is this: flawed and weak though he may be, Brown's protagonist is afraid of the universe of madness he glimpses when he gets close to Yolanda Lang. Argento's is drawn to it like a moth to the flame.

Luigi Cozzi, Argento's friend and sometime collaborator, has pointed out that *The Bird With the Crystal Plumage* owes a specific debt to Mario Bava's *The Girl Who Knew Too Much*: in Bava's film a young woman witnesses an attempted murder and is disturbed by the feeling she's missing something; she eventually realizes the woman she thought was the victim was actually the attacker. Conflated with the scene in *The Screaming Mimi* in which Sweeney sees Yolanda trapped between the doors, this is, of course, the set piece around which *The Bird With the Crystal Plumage* revolves. But Bava's influence on Argento is far more extensive than this.

Born in 1914, Bava was the son of a cinematographer, Eugenio Bava, and grew up surrounded by the cinema. Combined with his own interest in painting and fascination with special effects, Bava's background paved the way for a career in the Italian cinema that began when he was 19 and continued until his death in 1980.

Following in his father's footsteps, Bava quickly established a reputation as a fast, versatile and reliable cinematographer. Trouble on the sets of *The Devil's Commandment* (1956) and *Caltiki: the Immortal Monster* (1959) - in both cases, director

WHAT

MADE

MIMI

SCREAM

?

Be sure
you're
emotionally
mature
enough
to take it!

SCREAMING MIMI

starring

Anita **E**KBERG

Phil **C**AREY

Gypsy Rose **L**EE

FROM THE
BEST-SELLING
SHOCK NOVEL
OF ALL TIME!
(5 MILLION
READERS!)

with HARRY TOWNES · THE RED NORVO TRIO
Screenplay by ROBERT BLEES
Based on the book by FREDRIC BROWN
Produced by HARRY JOE BROWN and ROBERT FELLOWS
Directed by GERD OSWALD
A SAGE PRODUCTION · A COLUMBIA PICTURE

Screaming Mimi ad slick exploits the traditional recourse of lurid horror pictures with
reference to maturity.

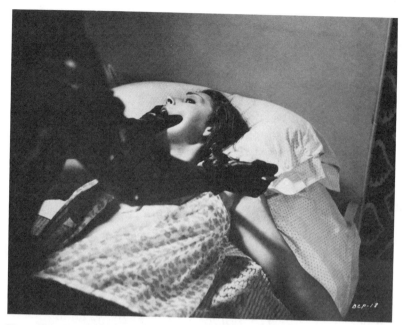

The sadist with black gloves: *The Bird With the Crystal Plumage.*

Julia (Suzy Kendall) is trapped by the unseen killer in *The Bird With the Crystal Plumage.*

Riccardo Freda's inability to get along with his producers - gave Bava his first directing experience, and in 1960 he directed his first film. *Black Sunday/La maschera del demonio* was an impressive debut, not least of all because it catapulted into the limelight Barbara Steele, sadomasochistic Madonna of the *cinefantastique*; it was Bava who observed that in certain shots her face took on an appearance that was scarcely human.

From Bava's painterly sensibility emerged a distinctive style that he brought to bear on a variety of subjects: horror, Westerns, science fiction, historical epics and James Bond-style spy thrillers among them. But one of its most successful applications was to the Hitchcockian thriller. His first foray into the form took place only two years after the release of *Psycho*, and the title - *The Girl Who Knew Too Much* (a literal translation from the Italian *La ragazza che sapeva troppo*) - goes so far as to pay obvious, tongue in cheek tribute to Hitchcock.

Bava's 1964 *Blood and Black Lace* (amazingly enough, a far more evocative phrase than *Sei donne per l'assassino* - six women for an assassin - and only slightly less indicative of the movie's content) begins to clear a path into the territory that Argento would later dominate. A fashion salon is plagued by a series of grisly murders connected somehow with a dead model's diary, reportedly chockablock with indiscreet gossip about drug abuse and sexual misbehaviour about the bad and the beautiful who populate the rarified world of Christian Haute Couture. The body count (modest by today's standards, but substantial at the time) is not so much a narrative consideration as a stylistic one: each new demise offers fresh opportunity for murderous invention as a maniac - clad in the soon-to-be *de rigueur* black gloves and shiny raincoat - face concealed by a filmy cloth that recalls Belgian painter René Magritte's eerie portrait of surreally swathed lovers - lovingly murders the elegant mannequins one by bloody one. Bava's colour sense owes a clear debt to his early interest in painting, though it is only intermittently evident, as when one model scurries to the lavish, cluttered apartment of her drug-addicted boyfriend, only to find death amidst alternating washes of red and blue light. For every surreally beautiful set piece, *Blood and Black Lace* contains at least one equally dull and conventionally photographed sequence whose function is to advance the story - most scenes involving the police, who are ineffectually looking into the matter, fall into this category - but despite this evident weakness it is a clear precursor of unusual things to come.

Hatchet for the Honeymoon ([1969] - *Il rosso segno della follia*, literally *"The Red Sign of Madness"*) dispenses with even the vestige of mystery plotting that *Blood and Black Lace* retains; while the latter conceals the murder's face both behind a literal veil and a plot twist, the former starts out by announcing the identity and motives of its maniacal murderer. *Hatchet for the Honeymoon* opens on a train hurtling towards the camera, then follows a black-clad man as he kills a young woman in her private berth. The sequence is calculated to disorient the viewer; by cutting back and forth between one- and two-shots of silhouetted figures in that corridor to create a warped sense of spatial relationships, the interior of the train is made to seem utterly alien. In the next scene we are given a series of close ups of the killer's chiseled face; he shaves (drawing a glittering straight razor across the flawless planes of his own flesh), dresses, and wanders through his palatial home. "My name is John Harrington," he says in a voice-over. "I am thirty years old. I am a paranoiac - an enchanting word; so civilized and full of possibility. The fact is I am completely mad... the fact remains that I have killed five young women..." There's no inverted *Roger Ackroyd* strategy in action here - the narrator isn't lying or concealing information as he does in Agatha Christie's notorious mystery (in which the narrator provides the reader with all the information about the killing of Roger Ackroyd that an astute puzzle-solver could want save that he himself is the murderer): John Harrington is a madman, a killer, and we the viewers know it from the start.

The owner of a fashion salon specializing in wedding dresses and other accoutrements of the wedding day, Harrington inhabits a space that's even more stylized than that of *Blood and Black Lace*. Though still firmly motivated by specific narrative events and points of characterization, Bava's visual style in

Hatchet for the Honeymoon is aggressively baroque. A delirious 360° swish pan accompanies the killer's waltz with his prospective victim; it's both the equivalent of the dizziness produced by the whirling dance and a formal indication of a disordered fictive space. Extreme, fetishistic close-ups of children's toys caught in a mechanical frenzy are closer looks at real objects belonging to the killer - he's preserved the relics of his own childhood because of his obsession with the past. The distorted, fun-house imagery that accompanies the murders both reflects Harrington's disordered state of mind and is the literal reflection of the action in the warped blade of a meat cleaver. Though its supernatural aspect, involving the return from the grave of Harrington's understandably vindictive wife, takes *Hatchet for the Honeymoon* out of the realm of the *giallo* proper, it displays - still in an undeveloped form - many of the mannerisms incorporated into Argento's films, and there's no question but that it constitutes a clear influence on the development of his aesthetic. Bava's *Five Dolls for an August Moon* (1970) was, in his words, "a pathetic version of [Agatha Christie's] *Ten Little Indians*," and his last psychothriller, *Twitch of the Death Nerve* is another matter still. Called originally simply *L'Antefatto*, it was made after both *The Bird With the Crystal Plumage* and *The Cat O'Nine Tails*. Violent and convoluted (far more so on both counts than Argento's first two films), it begins with a wheelchair-bound old woman hanged by her husband (he's stabbed to death moments later by an unseen assailant) and ends with a ruthless couple shot-gunned to death by their children, who giggle "Gee, they're sure good at playing dead, aren't they?" before skipping off to play. In between, various grasping heirs, inquisitive neighbours, and young people with an unerring sense of the wrong place to be at the wrong time find themselves dispatched by miscellaneous brutal means: by axe, by spear, by garrotte, bye-bye. Though this kind of black comedy is antithetical to the dreamy and oh-so-serious viciousness of Argento, it prefigures the dominant trend in the American horror cinema of the late 1970s and '80s: the body-count picture. Retitled *Last House on the Left Part 2* by its American distributor when it was re-released in 1974 in an attempt to make it appear a sequel to Wes Craven's *Last House on the Left*, *Twitch of the Death Nerve*'s most influential descendant was *Friday the 13th*, directed by *Last House on the Left*'s producer, Sean S. Cunningham. In fact, both *Friday the 13th* and *Friday the 13th Part II* include among their rosters of amazing mayhem an effect which debuted in *Twitch*: squirming lovers impaled in a final embrace on a spear driven through both their bodies.

Argento and Bava worked together only once, at the end of the older director's career; the project was the last undertaken by Bava before his death of a heart attack at the age of sixty-six. Calling on his years of experience in creating cinematic illusions, Bava created a number of special effects sequences for Argento's *Inferno*, including the eclipses and the sequence in which Rose Elliot - exploring the damp basement of her apartment building - finds that what appears to be a puddle is actually the portal to a vast, submerged ballroom of the dead. Though his name doesn't appear on the finished print, Bava has been publicly credited by Argento for his work on the film. In addition, Argento has maintained a close professional relationship with Bava's son Lamberto. Lamberto Bava began his career as his father's assistant, and went on to direct several films of his own before becoming Argento's assistant on *Inferno*; he did the same on *Tenebrae* and *Creepers*, and in 1985 Argento produced Bava's *Demons*, a supernatural nightmare set in a rundown movie theatre whose patrons are besieged by the slavering legion of the undead.

Argento's debt to Bava is most apparent in *The Bird With the Crystal Plumage*, whose *mise en scène* - while far more sophisticated than that of the average low-budget thriller - only indicates the direction the director will take later in his career. Like *Blood and Black Lace* and *Hatchet for the Honeymoon*, the visual style of *The Bird With the Crystal Plumage* is conspicuously inconsistent. Scenes involving the police are tolerable at best, tending towards wooden exposition; they make a fine argument for Hitchcock's contention that the reason people in his movies don't go to the police for help is that the police are boring. Argento's solution to this problem has been in large part

Daria Nicolodi in Mario Bava's *Shock*.

to all but eliminate the police from his subsequent films, following Hitchcock's lead. But for all its flaws, *The Bird With the Crystal Plumage* is unusual enough to have suggested that its director was capable of bigger and better things. Even relatively unsympathetic contemporary viewers admitted the skill of certain elements, foremost among them the remarkable scene involving the double glass doors.

The power of this image transcends its function within the narrative: even as it haunts Sam Dalmas - bits of the scene literally displace the chronologically appropriate images whenever Dalmas thinks about the incident - it also haunts the viewer, lingering long after the details of the story have been forgotten. Its resonance isn't just a matter of pure visual beauty. Though *The Bird With the Crystal Plumage* was shot by Academy Award-winning cinematographer Vittorio Storaro, its budgetary constraints show and in recent years the circulating prints have faded substantially. Though not unattractive, the film couldn't stand alone on its appearance. You have to look instead to the subtle way in which the imagery of gallery sequence disorients the viewer, setting up one set of expectations and then subverting them in a manner both unsettling and memorable.

Like the movie viewer who sits in a darkened theatre and watches glowing two-dimensional images flicker before his eyes, Sam Dalmas walks along a nighttime street, enveloped in his own cloak of darkness. His attention is engaged first by the light, the light emanating from the art gallery whose glass-paned façade allows it to spill onto the street. Through the glass, framed by the metal strips that define the doors, Dalmas can see figures, flattened and remote. This moving image is tantalizingly incomplete; Dalmas crosses the street to get a better look. It seems that he is about to lose his status as surrogate voyeur - the logic of filmic space (the gallery is across the street, Dalmas is moving towards it) dictates that he is about to become part of whatever event is taking place within. But that's not what happens. Dalmas passes through the first set of glass doors and is trapped: he has been made doubly a spectator. The inner doors keep him separated from the woman

53

bleeding within the gallery while the outer doors set him apart from the action on the street, the action of which he was a part only seconds before. To the passerby Dalmas tries to hail for assistance, Dalmas is as remote an object as Monica Ranieri is to Dalmas - the man gestures that he can't hear Dalmas, then shuffles away, apparently deaf to Dalmas' pleas that he call the police. Though the police do arrive some moments later, it's as likely that they were called by Monica's husband (whom we will later learn had left the gallery only moments before) as by the passerby. And even after the police arrive and open the glass doors, Dalmas remains where he is; he ventures into the gallery only at Inspector Morrosini's behest, as Monica is about to be taken out on a stretcher - when there's no longer any scene of which Dalmas can be a part. But Argento still isn't through. Dalmas never gets into the action, but the action - the miasma of violence and insanity that produced the scene in the gallery - comes out to get him.

Like the grasping hand, the flesh-gun, and the slobbering monster that emerge from television sets in the far more explicit imagery of *Poltergeist* (1982, Tobe Hooper), *Videodrome* (1983, David Cronenberg) and the ludicrous *Terrorvision* (1986, Ted Nicolau) respectively, or the movie star who steps down from the screen in Woody Allen's 1985 *The Purple Rose of Cairo*, the meat cleaver that almost splits Dalmas' skull as he walks home is a spectre from the safe world of the insubstantial image that has taken on a disturbingly concrete aspect. This is far from the only reference in *The Bird With the Crystal Plumage* to the world of the two-dimensional image: Consaldi's paintings; the photographs shot, developed, and lovingly printed by the killer; the freeze-frames that halt Dalmas' obsessive memories of the attack and turn them into mental snapshots; the line-up of the usual suspects at the police station (even if its star, "Ursula Andress," belongs - as Morrosini points out with some irritation - with the transvestites, not the perverts); the frequent isolation of images in windows, doorways, and the odd-shaped frames formed by the surrounding architecture. The glass door scene is the most sophisticated working out of this reference, but it's far from unique.

Surprisingly enough, *The Bird With the Crystal Plumage* wasn't greeted with too much hostility when it hit American shores in the summer of 1970. *Variety*, in fact, was positively ecstatic in its own inimitable way. It dubbed Argento "a garlic-flavored Hitchcock"; the inevitable comparison spiced up, as it were, by a culinary adjective drawn from the then-current vogue for designating westerns spaghetti [Italian], sauerkraut [German] and so on. Its reviewer also praised the skill with which this "deftly executed thriller" was constructed. Most other writers were more reserved in their praise, turning in mixed reviews that all but apologized for the subject matter while admiring the quality of the execution. "Like almost everything else in the film, the title is wonderfully fancy and eighty percent irrelevant," commented the *New York Times'* Roger Greenspun. "But like almost everything else in the film, it reflects an elegant, enterprising, occasionally desperate sensibility much given to fabricating sequins out of *non-sequiturs.*" *The Christian Science Monitor's* David Sterritt allowed that "Mr. Argento's feel for the formal visual possibilities of his scenes takes a fair share of the curse off [the violence] of all but the one or two most gristly sequences. The emphasis is on decor, lighting and a quasi-abstract use of camera angles - almost never on the gruesome actualities of the admittedly seedy plot." Even such qualified approval wasn't universal. "Having trashed the Western movie genre," wrote dissenter Richard Cohen in *Women's Wear Daily*, "it is apparently time for Italian filmmakers to turn their knock-off talents to the crime melodrama done in the fashion of Alfred Hitchcock... Argento gets in a lot of the little touches but, like the Italian makers of Westerns, he gets them all cockeyed." What makes this statement interesting is that for all its narrow-mindedness (its Hollywood-centricity, grounded in the notion that there's one right way to make movies, and that's the way we make them in America), it contains a perceptive linkage: that of the *giallo* and the Italian Western, for the two forms bear much the same relationship to their American counterparts.

In this context, one is of course assuming that it's fair to speak of "the crime melodrama done in the fashion of Alfred

Hitchcock" as an American construct. On the surface that may seem a dangerous assumption, since Hitchcock is not only British by birth, but spent the first 20 years of his career working within the film industry of his native country. But with a handful of exceptions - *Blackmail* (1929), *The Man Who Knew Too Much* (1934), *The Thirty-Nine Steps* (1935), *Sabotage* (1936) and *The Lady Vanishes* (1938), all best known to film students and serious movie buffs - these are not the films that come to mind when one invokes "Hitchcock." Most people are thinking of *Shadow of a Doubt* (1943), *Spellbound* (1945), *Notorious* (1946), *Strangers on a Train* (1951), *Rear Window* (1954), *The Man Who Knew Too Much* (1956), *Vertigo* (1958), *North By Northwest* (1959), *Psycho* (1960) and *The Birds* (1963)... Hitchcock's American films. American in that they were produced by major American studios (Universal, RKO, Warner Brothers, 20th-Century Fox, Paramount, M.G.M. *et al.*) and that their iconography was that of 'America' - American small towns, American cities, American tourists lost abroad in the maelstrom of decadent European and Third World cultures, American Freudianism of the 1950s: yes, the examples are simplistic and liable to exception, but the broad cultural outlines are there. That the Western is the quintessential American form is a notion liable only to revisionist debate, a debate made conceivable only by the far-reaching cultural power of the American version of the material. There may well have been films about cowboys and settlers made in countries other than the United States that date back to the earliest years of the motion picture industry, and the European Westerns of the '60s have had their own profound impact on the history of the cinema. But the iconography of the Western is that of the civilization of the 19th-Century American western frontier by way of the dime novel and the Wild West Show that made legend out of history even as the events unfolded.

In his study *Spaghetti Westerns*, Christopher Frayling refers to the ongoing redefinition of "the dominant 'codes' of Hollywood... and questioning [of] the values which these 'codes' had traditionally been held to represent." The point, of course, is that Italian Westerns signify precisely because of their rela-

Reggie Nalder, that face that launched a thousand gasps, in *The Bird with the Crystal Plumage*.

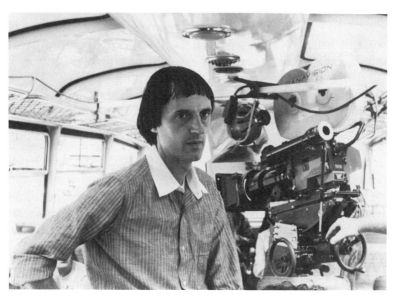

Argento on the set of *Creepers*.

tionship to American Westerns, and the same is true of the *giallo* and the Hitchcockian thriller. Frayling also points out that this redefining process, which reached its apotheosis in Sergio Leone's *Dollars* trilogy - *A Fistful of Dollars* (1966), *For a Few Dollars More* (1967) and *The Good, The Bad and the Ugly* (1969) - is also evident in the work of many other filmmakers working within the genre, both pre- and post-Leone. Their work may be less consistent and the reworking less structurally complex, but the very fact of working with a genre defined in relation to another makes revisionism an inevitable part of the mix.

In the same way, Argento's *gialli* aren't unique just because they exist in a dialectical relationship to other thrillers, but because the relationship is a continuing and informed one. Many thrillers have been produced by the Italian film industry under the guidance of many directors; they run the gamut from conventional and/or badly made to intermittently interesting (Bava is an obvious example) to simply extraordinary. But like Leone's, Argento's work consistently stands out.

In light of the obvious similarity between the way the Western and the Hitchcockian thriller were transformed by Italian filmmakers, Argento's background as a critic (he has described writing about film as "studying film - like a University") becomes clearly significant. More significant still was his first job in movies. With Bernardo Bertolucci - his contemporary, already noted as the director of *Before the Revolution* - he was commissioned to write a story outline for Leone, the outline for what was to be Leone's ultimate statement about the Western: *Once Upon a Time in the West.*

"On the first day *The Good, The Bad and the Ugly* was shown in Italy," Bertolucci relates, "I met Leone - in the projection booth. The next day he called me to write a movie. I wrote a huge treatment, about 300 pages , full of quotes from all the Westerns I love. Some of the quotes even Leone did not recognize." Slightly more careful to stress the collaborative nature of the project (the completed credits attribute the screenplay to Leone and Sergio Donati and the story to Bertolucci, Leone and Argento, in that order), Argento elaborates:

"We worked with Sergio Leone for six months on this picture. Before writing we saw all the famous Westerns we could, to remind ourselves. I remember we saw *Johnny Guitar* three times, and John Ford's *The Searchers*. For one month, from morning until night, we watched these pictures in the screening room; sometimes Leone stopped by and said, 'Just watch - don't sleep!'." The result, a positive compendium of classic Western images and themes, was indeed Leone's last Western, and it was grandiose, endlessly allusive and even definitive; this was, after all, the Italian Western containing footage shot in Monument Valley - John Ford country - whose weird geographical features were until then the true sign of the real thing, the American Western.

With this experience behind him, Argento began working fairly regularly as a collaborator on screenplays in a variety of genres. With the Western and the war film holding sway as the Italian cinema's best sellers in the late '60s and early '70s, much of Argento's work was in those areas. They include *Scusi lei e'fa vorevole o contrario?* (1966, Alberto Sorvi), *Today It's Me, Tomorrow It's You* (1968, Tonino Cervi), *Commandos* (1968, Armando Crispino), *Les héros ne meurent jamais* (1968, Maurizio Lucidi), *La Légion des damnés/Battle of the Commandos* (1969, Umberto Lenzi) and *Five Man Army* (1970, Don Taylor). He dabbled in other subject matter as well, witness *L'Enfer avant la mort* (1968, Alfio Caltabiano), *Le stagione dei sensi* (1968, Massimo Franciosa), *Sexual Revolution* (Riccardo Ghione) and *Metti, una sera a cena/Disons un soir a dîner/One Night at Dinner/The Love Circle* (1969, Giuseppe Patroni Griffi), whose relatively large budget and well known international cast - including American Tony Musante, French Annie Girardot and Spanish Florinda Bolkan - constituted a professional step up from his previous credits. But for the screenplay for the film he intended to direct, Argento gravitated towards the thriller.

Argento has often expressed his admiration for the standard icons of the mystery genre. In particular, he admires Sir Arthur Conan Doyle's Sherlock Holmes stories, singling out *The Hound of the Baskervilles*, with its eerie supernatural overtones (dispelled in the end, of course, by the cold light of Holmes' reason), and the notorious *Final Problem*, which introduces arch-fiend Professor Moriarty in terms of such lofty and pervasive evil that it's hard to avoid reading Holmes' remarks in terms of some paranoid fantasy. Indeed, Nicholas Meyer did just that, and most convincingly, in *The Seven Percent Solution*, blaming it all on the great detective's cocaine addiction. Argento also cites Dashiell Hammett and Cornell Woolrich, black princes of the *Série Noire* and pioneers of hardboiled prose, along with French writers Pierre Boileau and Thomas Narcejac. Little-known in the States, their complex thrillers betray a debt to the dark world of American pulp novels. Several have been adapted for the screen, including *The Woman Who Was No More*, which became Henri-Georges Clouzot's *Diabolique*, and *The Living and the Dead*, which Hitchcock made into *Vertigo*. The thematic constants linking these works are apparent: urban paranoia, cynical nihilism, and the uneasy conviction that there's something very wrong at the core of the world, something of which any given act of violence or perversity is just the tip of the iceberg.

In a distillation of the rational methodology of detection, Sherlock Holmes reworks Occam's razor for the faithful Watson, baffled (as ever) by the apparently impenetrable surface of some bizarre event. "When you have eliminated the impossible," Holmes purrs patiently (in *The Sign of the Four*), "whatever remains, however improbable, must be the truth." This is the essence of the code of the classical mystery, both in literature and film, but it is diametrically opposed to the assumptions underlying Argento's work, hence the irony with which it's cited not once, but twice in *Tenebrae*. A more apposite model of detection may be found in Robert Aldrich's film of Mickey Spillane's *Kiss Me, Deadly* (Spillane is, significantly, also invoked in *Tenebrae*). "You find a little thread," coos Aldrich's Velda to a singularly stupid and unimaginative Mike Hammer, "and it leads to a string. You follow the string till you find a rope, and from the rope you hang by the neck until..." Until indeed... what following the thread, the string and the rope doesn't do is lead to a solution, a way of righting the wrong that has disrupted the flow of an otherwise orderly universe, because no such solution is possible. This is the network of ideas informing Argento's films, and the ferocity with which it's worked into each of his *gialli* is awesome.

Argento scored a hit his first time out. *The Bird With the Crystal Plumage* drew audiences and suggested - at least to some critics - that he was a talent to watch; the stage was set for him to move on to bigger and better things. And while to the mainstream mentality "bigger and better things" implies escape from the genre ghetto, Argento was happy to go on to bigger and better thrillers.

THE CAT O' NINE TAILS and
FOUR FLIES ON GREY VELVET

"That's right, smile. Smile. A man is dead."
- Righetto, the photographer (*The Cat O'Nine Tails*)

"I want so badly to see you die slowly. Painfully."
- Nina Tobias (*Four Flies on Grey Velvet*)

The worldwide success of *The Bird With the Crystal Plumage* simplified the financing of Argento's second film, whose title - *The Cat O'Nine Tails* - may well be the most irrelevant he ever concocted, though *Four Flies on Grey Velvet* provides stiff competition. The picture that was "nine times more suspenseful" than *The Bird With the Crystal Plumage* - or so claimed the copywriters who conceived the American advertising campaign - was set against a backdrop of genetic research and industrial espionage, but its underlying thematic concerns are very much in line with those of its predecessor: the almost limitless potential for corruption within the human soul. Formally, both *Cat* and *Four Flies* represent substantial advances over *The Bird With the Crystal Plumage*: they elaborate on its structural experiments and bring them to the forefront.

Cat opens as Franco Arno (Karl Malden), a blind former newspaperman who now creates crossword puzzles, walks along the deserted street in front of the Terzi Institute with his little niece, Lori. His attention caught by the word "blackmail," spoken by a man in a parked car, Arno directs Lori to take a look while he pretends to fumble with his shoelace.

The following day Arno learns from a sleek, impatient reporter - Carlo Giordani (James Franciscus) - that someone tried to burgle the Institute the night before. Within hours, Doctor Calabresi - one of the two men in the car, the speaker whom Lori saw - is pushed to his death in front of a train. Arno and Giordani pool their talents and apply them to uncovering the

FROM THE MASTERS OF TENSION WHO GAVE YOU "THE BIRD WITH THE CRYSTAL PLUMAGE" —THE PICTURE THAT OUT-PSYCHOED 'PSYCHO'!

"Cat O'Nine Tails"

It's nine times more suspenseful!

NATIONAL GENERAL PICTURES PRESENTS
A FILM WRITTEN AND DIRECTED BY DARIO ARGENTO
STARRING **JAMES FRANCISCUS · KARL MALDEN**
AND **CATHERINE SPAAK**
"CAT O'NINE TAILS" · Produced by Salvatore Argento For Seda
Technicolor® Techniscope® A National General Pictures Release

American ad slick for *The Cat O'Nine Tails.*

64

mystery that surrounds the Terzi Institute. They focus their attentions on several individuals, including Doctors Braun and Casoni (respectively a high-living homosexual engaged in industrial espionage and a brilliant but possibly unstable *wunderkind* who left his last position under a cloud); Anna Terzi (Catherine Spaak), adopted daughter of the Institute's founder; and Bianca Merusi, Doctor Calabresi's fianceé and Braun's partner in crime.

They also look into the activities of the Institute itself, and learn its two current projects are the development of a drug related to genetic illness and a study of the implications of the XYY chromosome configuration. Casoni explains that individuals with this configuration appear predisposed to criminal behaviour. Their inquiries prompt the killer to murder again and again; before they unmask him as Doctor Casoni - who learned he had the unfortunate genetic pattern, broke into the Institute in order to alter his records and conceal the fact, then killed ruthlessly to cover his tracks - Giordani and Arno have both survived attempts on their lives, Lori has been kidnapped, and many secret sins and crimes have been brought blinking into the daylight.

The Cat O'Nine Tails is even more relentlessly convoluted than *The Bird With the Crystal Plumage*, and this summary doesn't begin to cover the twists and turns of the plot. Bianca Merusi discovers the motive for her fiancé's murder and is willing to tell Arno what she has learned, but is murdered before she can do so; Giordani and Arno violate her grave in order to recover a locket - in which they rightly suspect she hid some vital evidence before she died - but are forced to turn it over to the killer when he reveals that he has kidnapped Lori. The Terzi Institute's drug project is part of a subplot involving Bianca and Braun (who are selling information about it to a pharmaceutical company), and Braun is betrayed by a man who hopes that Braun's imprisonment will cause his lover - whom Braun seduced - to abandon him; if this doesn't happen, the informant tells Giordani, he will kill himself. Anna and Giordani become lovers, and when she's slow to drink a glass of milk that proves to have been poisoned by the killer in an attempt to silence Giordani, he suspects she may be the maniac he seeks... these and many other incidents complicate the narrative.

Argento's original screenplay, from a story by Argento, Luigi Collo and Dardano Sacchetti, gives an overall impression of derivativeness even though it's in no way indebted to a single work - or specific combination of works - in the way *The Bird With the Crystal Plumage* is indebted to Brown's *Screaming Mimi*.

Luigi Co⌐ ⌐ mentions two direct influences, saying that "the concept ⌐ the double 'Y' chromosome came from a British thrille⌐ called *Twisted Nerve*. Another idea was borrowed from an ⌐d Siodmak thriller, *The Spiral Staircase*." The *Twisted Nerve* connection is tenuous at best; the 1969 film does indeed explain schizophrenic behaviour by way of the notion of chromosomal imbalance, but that notion can hardly have been said to have originated with the Boulting brothers (John produced, Roy directed and co-wrote the screenplay with Leo Marks, who also wrote Michael Powell's *Peeping Tom*); and anyway, *Twisted Nerve*'s lunatic protagonist has nothing in common with Dr. Casoni. In fact, *The Cat O'Nine Tails* makes a fairly sophisticated use of this at best dubious scientific notion; rather than blaming Casoni's mania on his genes (as *Twisted Nerve* does), it suggests he's driven himself to acts of insane violence by brooding about the matter. This is the difference between being possessed by the devil and being driven to hysterical fit by *fear* of demonic possession, and the difference isn't inconsequential.

Cat's debt to *The Spiral Staircase* is even less significant: Siodmak's film concerns a psychotic killer who preys on the handicapped, and revolves around a mute girl slated to be his next victim. Arno is handicapped - blind - but it's not his disability that makes him Casoni's target. If anything it's his abnormal *ability* that singles him out. It's Arno who first deduces that Calabresi's death by speeding train might not have been an accident; he goads Giordani into finding out whether the newspaper photograph of the event is a blow-up from a larger picture. His reasoning is that if it's been cropped there might be something interesting in the remainder of the frame - and there is. Giordani may be able to see *physically*, but he's blind to the possibilities suggested by Arno, whose only access to the world of images is through the eyes of little Lori. It's Arno who likes to solve puzzles ("You must have been one hell of a newspaperman," comments Giordani, with some understatement) and it's Arno who picks up the trail that leads to the solution. It's even Arno who overpowers Casoni on the roof of the Terzi Institute and pushes him to his death in an elevator shaft after the athletic Giordani has been stabbed, beaten, and left for dead elsewhere on the premises. Franco Arno is no conventional cinematic cripple, existing solely to be terrorized like Audrey Hepburn in *Wait Until Dark*. Superficially, he's handicapped because the plot demands it, but his *blindness* is part of the subtext of *The Cat O'Nine Tails*, a film constructed on a framework of allusions to seeing and sightlessness that will be enumerated later. By extension, *The Cat O'Nine Tails* - like all of Argento's films - is about the impossibility of seeing (or knowing, since "see" is widely used to signify understanding or knowledge) anything in a world in which all perception is by its nature fragmentary or distorted. This is, of course, a notion clearly present in *The Bird With the Crystal Plumage*. But unlike *Bird*, *Cat* didn't perform well at the American box office, despite the truly thrilling viciousness with which it unfolds.

It's been argued that this was due in large part to the cavalierness with which Argento discharged the film's narrative; Riccardo Menello, for example, claims (in an otherwise laudatory article in *Photon* No.25) that the "reason that *The Cat O'Nine Tails* is so weak in many places is that Argento is still struggling [presumably unsuccessfully] with things like plausibility... and character development. In *The Bird With the Crystal Plumage*, story and script dictate the film's visual style, while in *The Cat O'Nine Tails* story and screenplay are in conflict with technique and it's often those scenes least tied to the plot that succeed most." Even leaving aside the dubious contention that in *Bird* visual style is wholly subsidiary in importance to the matter of getting the story told, this statement isn't compelling. *The Cat O'Nine Tails* is confusing,

Puzzles within puzzles: blind Franco Arno (Karl Malden) at work. *The Cat O'Nine Tails*.

Franco Arno (Karl Malden) turns the tables on the XYY chromosome killer (Aldo Reggiani) in *The Cat O'Nine Tails*.

implausible, weak in one principal respect: it's not linear. And that's a weakness only if narrative linearity is its goal. But *The Cat O'Nine Tails* is conceived - to use the metaphor supplied by Arno's profession - as a crossword puzzle in which catching onto the tricks concealed within the clues is as important as finding the solution. To continue the analogy, *The Cat O'Nine Tails* is a cryptic, a puzzle whose clues are based on puns, anagrams, rebuses, complex word associations and double entendres: "WORL" = "World Without End," rather than dictionary-style definitions "Servant" = "Esne," of which the most obscure are still straightforward. Unlike the thriller that's spoiled if the ending is revealed prematurely, *The Cat O'Nine Tails* is infinitely more fun to watch once one knows Casoni is the killer.

"*The Cat O'Nine Tails*, written and directed by Dario Argento, is a sleazily sick and senseless murder mystery designed chiefly to provide close-ups of the death throes of several people who are garrotted... This vomitous offering comes from the Italian writer/ director who made his debut with *The Bird With the Crystal Plumage*, an equally badly dubbed flashy-stylish murder mystery that had some popularity last summer among famished thriller nuts, ready to settle for cheap," ranted Judith Crist in *New York* magazine (June 7, 1971) with breathless indignation, and she wasn't alone. While even unsympathetic reviewers noticed the stylishness of *The Bird With the Crystal Plumage* (several revised their relatively high opinions of *Bird* in the light of *Cat*, though the reviewer quoted above never much cared for it, either), *The Cat O'Nine Tails*' notices were grotesquely plot-heavy, rife with gasping enumerations of the quality and quantity of its repellent elements, among them homosexuality, incest, grave-robbing, child-torture, blackmail, adultery, and murder, murder, murder.

The Cat O'Nine Tails opens with a tracking shot of the roof of the Terzi Institute; the camera glides through the darkness past strange shadowy forms as an Ennio Morricone lullaby croons softly and the credits are superimposed over various parts of the screen. The shot is unsettling when it's deceptive ("Where am I supposed to be?" asks the viewer drawn into identification with the camera-I point-of-view), and equally unsettling when it chooses to inform. The pan ends on the edge of the roof of a high building; it peers down at the pavement below. "What the hell am I doing up here?" the hapless viewer may well wonder. Only after seeing the entire film is one likely to realize that the shot had to do with the burglary at the Institute, and even then it's troubling, for the actual crime takes place chronologically after the scene that follows the credits sequence.

This temporal displacement works hand-in-hand with the fact that the shot immediately following the final credit is nothing less than a visual taunt: it's a close-up of the white tip of Arno's cane tapping against the kerb, followed by a long shot of Arno as little Lori guides him along the pavement. Arno's obvious blindness mirrors that of the audience, tantalized by the strange shot as he is tantalized by the sentence fragment that he hears from the parked car he and Lori pass. "...I have no choice; I'm not interested in blackmailing you. I have to pass on the information." The alert viewer may catch a glimpse of one man's face as the camera glides by; his companion, the person being addressed, is shrouded in shadow. Since it's the hidden person who has something to conceal - about whom there is some information that must be passed on (presumably for the greater good) and which could provide the basis for blackmail - it's his/her face one wants to see. It's only natural that this is precisely what is scrupulously concealed.

Arno and Lori return home; she's put to bed and he sets to work constructing a crossword puzzle. His method is ingenious: he works on a metal grid that holds blocks, onto which raised letters are printed. Arno removes his glasses and gazes sight-lessly into space as he manipulates the cubes. A sound startles him and the image is momentarily replaced by another: a close-up of a man lying face down on the ground. This shot is seriously puzzling, since Arno is blind - otherwise it would be read automatically as a flashback to something of which he has been reminded by the unidentified sound.

Over a series of alternating shots of Arno and the man on the pavement, Argento reveals an action taking place in simulta-neous time (and contiguous space - the Terzi Institute is

The XYY chromosome killer (Aldo Reggiani) keeps his appointment with destiny.

The XYY chromosome killer (Aldo Reggiani) runs true to type in *The Cat O'Nine Tails*, and Carlo Giordani (James Franciscus) pays the price of curiosity.

directly behind Arno's apartment and from his window one - if not Arno - can see that there's a disturbance there): a robbery in progress. The man on the pavement is the night watchman; the point-of-view in the shot that of the thief who has knocked him out with a blow to the head. The "flashback" is in fact a view that's the product of some kind of second sight; a sight that emanates from some strange space to which normal individuals have no access. The alternating shots don't lend themselves to explanation as some gratuitous structural device, for Arno is clearly reacting to something at the same time that the action unfolds in the intruding shots. He sees them, perhaps, in his mind's eye - but they're incomplete, inconclusive, as the images surely would not be if Arno were imagining them, making them up out of whole cloth. It's left for Giordani the next day (who initially bumps into Arno and berates him for not looking where he's going) to tell Arno what has gone on at the Institute. The viewer, meanwhile, has seen the crime committed in some detail: the entry through a window, the stealthy passage through the darkened corridors, the picking of the lock and so on, in an extended subjective sequence. What has not been seen - concealed in the blind spot of the camera-as-thief point-of-view (which is to say, what happens behind the lens) is the thief's face, as well as the object that has been stolen. The *how* of the crime has been explored at length, while the *why* and *by whom* remain tantalizingly obscure.

This back-and-forth game provides *The Cat O'Nine Tails* with the visual expression of its overall thematic motif: it's no wonder Casoni is represented by the vast iris of his eye. Righetto the photographer at one point speaks directly into the lens of the camera; so does Lori when she is lured from the friends' home where Arno has sent her for safekeeping. To whom do they speak? The shot of Righetto talking is matched by one of Giordani; the restoration of internal cohesiveness is effected, though there's a lingering distance created by the unusual device of address to the camera. The shot of Lori, by contrast, has no such follow-up. This is, it's true, a tactic whose specific purpose is to prevent the viewer from learning prematurely who the killer is; but it's also a disjunctive strategy reinforcing the notion that the process of seeing is fraught with difficulty. In this respect the conclusion of *The Cat O'Nine Tails* is particularly striking. Cornered by Giordani, Arno and the police in the Terzi Institute, where he has hidden the kidnapped Lori in a concealed recess, Casoni goes truly mad; he's overcome by a blood lust no longer channelled by the need to hide the proof of his genetic imbalance or the murders he's committed. He beats Giordani bloody and prepares to slit the child's throat; Giordani thwarts the action by hurling himself into the blade's path. When the three are last seen, Lori - bound and gagged - is cowering in a corner, Casoni is staggering to his feet, and Giordani - Casoni's knife buried in his flesh - is unconscious or perhaps even dead. In the next scene Arno, armed with a sword cane, confronts the wounded Casoni on the roof. "Where's Lori?" he demands, prodding Casoni with the deadly tip. "Dead. I killed her," Casoni sneers in reply. After Casoni plunges through a skylight to his death in the elevator shaft below, Lori's voice is heard calling her uncle's name as the credits begin to roll. Is she really alive, or is this a memory, wishful hearing? We never see Lori alive and well, nor do we see Giordani. He may well be dead; there's no way of ever knowing. There was no shot of Casoni killing her, but he could have done so between one shot and the next; he claims to have done so. On the other hand, there's no reason to assume that Casoni is not a vicious liar as well as a killer. The sound of Lori's voice provides no conclusive evidence either way; it could be the voice of a living child (and Arno, of course, has never seen Lori - for him her voice is his perception of her), and equally could be an echo of the past - an aural memory of a dead little girl. The viewer is left with only the image of the narrow sides of the elevator shaft. All in all, it's an ending whose inconclusiveness is both breathtaking and sadistic. In another kind of thriller this ambiguity would constitute a flaw, a failure to pay off; in *The Cat O'Nine Tails* it's the logical extension of the film's consistent refusal to admit the possibility that there are any satisfactory solutions to any mysteries.

In this respect there is a certain metaphysical logic to the picture's curious title. Giordani, blinded by his conviction that there is a logical explanation for the problem at hand and that he (contrary to the film's internal evidence) is the man who could find it, jots down all the leads in the Terzi Institute case. They number nine, like a "cat with nine tails," he observes (a weird simile that makes no sense at all; where did he study journalism?). "A cat o'nine tails - like the old naval whip," Arno responds, and his view of the matter is overall the more correct one. Giordani thinks the clues - or at least one of the clues - will lead him to an answer; Arno knows that all together they constitute little more than an opportunity for self-torture.

Four Flies on Grey Velvet concludes the "animal trilogy" (an allusion to titles alone) comprised by Argento's first three films. Like the preceding two, its name is a fanciful, eye-catching construct that is only scarcely connected to the film itself; like the bird with the crystal plumage, and the metaphorical cat, the four flies are a clue of sorts. Also in common with the films that precede it, the protagonist of *Four Flies on Grey Velvet* finds himself sucked into a world of darkness and insanity by what appears to be the sheerest accident. But there's an important difference: *Four Flies'* Roberto Tobias stands apart from *Bird*'s Sam Dalmas and *Cat*'s Giordani and Arno because his involvement isn't accidental. And while Dalmas, Arno, and Giordani are excited by the aura of madness that surrounds the murderers they hunt, and their actions may well spur those killers on to further acts of violence, they *aren't* murderers themselves. Even Arno can't be held fully responsible for Casoni's death - it's his push that sends Casoni crashing through the skylight, but Arno can hardly have been expected to know the skylight was there - he's a blind man on a strange roof.

Roberto Tobias kills a man; at least he thinks he does and never learns otherwise, which amounts to pretty much the same thing. He's a transitional protagonist who bridges the gap between the relative innocents - Dalmas, Arno, Giordani - and the relatively guilty - *Deep Red*'s Marc Daly and, most spectacularly, *Tenebrae*'s Peter Neal.

After rehearsing with his band, Roberto Tobias (Michael Brandon) leaves the studio and sees a man, a stranger who has

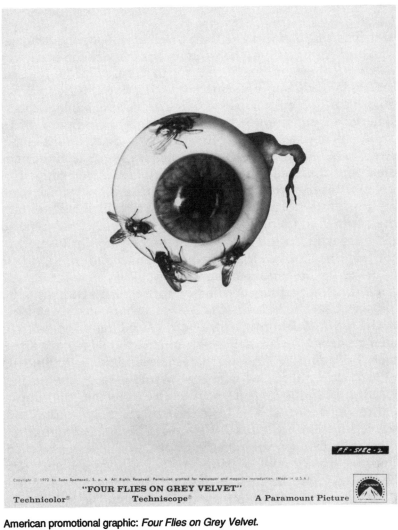

"FOUR FLIES ON GREY VELVET"

Technicolor®   Techniscope®   A Paramount Picture

American promotional graphic: *Four Flies on Grey Velvet.*

been following him for some weeks. Roberto follows the stranger, who leads him through the winding streets of Rome until they reach an apparently deserted theatre; once inside, Roberto confronts the stranger and in the ensuing struggle the stranger falls to the ground, stabbed with his own switchblade. Roberto is horrified, and there's worse to come: a masked figure with a camera is in one of the balconies taking pictures of the entire scene. Confused and frightened, Roberto flees. It soon becomes apparent that the masked photographer is determined to torture Roberto, though he cannot figure out why; the dead man's identity card is sent to him in the mail, photographs of the scene turn up hidden among his belongings, the masked man breaks into his house at night and makes vague but chilling threats in a strained whisper.

Desperate, Roberto confides in his wealthy, high-strung wife Nina (Mimsy Farmer) and his eccentric friend Godfrey (Bud Spencer/Carlo Pedersoli), who lives in a shack on the outskirts of the city and eats raw fish. Godfrey (God, for short) advises hiring a detective; Nina suggests Roberto should see a psychiatrist. The detective, Arrosio (Jean-Pierre Marielle) stumbles on a lead but is murdered before he can tell Roberto what he's learned. The Tobias' maid - who has also unearthed the puppet-figure's identity and tries to use the information for blackmail - meets the same fate. Also slain is the stranger from the theatre, whose *apparent* death at Roberto's hands was staged. He tries to extort more money from his partner, the photographer, and is beaten to death for his audacity. Afraid for her safety, Roberto sends Nina away. Her cousin Dalia (Francine Racette) - with whom Roberto has a brief affair - is murdered shortly after. Using a special camera, the medical examiner takes a picture of the last image retained on Dalia's retina. It's something of a puzzle: four flies arranged in an arc.

Roberto buys a gun and awaits his tormentor in his darkened house, but the first person to arrive is Nina. Roberto is worried about her until he notices the pendant swinging around her neck. It's a lucite disk containing a fly.[1] Before Roberto can

[1]For the record, according to Cozzi the fly was originally to have been

collect himself, she has his gun. Nina is insane, driven mad by a sadistic father who had her committed to an insane asylum for no better reason than that he would rather his only child have been a boy. Unable to avenge herself on her father, who died while she was still incarcerated, Nina married a man who was the image of her father - Roberto - and took out her maniacal hatred on him instead. Only Godfrey's fortuitous arrival saves Roberto from certain death, and the fleeing Nina dies when she drives her car into the back of a truck.

"A murder story that runs off in all directions applying the whammy to a young man who is pushed into a series of murders by someone who is trying to drive him nuts by anxiety or shock. Or something," summarized reviewer Wanda Hale in New York's *Daily News*, leaving *Women's Wear Daily's* Howard Kissell to comment that "Dario Argento, who wrote and directed *Four Flies on Grey Velvet*, shows absolutely no evidence of storytelling ability, cinematic imagination or gifts for character delineation," by way of dismissing the film completely.

Coming off the worldwide financial success of *The Bird With the Crystal Plumage* and the European success of *The Cat O'Nine Tails* (which was released in the United States by National-General Pictures, an exploitation house on whom the film's poor US showing could be blamed in a pinch), Argento found a major American distributor for *Four Flies on Grey Velvet*: Paramount Pictures undertook its worldwide distribution. As is always the case in such arrangements, with the Studio's involvement came certain problems, including Paramount's demands regarding principal casting, which had to be acceptable to them in terms of the American marketplace.

---

a crucifix; the swinging cross looked like a gate on the eye-machine's image, and poor Roberto wasted a lot of time looking at fences. Cozzi also claims that the idea for the camera that photographs the last image on the dead woman's eye came from a newspaper account. Though the superstitious notion that dead man's eyes can convict a murderer was popular during the 19th century and survived into the early 20th (leading some Depression-era gangsters to shoot out their victims' eyes), it's weird science of the most egregious kind.

Luigi Cozzi's account of the tribulations involved in filling the central role of Roberto Tobias is both amusing and provocative; the range of actors considered and/or approached to undertake the role is so wide that one is hard put to imagine its parameters:

> In the beginning it was to be Tony Musante, star of *The Bird With the Crystal Plumage*. But he wanted an extremely high price to do the picture. Dario tried next for Terence Stamp, who agreed providing some changes were made in the character. When Dario refused these alterations, Stamp bowed out and Tom Courtenay was approached. Paramount vetoed this choice and offered to sign either John Lennon or Ringo Starr, neither of whom Dario believed would be good for the role. Jean-Louis Trintignant was asked but had to refuse due to other commitments. Paramount suggested James Taylor, the American pop-singer, whom Dario almost signed, then changed his mind when *Two Lane Blacktop* proved to be a box office flop. Michael York was then signed for the role but, a few days before shooting was to begin, York cabled that production on his *Zeppelin* had been delayed and he could not come as scheduled.
>
> Argento could not wait and was forced to seek a substitute. Then he remembered Michael Brandon, a young actor he had seen in *Lovers and Other Strangers*. People had commented that Brandon and Dario looked somewhat alike and, indeed, he was ultimately signed for the role although nobody (including Dario) was ecstatic about the choice.

What's the phrase... consider the possibilities? A group of more dissimilar performers can hardly be imagined. You can see some of the logic, especially in suggesting real pop musicians for the role of rock drummer Roberto. But Beatles John Lennon and Ringo Starr? Mellow James Taylor? French Jean-Louis Trintignant, of Bernardo Bertolucci's *The Conformist* would have come with some interesting art cinema baggage, as would British Terence Stamp, whose sexual ambiguity in Pier Paolo Pasolini's *Teorema* would have been particularly *apropos*. And as to Tom Courtenay, best known as the timid, daydreaming protagonist of John Schlesinger's *Billy Liar*, odds

Spatial disorientation in *Four Flies on Grey Velvet*.

The sadistic, androgynous puppet character of *Four Flies on Grey Velvet*.

are he could have done some interesting things with Roberto's horror at having his real world taken over by an unfathomable nightmare. But with pallid, twitchy Mimsy Farmer already cast as Nina, it's hard to believe that no one was happy with Brandon. The physical similarity of Farmer and Brandon - both built along conspicuously slender, small-framed lines - initiates the incest subtext that culminates in the revelation that Nina married Roberto because he looks exactly like her father. This resemblance, by the way, must be taken as genuine (as it would not have to be if the only evidence of its existence were Nina's remark through clenched teeth: "You... you were so like him."): the attention of Arrosio, the detective, is immediately caught by the "striking resemblance" when he examines Nina's family photograph album.

It's also interesting that Brandon does indeed resemble Argento quite a bit, particularly in light of the fact that *Four Flies* was the first of his films in which (according to Cozzi) Argento didn't himself appear anonymously as the black-clad killer; with Brandon standing in for him on screen it appears he was content to turn over the job to Cozzi, who lurked behind the puppet-man's smiling mask.

Many writers have observed that Argento's work is, for that of a horror filmmaker, remarkably free of religious underpinnings. It doesn't abound in things men aren't meant to know and the spectre of eternal justice setting right the scales in the end - the vampire vanquished, the monster/mutant/madman consigned (or returned) to his grave - either through the inspired actions of the human community or some serendipitous natural agent, is conspicuous by its absence. The chaos that disrupts the lives of Argento's protagonists reigns supreme, even if its specific eruptions are quelled - Dalmas and Arno escape physical harm but are irrevocably touched by madness, Giordani only barely (if at all) survives the physical onslaught as well. In this respect (as Canadian writer David Soren has observed in *Photon*) *Four Flies on Grey Velvet* is something of an aberration among Argento's films. If not in any conventional sense, *Four Flies* has a distinctly Christian subtext that finds its protagonist suspended between heaven and hell. Nowhere is this more evident than in the character of God.

"God was a tallish, scrawny old man with a short but tangled beard, stained with nicotine," wrote Brown in *The Screaming Mimi*. "His full name was Godfrey... he was a little cracked, but not much." Argento eliminated the character from *The Bird With the Crystal Plumage*, but he was too good to let go forever, so Argento moved him in to the outskirts of the metallic jungle that is the home of Roberto and Nina Tobias. Though the physical description is no match for beefy Carlo Pedersoli (veteran of many spaghetti Westerns and a very popular Italian character actor, appearing under his *nom d'écran*, "Bud Spencer"), the underlying conception is the same. When *Screaming Mimi's* Bill Sweeney wants "to commune with God" he takes a taxi to Bughouse Square where all the bums sleep on warm nights; God there counsels him that "a guy can get anything he wants, if he wants it badly enough," if he concentrates "all [his] efforts, direct and indirect, to that one object." It's an interesting message, advice from the god of the American work ethic, a message that implies a fundamental fairness in this world and the next - as you sow, so shall you reap. Roberto Tobias must take his troubles to a god of disgusted resignation in the face of chaos (who is nonetheless heralded on the soundtrack with a burst of Handelian - by way of Morricone - rejoicing and remarks that if he must be called "God," he would like to be called "God Almighty") who has little to offer in the way of positive thinking. He sends to Roberto a guardian angel - the dishevelled professor, with his extensive supply of biblical wisdom - who is to look out for "anything strange, like blackmailers, murderers or the like." But when he spots them all he's supposed to do is tell his decidedly un-omniscient lord. God chooses to associate himself with the iconography of death - death in its grossest, most unenlightening form - when he arranges a meeting with Roberto at the showroom of the Fifth International Exposition of Funerary Arts, whose displays include a musical coffin, a heart-shaped coffin with red crushed-velvet interior, a gold *faux*-Egyptian sarcophagus, and an Art Deco coffin with folding door flaps. "Death," he sniffs, "is a commercial necessity," a far cry from the notion of physical

Roberto Tobias (Michael Brandon) realizes he has killed a man he doesn't even know.

Pervasive violence in the paranoid world of *Four Flies on Grey Velvet*: Roberto Tobias (Michael Brandon) attacks the mailman.

death as the moment of liberation of the soul. It's the way in which "worms make a living." And, as Soren rightly points out, God "becomes... the heroic divinity of an Aeschylean tragedy, arriving as a *deus ex machina* to save Roberto's life" when his appearance distracts the hysterical Nina.

It's in this scene that the undercurrent of violent hysteria that informs *Four Flies on Grey Velvet* breaks through the surface, and the best God can do is deflect its fury. While this religious structure is hardly worked through so thoroughly as that of, say, Larry Cohen's *God Told Me To/Demon* (1977), it's unique in Argento's filmography. Just as Roberto is a transitional hero, so the entire milieu of *Four Flies on Grey Velvet* represents an interim landscape; it bridges the relatively stable worlds of *The Bird With the Crystal Plumage* and *The Cat O'Nine Tails* and those of *Deep Red, Tenebrae, Creepers* (in which even the insect kingdom seems in the grips of some collective insanity) and the spectacularly deranged diegeses of *Suspiria* and *Inferno.*

Four Flies on Grey Velvet takes from *The Cat O'Nine Tails* some surprisingly specific material, particularly apparent in the way it uses certain sexual motifs; in this respect the films appear almost a pair. Incest, for example, plays a part in each film. While it's not utterly essential to the plot (some other form of aberrant sexuality could have been substituted), it is of considerable formal importance. In *Cat*, the fact that Anna Terzi may be sleeping with her adoptive father is not a narrative linchpin - its only real function on this level is to add to Giordani's suspicion that she may be the murderer he and Arno are seeking. But it adds immeasurably to the film's overall atmosphere of sick perversity by casting an unhealthy shadow over Arno's relationship with Lori, for the two pairs - Anna/ Terzi and Lori/Arno - reflect one another structurally. Even Lori's nickname for her uncle (to whom she is not actually related, as Anna is not related by blood to Terzi; "I don't have any relations and Lori's all alone in the world, so we find that we need each other," Arno explains to Giordani as the child perches on his lap) takes on a faintly corrupt cast in this context; she called him "Cookie," "because he's so sweet." Such nicknames - "Sugar," "Honey," "Cupcake" - have a distinctly sexual (if infantilely fixated) edge; the notion that someone is so sweet that one wants to eat him/her up is also charged. *Four Flies*, of course, is driven by the notion that Nina has married her father in Roberto's guise, and there's a further link to the incestuous couplings of *Cat* through a tantalizing fragment of conversation between Arrosio and a doctor at the Villa Rapidi, the mental institution to which Nina was confined as a child. "After the father died," says the doctor, "all symptoms of emotional disturbance disappeared. It was our opinion that the patient was completely cured. However, there's one important point I would like to emphasize - we suspected the man wasn't the patient's real father."

Further, *Four Flies* is riddled with allusions to a gender fusion/confusion which is, structurally speaking, incest's correlative[2]; both involve effacing certain formal lines. If incest crosses a manmade boundary, that of the family (yes, it's a fact of nature to be born of a certain man and woman, but the definition of an incestuous relationship varies wildly from one culture to the next: it may or may not be incest to sleep with a cousin, a step-sibling, or a spouse's sibling, depending on local custom - these distinctions are societally generated), then gender confusion addresses a more fundamental division: that between men and women. Nina's father, disgusted that his only child was a girl, ignored the facts of nature and raised her as a boy - her mind didn't fare well under the strain. This spectre is raised as early as in *The Bird with the Crystal Plumage*, when one assumes that the killer in the black slicker must be a man, only to find that it's pretty Monica Ranieri, who has made herself over as the mad*man* who attacked and nearly killed her as a young woman. The transvestites of the St. Peter's club in

[2] This is a purely structural theory of incest, it must be emphasized, a literary construct that has nothing to do with incest and its ramifications in real life. This line of thinking owes a substantial debt to John T. Irwin's *Doubling and Incest/Repetition and Revenge* (Johns Hopkins University Press, 1975), a structural analysis of the works of William Faulkner.

The Cat O'Nine Tails, where homosexual Dr. Braun spends his leisure hours, evoke the same confusion. But while they're scattered through *Bird* and *Cat*, *Four Flies on Grey Velvet* abounds in such references and so lays the groundwork for *Deep Red* and *Tenebrae*, whose sexual landscapes are veritable minefields.

Mimsy Farmer and Michael Brandon - and, to a lesser degree, Francine Racette as Nina's cousin Dalia - are all conspicuously androgynous figures, slender, small-hipped, and almost child-like in their silhouettes. Both women are flat-chested, and Nina's hair is cropped very short as well. Roberto's longish hair isn't unusual for the period (nor, for that matter, is Nina's short 'do), but in combination with his smooth, hairless chest and startlingly unmuscular body it provides a reading that doesn't abound in conventionally "masculine" signifiers. Into the equation one can add the figure of Arrosio, the homosexual detective. Far from concealing his sexuality, he makes it a point of honour. "You think this fairy is going to jump on a chair and scream bloody murder if he sees a mouse, right?" he taunts Roberto (who seems to have been expecting a different kind of dick), then asks, "I don't suppose you've ever had a homosexual experience?" This isn't to say homosexuality and androgyny are the same thing - they aren't - but that they form part of the same system of allusions in this film, linked by Nina's voice-over recollection of her wrathful father. "I wanted a son! Not a weakling like you!" his hectoring voice asserts; he could be speaking equally to a daughter (inherently weak because she's female) or a son who's been deemed "unmanly." There are also such details as the killer's sexless puppet mask (it's an ironic detail that both the speaker and the listener have been identified with this mask, though the viewer is not at that moment aware of the fact) and the photograph of the child whose sex cannot be guessed, glimpsed when Nina's partner calls her to demand more money, and the sign on the door of the public rest room where Nina kills Arrosio: two small circles, one containing the silhouette of a woman, the other of a man. Mad Nina, caught between conflicting gender messages, trapped in a displaced Oedipal triangle, is the nexus of this disordered state: all roads lead from her, and all roads lead back.

This idea of circularity is introduced by a cluster of images at the beginning of the film: a high-angle shot of Roberto's drum kit, the rim of a cymbal, the steering wheel of Roberto's car, a bizarre point-of-view shot from inside an acoustic guitar (the image, the guitarist's hand strumming the strings, is framed by the circular sound hole), and a remarkable shot of three perfectly round pieces of confetti - one red, one yellow, one blue - arranged on the black lens of a pair of sunglasses. The camera itself describes circles in movement, notably when it does a series of giddying 360° swish pans around the padded cell that Nina recalls in her nightmare flashbacks. Though *Deep Red* and *Tenebrae* manage to take these concerns a little further (notably in some transsexual casting), *Four Flies on Grey Velvet* betrays a remarkable view of the sexual world as some kind of nasty moebius strip that can turn nowhere but back on itself.

One of the paradoxes of Argento's work is that despite his overt experimentation with the language of the cinema - that of images - his films are riddled with images that allude in no uncertain terms to the world of words. Sam Dalmas, Carlo Giordani, and *Tenebrae*'s Peter Neal are writers; *Inferno* and *Tenebrae* open with images of huge books whose pages fill the screen. Franco Arno - a former writer - constructs crossword puzzles, while *Creepers*' headmistress seems afloat in a sea of words that are projected on the back wall of her classroom and even on her own body. Newspaper headlines, notes, and lists litter the lives of his protagonists. *Four Flies on Grey Velvet*, again acting as a link between the films which display the less developed form of this concern and those that are utterly obsessed, offers a number of images imbued with a notion of words as almost mystical objects. *Bird* and *Cat* have writers as their protagonists. But *Inferno* valorizes words themselves - one of the keys to the power of the Three Mothers lies in the discovery of the name *written* in the cellar. And *Tenebrae* is about words that *hurt*: "On page 46 I learned to kill, and you taught me," whispers the razor-killer to the horrified Peter Neal. *Four Flies* is somewhere in between. When the Tobias maid attempts to blackmail Nina, she does so from a telephone

Killer and victim: Roberto Tobias (Michael Brandon) and Carlo Marosi (Calisto Calisti):
Four Flies on Grey Velvet.

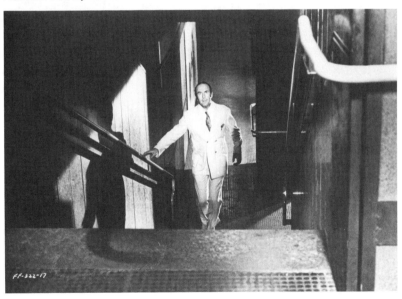

Detective Arrosio (Jean-Pierre Marielle) on the trail of the killer in *Four Flies on Grey Velvet.*

booth. As she speaks, the camera pans up to the top of the booth, to several small holes, from one of which emerges the telephone wire. It pans down the wire, beneath the pavement from one bundle of cables to another; through an electronic line switching unit and to yet another wire - this one connected to the killer's phone. This obsessive tracing of the path of the maid's words (heard continuously over the images) suggests their constitution as physical entities,[3] an idea taken to a logical extreme in the final confrontation between Roberto and Nina. "I want so badly to see you die slowly... painfully," she hisses, gesturing to Roberto with his own gun (one might invoke again the Lacanian model of possession of the phallus granting access to the power of speech here, but it's almost too obvious to mention) while he cowers against a wall. "Why?" he asks. "Why? Because you're so much like him!" Nina laughs, and a close-up of her cavernous mouth is followed by a slow-motion shot of a bullet; the sound of a shot bridges the two images. Nina's words, it would seem, are words that can truly kill; her pathological hatred of her father is not only articulated but resolved into steel pellets that carry a deadly message. *Tenebrae* may be the more explicit exploration of the notion that words can kill (and it's Peter Neal who, when the police question him because pages of his book were found at the scene of a crime, asks whether the president of Smith and Wesson is interviewed whenever someone is killed with one of their guns), but *Four Flies on Grey Velvet* corners the market in literal-mindedness. Nina's words cut like knives, sting like lashes, smart like bullets because they *are*.

[3] It also illustrates one of Argento's obsessions: "When I work in a place that's strange to me, I spend hours looking at everything, seeing where the wires at the base of the wall go. I explore the smallest corners so that I don't find myself with phantoms jumping out at me. There is, therefore, a very subtle way of generating fear; by making everything clear, by showing everything...An atmosphere can be created in this way, full of transparent things, impalpable, horrifying. Because there will always be a pen on the table and, beside the pen, a little black hole that I want to go into with my camera." Quoted by Christophe Gans in *Starfix* No.5, June 1983.

Yet even as Argento invokes the power of the spoken and written word, his films are fully articulate within their own language system. In certain scenes in *Four Flies*, for example, he uses striking editing patterns (Argento is, of course, not himself an editor, but these scenes were shot with an eye to the form in which they ultimately appear) that are both the carriers of narrative information and cinematic *tour de forces* in their own right. In one such scene, Roberto drives to Arrosio's office. Shots of Roberto in his car (taken from inside) alternate with point of view shots of: 1) a wide staircase in a kind of mall; the camera tilts up as though it were about to pan up the stairs, 2) a sign on the wall - track in - "G. Arrosio: Private Eye," 3) a smaller flight of stairs, up which the camera pans, 4) a hallway lined with office doors; the camera pans past them, and 5) a doorknob to which is affixed an eye - track in to a close-up. This resembles a sequence in *The Cat O'Nine Tails* in which shots of Arno - who's thinking about going to see Giordani - are alternated with shots of increasing length of Giordani in his office; finally the two men appear together in frame. The first shot of Giordani suggests one is watching Arno's thought processes - he's envisioning Giordani and we share the image[4] - but by the last shot it's clear that the sequence has been used to elide diegetic barriers both temporal and spatial. But the sequence in *Four Flies* is not only disorienting; it's funny as well. Because of the match on sound (the car's engine, which is heard over all the shots) and action (in the shots of the car it's moving forward; the point of view shots retain a forward momentum) it looks as though Roberto is driving around indoors. However it may look, one knows that can't be the case, so an alternate reading is proposed: Roberto's thoughts have been made visible - as he drives, he imagines the street, the building, the hallway where Arrosio's office is located. And finally, there's a narrative ellipsis - Roberto reaches into frame to turn the weird doorknob with the eye. It's a flashy device, to be sure, but makes some

---

[4] The awkwardness here is Arno's blindness; the tip-off is that Arno has never seen Giordani, so we must be seeing two "real" images overlapped.

sort of sense and seems ultimately reasonable within the generally peculiar parameters of the film's style. The same can be said of the sequence in which the blackmailing maid waits in the park where she has told Nina to meet her with the money that will buy her silence. As she sits on a bench overlooking a playground, smoking her cigarette, the cheerful piped-in music is suddenly absent; the children vanish, as do a pair of lovers kissing in the bushes. The sky is unnaturally dark, the noises made by a running squirrel and the nearby fountains is menacing, amplified. The explanation: sunk deep in her thoughts, the maid has lost track of time and the hours have slipped by without her noticing their passage. But once again the effect is startling, reminiscent of a bad dream in which an ordinary space turns into something else without warning; the park is suddenly threatening, a gloomy maze. Bushes thwart her attempts to find a way out, the gates have been locked, voices whisper in the darkness and help lies tantalizingly near yet hopelessly out of reach on the other side of a high stone wall.[5]

And if the maid's reality seems in this sequence to degenerate into a bad dream, then Roberto's nightmares - another conspicuous feature of *Four Flies on Grey Velvet*'s mode of speech - have a disturbing tendency to spill over into his reality.

During the course of the film, Roberto has four dreams, or rather, four variations on a single dream. Suggested by a story told by his friend Andreas (the psychiatrist Nina wants him to see), it begins always with dazzling light, sometimes an extreme long shot of milling crowds in a Middle Eastern courtyard, sometimes with a close-up of a white-clad executioner against a blinding sky. Colour bleeds into the image until it's merely bright, rather than bleached to sparkling whiteness. A

[5]This is the scene to which Cozzi alludes when he mentions the influence of Cornell Woolrich on *Four Flies*. In Woolrich's *Black Alibi* (filmed as *The Leopard Man* by Jacques Tourneur and *auteur* producer Val Lewton), young Conchita de Contreras comes to her death in a deserted church yard under identical circumstances: she is accidentally locked in and is killed even though she manages to reach an outside wall, because it's too high for her - or the man she has contacted on the other side - to climb over.

Roberto Tobias' haunting dream: *Four Flies on Grey Velvet*.

Roberto and Nina Tobias (Michael Brandon and Mimsy Farmer) and the secret of the four flies on grey velvet.

condemned man kneels on the ground; the executioner holds a stiletto in one hand and in the other a gleaming sword that he begins to swing in a great arc... When Roberto wakes from the first dream the sound of the swinging sword is still there, and so is the puppet-faced man who threatens him in the darkened house. "I could kill you now, but I won't... I'll wait. Who's going to help you? The police perhaps? You can't ask anyone... you're all alone." The lights don't work, the cat hisses in the blackness, the eerie puppet-man's garrotte appears as though out of nowhere. "Maybe it's all a bad dream," suggests Nina when Roberto awakens her, and when he pours out the whole dreadful story of the accidental murder and his torment at the hands of the stranger she suggests he talk to their friend Enrico, the psychiatrist. If it's not a dream, then perhaps the entire business is a hallucination. But it happens again: this time Roberto's dream segues into the sound of shattering glass, footsteps, the cat making some racket. When he investigates he finds that the house has been ransacked; pillows are slashed, things broken, a note that reads "It was so easy," tucked under the corner of an ashtray. The dream was shorter than the first one; the executioner's blade came closer to the throat of the soon-to-be dead man. The third dream is shorter still and concludes as the blade reaches the dead man's neck; Roberto wakes to Dalia trailing her fingers across his throat. The fourth and final Arabian dream is only three shots in duration; Roberto dreams it when he dozes off in his darkened house, as he waits for the killer to arrive. He is awakened - from the image of the severed head, lopped off by the glittering sword, bouncing on the white, white ground - by the sound of the telephone shrieking "out against the dread silence of frustration and terror," to use Riccardo Menello's phrase. It's God calling; he offers to come over but is cut off (how apt the phrase) in mid-sentence as the line goes dead. The progress of these dreams charts the process by which Roberto's reality dissolves into a nightmare of death and retribution, or perhaps simply that by which all his dreams run together into one continuing dream whose landscapes - ranging from the Middle Eastern courtyard to bizarre Roman back alleys - are really *one* landscape full of hidden pitfalls and vicious surprises. Beginning with *Deep Red*, Argento's films become full-length nightmares whose diegeses are disturbed from the outset; whose oneiric qualities are consistent, achieved by way of subtly (and not so subtly, in the cases of *Suspiria* and *Inferno*) disordered compositions, colour values and angles. *Four Flies* indicates the path these later films take in terms of those that precede it; their relatively orderly landscapes are juxtaposed with moments of emerging irrationality.

As had been the case with *The Bird With the Crystal Plumage*, both *The Cat O'Nine Tails* and *Four Flies on Grey Velvet* were scored by Ennio Morricone, one of the most prolific Italian composers of music for films. By 1970, Morricone had achieved some measure of fame as a result of his eccentric, hyperkinetic scores for Sergio Leone's Westerns, but the body of his work wasn't (and isn't) so distinguished as that he created for the "*Dollars*" trilogy and *Once Upon a Time in the West*. In his study *Spaghetti Westerns*, Christopher Frayling remarks that Morricone's other compositions had "seldom matched up to his Leone scores - in either invention or appropriateness... it seems clear that the relationship between director and composer in this case proved unusually fruitful, on a par with the relationship between Franju and Jarre, Truffaut and Delerue, Fellini and Rota, or Demy and Legrand." Or, he might have added, Argento and the members of Goblin, with whom the director was on a far more sympathetic wavelength than he was with Morricone. "In fact," Frayling remarks in another context, not unrelated to the present one, "some of Morricone's musical themes and ideas, after rejection by Leone, tend to turn up - rearranged by Bruno Nicolai [credited as "Music Conductor" on *Bird* and *Cat*; "Orchestra Conductor" on *Four Flies*] - in other Italian Westerns where they simply become intrusive." The score for *The Cat O'Nine Tails* comes to mind; it actually does sound like a Morricone Western soundtrack, with its reedy accompaniment to female voices crooning an incongruous lullaby. Though not actively deleterious to the film, *Cat*'s score is not its strongest point, and often lapses into painfully conventional "suspense music." It's been reported that when Argento was in preproduction on *Four Flies* he approached the British hard-rock band Deep Purple to do the score; the band's touring commitments made this impossible and he found himself working with Morricone again. The result, though again not truly damaging, wasn't precisely inspired. Morricone took a cue from Roberto's profession and added some jarring rock to his usual formula; this wasn't a particular asset because it's very bad rock indeed. It is, however, an integral part of the film's grossly amusing credits sequence, which juxtaposes the image of a throbbing heart against a black background (silent, except for the familiar thump-*thump*, thump-*thump*) and shots of Roberto rehearsing amidst a virtual cacophony of screeching guitars and jangling drums. With the conspicuous exception of this witty montage (which does not - unlike the credit sequence of *Deep Red* - establish the tone for the rest of the film), Morricone's score for the film is simply not very interesting. This undistinguished aural element ended with *Four Flies*; *Deep Red* was Argento's first collaboration with Goblin and set the tone for his future endeavours.

Ultimately, one doesn't want to make inflated claims for either *The Cat O'Nine Tails* or *Four Flies on Grey Velvet*. They aren't without points of interest in and of themselves - speaking both in thematic and structural terms - but it's principally because they indicate certain directions Argento would explore in his later, more thoroughly developed films, that they resonate as powerfully as they do. With *Four Flies on Grey Velvet* a phase in Argento's career came to an end. The style of editing that produced visual tropes on the order of the maid's short day's journey into night was abandoned, the soundtracks were composed in order to take on a new relation to the images, the images themselves grew richer, brighter, and more ambiguously constructed. Four years after the release of *Four Flies* - with Argento's sole digression into another genre in between - came the first of his new films, *Deep Red*.

LE CINQUE GIORNATE and DEEP RED

"It's like having a madman in the house."
- Amanda Righetti's maid

Having made three *gialli* in as many years, Argento began work - again with Luigi Cozzi - on a film that was to be a substantial change of pace. Before the film's release, Cozzi offered this account in *Photon* magazine:

Four Flies was still being edited when Dario began work on his next film, to be titled *The Five Days of Milan* [*Le cinque giornate*]. It's a comic venture set during a revolution that took place in 1848. As I write this, shooting has just been completed and the film is slated for release at Christmas 1973. Dario chose to do a comedy because he feared that audiences might be getting somewhat tired of the usual thriller formula, especially due to the tremendous volume of imitators who have been making pictures so similar to his own. Nevertheless, *The Five Days of Milan* has been shot in the style of *The Wild Bunch*, containing much violence and blood, plus every comedy idea that Dario and I could think of.

The film is aimed almost entirely at the Italian market and, as some releasing companies have already refused it, I doubt that it will be released in the United States.

Argento's concern that the public may have been tiring of *gialli* was understandable. Film is a trendy medium, worshipping at the altar of the box office; one commercial hit inevitably spawns a slew of imitators. Italian cinema, lacking Hollywood's dense multi-studio structure and with a great deal of power concentrated in a very few hands, is simply more so: a hit unleashes a veritable flood of imitations in record-breaking time. "Italy's cinema," wrote Paul Hoffman in *The New York Times* in 1974, "is governed by the law of the *filone* - an Italian word meaning "streamlet." One successful spaghetti Western generates a flow of imitations until the public gets tired and the *filone* dries up."

By the time Argento had completed *Four Flies on Grey Velvet*,

95

the *giallo filone* had indeed overflowed its banks, glutting the market with thrillers whose outlandish titles were the only interesting things about them. Nevertheless, *Le cinque giornate* was not the answer.

In tone and style it owes a great deal to the caustic, cruelly jocular world of the spaghetti Western. In fact, it almost *is* a spaghetti Western; set in the American frontier and dressed with a few more horses, the story would pass muster as a town-bound Western with no trouble at all.

Le cinque giornate opens on convicts sleeping on the floor of a filthy prison. Cainazzo (Adriano Celentano), an attractive young man, is attacked by a rat as he dozes. Without waking, he kills it and casts the body aside. The dead rat winds up in another prisoner's mouth and precipitates a scene, interrupted by the explosion of a cannon. The cannonball shatters the prison wall and Cainazzo escapes to the streets of Milan.

His picaresque journey through the chaotic city begins when he quite literally runs into a thief making the best of the anarchy that's already taking hold of the city. The fortunate Cainazzo escapes death on several occasions, acquires a side-kick - good natured baker Romolo (Enzo Cerusico), who eventually dies in front of a firing squad for trying to save a young woman from being raped - and encounters ruffians and travelling entertainers, philosophers and pregnant women, opportunists and idealists, soldiers and revolutionaries as the uprising slowly degenerates into a corrupt outpouring of mass violence.

Le cinque giornate is an extraordinarily awkward film, crude and conventionally photographed (by Luigi Kuveiller, who shot the gorgeous *Deep Red* only two years later); in stylistic terms it could easily have been Argento's first film, rather than his fourth. To choose only the most obvious example, the use of accelerated motion for comic effect when Cainazzo and Romolo, (whose combined knowledge of birthing babies would fit on the head of a pin) must assist a woman in labour - is primitive and obvious. Argento demonstrates no natural flair for comedy, and the old theatrical joke about dying being easy while comedy is hard comes to mind. Argento didn't cut himself any breaks with the subject matter; the film's cynical and defeatist politics militate against levity, and the mix of earthy humour and savage violence successfully juggled by directors like Leone and Peckinpah isn't as easy to pull off as it looks.

As Cozzi had predicted, *Le cinque giornate* was not shown in the United States or Great Britain. In fact, as Argento told writer Martin Coxhead, "It was shown only in Italy, not anywhere else. It was a very Italian film, absolutely... I wanted to make it specifically for my country and my people. It was a rebellious film, dealing with uprising... A revolution seen by people who have nothing, a revolution against the bourgeois. It was a violent, absurd film, like the [student] riots in Paris in May 1968."

The idea of aiming a film at an exclusively Italian audience was not necessarily commercially unwise. Italy is a country with a great tradition of movie-going. At the time *Le cinque giornate* was produced, "Italians alone represented half of the entire movie-going audience in the [then] nine-country [Belgium, France, Italy, Luxembourg, the Netherlands, West Germany, Denmark, Ireland, and Great Britain] European Common Market. In 1972, 553,000,000 tickets were sold in Italy - about 10 for every man, woman, and child in the country - against 183,000,000 in France, 163,000,000 in Britain, and 150,000,000 in West Germany," to again quote Hoffman from the *Times*. The problem was simply that the Italian public was not at all taken with *Le cinque giornate*. The film was both a popular and a critical disaster. For his next project, Argento returned to the genre with which he'd been so successful. The result was his first fully developed work, *Deep Red/Profondo rosso*, and the difference in quality between *Deep Red* and the films that preceded it is truly startling. Between *Bird* and *Flies* Argento developed steadily as a technician and stylist, experimenting with increasingly unusual shot compositions and camera movement. *Le cinque giornate* was a step in a very different direction, so it's not really surprising that it doesn't build on the foundations laid by the *gialli*; it's a detour. But *Deep Red* is a quantum leap in all respects. Its stylistic vigour, thematic denseness and emotional intensity are all striking;

Italian poster art for *Le Cinque Giornate*.

even the title suggests *Deep Red* is a different order of film from Argento's first *gialli*: shunning their precious obscurity, it's brief and evocative, particularly in the original Italian. "Deep"/ "profondo," suggests a cry from the pit, *de profundis*, out of the darkest night of the soul. "Red"/"rosso," a colour whose connotations are overwhelmingly violent: to see red is to be blinded by blood lust, to be enticed into momentary madness by the flash of crimson, like the bull goaded into charging to his certain death by the matador's cape.[1] *Deep Red* ends with the image of its hero's reflection as he gazes into a pool of blood, stunned by the things he's seen and done; in the red depths he's discovered a world of thought and action he never dreamed existed and through whose scarlet veil he'll always see. It's a scary image, and one that lingers.

Deep Red's screenplay by Bernadino Zapponi (co-author of Fellini's *Roma* and *Satyricon*) from a story by Argento, is far denser and more richly textured than those of Argento's first three films. An English pianist, Marc Daly (David Hemmings), lives in Rome, where he teaches music and composes, both on his own and with a local jazz ensemble. Returning home one night, he pauses in the piazza in front of his apartment building to speak with a friend and fellow pianist, Carlo (Gabriele Lavia), who is very drunk. A scream diverts Marc's attention and he sees - to his horror - his downstairs neighbour Helga Ulman (Macha Meril), a noted psychic, being murdered by someone whose face is hidden by Helga's bloody body. Helga is shoved halfway through a window as Marc watches; by the time he reaches her apartment she is long dead. The police are summoned, followed by a newspaper reporter, Gianna Brezzi (Daria Nicolodi).

Marc is haunted by the thought that he's seen something important - he thinks it's a painting that was in the hall when he arrived but has vanished by the time he thinks to look again. He confides his suspicion to Carlo, who drunkenly concurs that the painting must have represented something significant.

[1] It doesn't matter that bulls are colourblind and are reacting to the motion - it's the image that counts here.

Marc is forced to investigate the matter when his photograph, taken by Gianna, appears in the next day's newspaper with a caption suggesting that he was a witness to the killing and can identify the murderer; an attempt on his life proves that the murderer at least believes this is true.

Marc goes to speak with Carlo and comes face to face with Carlo's mother Marta (Clara Calamai), a deluded harridan haunted by the idea that she could have been a great actress. Her relationship with her son is clearly oppressive and destructive. Marc further learns that Carlo is a tormented homosexual who's drinking himself to death.

One of Helga's associates provides a tantalizing clue to the murder: just before her death, Helga had addressed a conference on telepathy and made contact with a "twisted mind" in the audience. This information leads Marc to an abandoned house with a haunted reputation, where he finds beneath a layer of crumbling plaster a child's drawing of a grotesque murder. The key to the mystery seems to lie somewhere in the past. The bloody trail eventually leads to a grade school archive and another version of the drawing, this one signed: it was drawn by Carlo. But after Carlo is killed fleeing the police Marc realizes that there must be more to the story, for Carlo was with him when Helga was killed. The real killer is Carlo's mother, who stabbed to death Carlo's father when he tried to commit her to an asylum. What Marc saw on the night of the murder was not a painting, but Marta's face reflected in a mirror hung among the paintings in Helga's hallway. Marc only barely escapes to enjoy the knowledge that he has indeed solved the puzzle: Marta attempts to kill him with a hatchet and actually succeeds in wounding him before her own death: the heavy pendant she wears slips into an elevator shaft when she trips over Marc's prone body and she is decapitated when the ascending car drags the thick chain through her throat.

Significantly, this story bears some striking similarities to that of *The Bird With the Crystal Plumage*. It begins with a crime, seen by someone who can't do anything to stop it. There is a clue, one which makes no sense until it's provided with the proper context; the context comes to light only after an investigation that nearly costs the protagonist his life. There is the first solution, close enough to pass for the truth except for some detail, and the *second* solution that overturns its predecessor and, with it, the protagonist's sense of the harmony of the world.

But while *The Bird With the Crystal Plumage* is a relatively self-contained film, *Deep Red* casts out allusions in all directions; the more you know, the more it resonates. One allusion in particular inflects the entire investigation aspect of the plot: the casting of David Hemmings as Marc Daly. Though Hemmings appeared in a variety of films, mostly during the '60s, he's irrevocably associated with one: Michelangelo Antonioni's *Blow-Up* (1966). In *Blow-Up* he plays Thomas, a photographer who thinks he may have photographed a murder; one of his pictures may contain the answer to a puzzle, but that answer is buried in the very grain of the film and Thomas' quest leads him from one question to another, each more perplexing than the one before. *Blow-Up* is the classic mystery with no solution, a mystery that seems to be about one thing - a murder and all that implies - and turns out to be about something else altogether - the ultimate impossibility of knowing. In *Deep Red* Hemmings' character is involved in a superficially less ambiguous situation: the body (actually bodies) here is as present as can be from the outset; no inferences need be drawn from grainy photographs. But *Deep Red* unfolds with a surprising complexity, and where better to start exploring its convoluted terrain than with Marc and his structural double, Carlo.

The notion of the *doppelgänger* - the double - predates psychoanalysis, reaching back through literary history at least as far as classical Greece in the estimation of psychoanalyst Otto Rank[2], whose study of the double makes much of the image of Narcissus staring at his reflection in a pool (which calls to mind *Deep Red*'s final image) and loving it as though it were another. But it's from psychoanalysis that the double gains its significance in contemporary thought. Rather than reading the

[2]*The Double* (Chapel Hill: The University of North Carolina Press, 1971) is his influential work on the subject.

reflection of Stellan Rye/Hanns Heinz Ewers' eponymous *Student of Prague* (liberated as part of an infernal pact and made free to bedevil him) as his "soul" in some religious sense or as a literal embodiment of the past he can't escape, the educated contemporary viewer immediately sees it as an aspect of the student's personality, some repressed part of himself. In this instance the aspect is malevolent, though this isn't always the case; the important thing is that the two parts are working at cross purposes to one another. In Edgar Allan Poe's *William Wilson* the double is the narrator's "better half" (a loaded phrase if ever there was one, implying femininity - you call your wife your better half, not your husband), the voice of decency and conventional morality who reasserts himself whenever Wilson No. 1 (the double has his name as well as his face) is in the midst of some particularly despicable act. That this voice is *"a very low whisper"* (italics in the original) can hardly surprise the modern reader: it is - to use the Freudian terminology that's an integral part of 20th-century language - the reedy voice of the superego (which embodies societal convention) trying to restrain the bellowing id, which can conceive the world only in terms of what it wants and when it wants it - *now*. In the figure of the *doppelgänger* Rank detects a particularly vivid working out of the "essential problem of the ego" which exists between the two, compelled to act by the id but restrained by the superego.

The most obvious use of the *doppelgänger* motif in the cinema is that exemplified by *The Student of Prague*: it's supernatural in origin (the student makes a pact with the devil) and fantastic in manifestation: the student's reflection literally vanishes from his mirror and skulks behind bushes and walls waiting for an opportunity to torment him. The same kind of thing happens in Bava's *Hatchet for the Honeymoon*: psychopath John Harrington's tormenting double is the ghost of Mildred, the wife he murdered. In *Deep Red* the *doppelgänger* relationship of Marc and Carlo is of a different order: each character is contextually real, and they don't bear a conventional doubling relationship to one another - they aren't siblings, lovers, namesakes or dead ringers for one another. But they're linked by circumstance and detail in a number of ways, and the linkage is so obsessive and pervasive that it demands structural resolution.

  Most obvious, of course, is that they're joined by profession - they're both pianists with a taste for American jazz, though neither is from the United States: Marc is English and Carlo, Italian. In one sequence - which opens with a close-up of four hands (two identical pairs) on a piano keyboard - they actually play a duet in which their respective parts are precise echoes of each other.[3] In addition, each is substantially defined by his sexuality, which for each character constitutes a point of disjuncture. Carlo is not just homosexual (like, say, Arrosio in *Four Flies*); he is sexually tormented. When Marc comes to the apartment of Carlo's lover, Massimo, Carlo is sardonically defensive: "Look who's here... you caught me in the act; good old Carlo... not only is he a drunk, but he has strange sexual tastes (the phrase "strange sexual tastes" is here translated directly from the Italian original; in the English language print, Carlo calls himself a "faggot," losing the subtle implications of the remark) as well."[4]

  Marc is the subject of a variety of implicit and explicit sexual allusions. The police inspector sent to the scene of Helga's murder suggests slyly that being a musician is no sort of

[3] This sequence doesn't exist in the American cut of *Deep Red*, but is in the longer, Italian version. Of all Argento's movies, *Deep Red* seems to have suffered the most extensive editing for US release, losing some 20 minutes of its 115 minute running time. Most of the deletions aren't of violent material; they seem to have been made simply to bring down the running time. Though none of the deletions completely obscures a narrative point, they do seriously interfere with the development of many subtexts. All scenes not present in the American cut will be noted.

[4] This scene was trimmed in the American print, which obscures the fact that Massimo - though dressed with cliched flamboyance - is presented as a sympathetic and stable character, rather than a contemptible pervert. In the longer version it is clear that Massimo truly loves Carlo and isn't afraid to say so, and that he puts up with a great deal of emotional abuse because he knows Carlo is tormented by some inner misery he can't express.

profession for a real man, while Gianna taunts Marc into arm-
wrestling with her, then gleefully beats him - more or less fairly
- every round and giggles at his dismay; when she assures him
that he is a "big... strong... man" there's no doubt but that she
means something else. It's Gianna too who needles him (in the
guise of friendly banter) as they walk away together from
Helga's funeral. "You may not believe this, but I don't have a
boyfriend right now," she says. "Me either." "I should hope not!"
she leers, leaving Marc to protest (in a situation in which any
protest seems too much) weakly "I meant a girlfriend," while
she goes on to ask why he can't keep his hands from shaking.
Artistic temperament, counters Marc, but the point is lost.[5]

Although they're the nominal centres of the narrative, both
Marc and Carlo are rendered helpless, ineffectual, at every
turn. The first time we see Carlo he is falling-down drunk,
collapsed in the piazza in front of Marc's apartment building;
he is in much the same state when we next encounter him at
Massimo's apartment. Carlo's only active contribution to *Deep
Red*'s considerable mayhem is to stab Gianna (whom he takes
by surprise in the darkened school building and who doesn't
die); when he confronts Marc moments later he can do little
more than threaten - even though he has a gun and Marc is
unarmed. Significantly, however, Marc can't actively save
himself in this situation - he stalls for time until the police
arrive and Carlo flees. Marc is humiliated by Gianna's car (both
by a faulty door and a seat that locks in a position so low that
he can barely peer over the dashboard;[6] it goes without saying
that Gianna always drives), is beaten and left for dead at the
burning villa (Gianna pulls him to safety), and is crippled by the
deranged Marta (her cleaver bites deep into his right shoulder;

---

[5] Once again, this scene has been trimmed to eliminate this entire
conversation; all that remains is a snippet in which Marc thanks
Gianna - with heavy irony - for running the photo identifying him as
an eyewitness to the murder.
[6] In the Italian version only. None of the shots involving the car serve
an essential function to the story; all of them make Marc look weak
and inconsequential.

Cheap and nasty American ad slick for *Deep Red*.

at the very least he won't be playing the piano again any time soon) when she confronts him at Helga's apartment after Carlo's death. Though his investigation drives *Deep Red*'s narrative, Marc is constantly presented not as an active force, but a reactive one. And if Carlo's entire perception of the world is coloured by the childhood trauma of his father's death (in which he was himself implicated when the bloody knife was passed to him), then Marc's is no less patriarchal: when Gianna asks why he became a pianist, he replies "Well, my psychiatrist would say that it's because I hated my father; because when I bang the keys I'm really bashing his teeth in." He's joking, of course, but it's a joke that conceals a grain of truth. Driven to violent - if impotent - extremes by the spectre of red death, Marc and Carlo are like Hammett's Continental Op adrift in *Red Harvest*'s Personville, whose very atmosphere is subtly and pervasively poisonous:

"This damned burg's getting me," [he tells an incredulous listener]. "If I don't get away I'll be going blood simple like the natives... A couple of days ago, if I thought about it at all, [an ice pick] was a good tool to pry off chunks of ice." I ran a finger down its half foot of round steel blade to the needle point. "Not a bad thing to pin a man to his clothes with. That's the way I'm begging, on the level. I can't even see a mechanical cigarette lighter without thinking of filling one up with a nitroglycerine for somebody you don't like. There's a piece of copper wire lying in the gutter in front of [the] house... thin, soft, and just long enough to go around a neck with two ends to hold on. I had a hell of a time to keep from picking it up and stuffing it in my pocket, just in case..."

But Marc and Carlo can't just take the next train out of town to escape the blood mania, because its origin is in the past that clings to Carlo and, by extension, to Marc. Well after she makes initial contact with the "twisted mind" in the audience at the parapsychological conference, Helga feels a sudden chill; she attributes it to some residual psychic energy that clings to the physical locale, like the white tape that remains after a body is gone. But she's wrong - the icy aura is the expression of a state

106

of mind and no mere change of venue can shake off its influence.

Marc and Carlo are the twin centres of *Deep Red*'s chaotic diegesis. Though they're far from the only manifestation of its disordered state, they're an extreme and logical example of the dualistic structure Argento often employs in his films; it is as though the overflow of hysteria and potential violence were so excessive that no one protagonist could embody it, so miasmic that the only way to deal with the volume is to divide it up. *The Bird With the Crystal Plumage* revolves around both Monica/Umberto Ranieri (symbolic Siamese twins whose mutual madness triggers the killings) and Sam Dalmas, whose investigation precipitates further violence. In *The Cat O'Nine Tails* the XYY killer begins by committing a crime whose motivation is, in retrospect, absolutely understandable: the theft of a document that could - through no fault of his own - ruin his promising career. But this first transgression paves the way for an orgy of (in the words of one particularly appalled reviewer) incest, homosexuality, grave robbing, child torture, mutilation, and murder; much of it necessitated by the persistent prying of the two journalists who nearly drown in the waves of violence that ripple outward from their initial point of inquiry. *Four Flies on Grey Velvet* posits Roberto and Nina Tobias (whose slender awkward frames suggest irresistibly that they're related by blood, even before we learn she married him because he's the image of her father) as twin generators/recipients of a tremendous amount of physical and psychological violence. Roberto kills a man and goes to great lengths to conceal the crime (though the viewer later learns the murder was staged, Roberto never does), while Nina pours her heart and soul into tormenting him, murdering repeatedly to further her project; their relationship is written in blood and blotted with guilt and fear. *Deep Red*, however, is the first film in which the levels of overt narrative sickness and structural perversity are evenly matched.

New York Times critic Vincent Canby, not content with registering his thorough dislike of *Deep Red*'s story, took the opportunity to single out its *mise en scène* for particular criticism; he declared Argento "simply a director of incomparable incompetence." This assessment just won't hold up in the face of the film's rigorous formal structure, and that structure asserts itself from its first moments - in fact, even before the film proper begins.

Deep Red's credit sequence establishes a distinctly uneasy, off-balance tone, and it does so by manipulating many of the same elements that inflect the film as a whole. The major credits appear as white type against a black background, accompanied by a bass-dominated score based on throbbing sequential notes.

The music theme segues into a child's thin voice singing a wordless tune, as an image fades in from black: there is a room and a Christmas tree; against the back wall two shadows struggle violently. There is a scream, and the shadows disappear. A knife, its blade smeared with blood, is thrown into frame left; into frame right walk a pair of child's legs and feet, clad in dazzling white socks and black patent leather shoes. The images fades back to black and the childish singing segues back into the rock score, which accompanies the rest of the credits. After "Directed by Dario Argento," the screen is black for several seconds; the music stops and there is silence.

When an image reappears, it doesn't fill the screen and is weirdly off-centre; the musical score is anachronistic mid-sixties jazz. The camera pans left, revealing the off-centre image as an image fragment. The camera continues to pan and the image vanishes and reappears as it passes behind a series of obstructions before coming to rest in long shot on a group of musicians, rehearsing in what appears to be an abandoned theatre. At a sign from the pianist (Marc, though he hasn't been introduced and won't be for several scenes), they stop playing. As he speaks, the camera tracks in from long shot to close-up: "Okay, that was fine, good... very good. Maybe too good; too precise, too formal... you need to throw it away, make it distinctive. Remember, this kind of jazz was born in... (he hesitates slightly) bordellos."[7]

[7]This entire scene is absent from the American print, whose first post-credit sequence begins with the track-in to the door that reads "European Congress on Parapsychology."

Already, having seen only the credits and two brief scenes (one of which is scarcely a scene at all - more a vignette), the viewer is disoriented. The vignette which interrupts the credits poses a slew of questions. What exactly happened? Something violent, certainly; there's a knife and there's blood. Is someone dead? Who? Who killed him or her? The child - was he or she (the legs and feet could belong equally to a small girl or boy) a witness to something dreadful? Or did he or she *do* something dreadful? Is the child singing, or are we hearing someone or something else - the radio, a record? When did this thing happen? The child's clothing (what little we see of it) doesn't look particularly contemporary, but the Christmas tree in the background signifies a special occasion, so perhaps it is simply a pampered child dressed up for a Christmas party. Did it even happen at all? Perhaps this is a dream or a fantasy of some kind. And why is this snippet of a scene so important that it interrupts the credits? If *all* the credits were superimposed over this scene it would be a conventional presentation (let's not bore the viewers with all these names - we'll give them a scene to look at in case they don't care about the director, screenwriter, producer...); but the first credits appear against a black background, underscored by their own theme music. The scene - which even has its own, very different music - is speaking out of turn; the credits are suspended for its duration, resuming only after the last echoes of the childish tune have faded away.

When the credits conclude there's a moment of suspended silence before the dark screen again gives way to an image. It bears no obvious relation to the bloody vignette, and when its fragmented space is resolved into something conventional (an ordinary space made to appear discontinuous because the camera's view is obstructed) it contains a group of adult figures, musicians rehearsing. They provide a source for the jazzy score, as unlike the music that accompanied the credits as is the childish singing, but they aren't shown in a series of close-ups that would make them into characters - they're just shapes. Even when one is singled out, he isn't given a name (no one calls out from off screen "Hey Marc, how did that sound?" or something of the kind); as soon as he's isolated by the camera's

Videocassette cover for *Deep Red*, retitled for maximum gruesome effect.

110

roving eye, it sets about (by way of a relentless inward track) making him into a fragment - when the scene concludes he is just a face, isolated in a shot that inverts the close-up which concludes the vignette - the child's feet. Perhaps *he's* the child of the previous segment grown up - the proximity of the scenes suggests such a reading, as do the formal matching of the inverted close-ups and the presence under both scenes of significant music that isn't part of the film's overall musical theme. This scene, which contains no answers, also raises another issue that - even if it doesn't register consciously - asserts itself throughout the film: that of a kind of pervasive, vague sexual uneasiness.

In his brief monologue, Marc hesitates (not once, but twice) before speaking the word "bordello." Why? He's not in mixed company (and the idea that if he were it would explain the matter presupposes that Marc's a very old-fashioned kind of gentleman), and it's probably safe to assume that most musicians know that the roots of jazz lie in Southern whorehouses: what is the problem here?

The third scene in *Deep Red* follows directly on the second, linked on the camera's tracking motion, which ends on a glass door reading "European Congress on Parapsychology." There is a cut to a long shot of an ante-room, then the camera tracks aggressively up to a set of heavy red drapes,[8] flings them open and proceeds down the centre aisle of an auditorium. Three people (two men and a woman) are seated behind a table on stage. One man is saying "... butterflies, termites, zebras; all these animals and many, many others use telepathy to transmit orders and relay information..." There is a cut to a high angle shot - apparently taken from the visible balcony - and then a series of cuts to the figures on stage and various members of the audience; one man whispers something to another who laughs, a man fiddles with what appears to be a hearing aid but is actually the ear-jack of a transistor radio, a sinister priest theatrically lowers his cigarette. Helga Ulman

[8] Drapes are a recurring theme in Argento's films, witness similar scenes in *Inferno* and *Four Flies on Grey Velvet*.

(the woman on stage), addresses the audience and provides a demonstration of her telepathic gifts, correctly naming a stranger in the audience and identifying some objects in his pocket. She can, she explains, hear a thought even as it is being formed, though she knows nothing of the future - her powers have nothing to do with magic.

A strange look passes over her face and she screams. "I can feel... there's in this room... I can feel a presence, a twisted mind sending me thoughts. Perverted, murderous thoughts... go away! You have killed and you will kill again! There's a child singing, and that house... blood, all blood. I'm scared... I'm scared." There is a cut to a point-of-view shot from the audience; the camera rises and begins to ease out of the row of seats towards a side door marked "WC"; this is followed by a cut to the centre aisle, as the camera tracks backwards and the red drapes pull closed behind it, completely blocking the view of the auditorium. All the while, Helga continues to speak in voice-over: "... we must hide everything, everything in the house... that's the way it was... No one must know - no one! Forget it; forget it... forever... forever..." Another cut takes us into the bathroom - there is the sound of hollow heels on the floor, and the sound of someone retching. The camera pans up from the sink (running water, round drain) to the mirror above: it's old and discoloured and the reflection in its mottled surface is undecipherable; a man asks if he should get some help but is rebuffed. Finally, there's a cut to Helga and one of her associates - Giordani - speaking in the now empty auditorium; the camera crouches behind a pillar. She says she'll write down all she heard that afternoon and give it to him the next day; she reveals also that she knows the name of the person whose mind she contacted. When she is stuck by another psychic chill, she dismisses it as a residual mental vibration.

Though this scene is extended and contains a great deal of information, it does little to clear up the questions remaining from the preceding two scenes. One thing seems clear: the vignette with the bloody knife happened at some time in the past and the perpetrator of whatever violence took place is still alive. He or she is in the auditorium, and Helga has glimpsed the secret sin of the past - it interrupts her routine psychic perceptions (of the man named Valgon, a first-time visitor to Rome who has three keys in his pocket...) as rudely as the earlier vignette disrupted the routine reading of the credits.

Throughout the scene, the camera constitutes an unsettlingly inconsistent witness. When the scene opens, it appears to be taking some character's point-of-view (it completes a track begun in the previous shot, suggesting that someone was present in both scenes), through whose eyes the viewer will take in the entire scene. But after it's tracked halfway down the aisle, this apparent point-of-view shot is disrupted by a series of shots taken from all over the auditorium: from both sides of the balcony, behind the on stage speakers, overlooking various segments of the audience. It's clear that no one person is in all these places. It pans from one spectator to another in close-up, tracks in on the back of Helga's head, leaps to a high angle over the stage and zeroes in for an extreme close-up of Helga's mouth as she drinks some water. The camera then resumes diegetic point of view status as when - as Helga points at someone in the audience - it rises from a seat and eases its way out. Instants later one sees the backwards track up the centre aisle and out of the auditorium, followed in turn by the point-of-view sequence in the bathroom. What's going on here? The viewer is kept constantly disoriented by the shifting "voice" of the camera (a characteristic of *film noir*), which moves back and forth between showing the scene in omniscient shots and shots clearly representing some specific viewpoint (between the third and the first person, to continue the literary metaphor) without discernible pattern. The camera seems to have become unhinged, operating in ways running counter to conventional notions about the role of the camera in the narrative process. Its movements don't contribute to some apparently "natural" perception of the scene, as they would if the camera either mimicked the motion of a single character with whom the viewer could constantly identify, or effaced its presence in long-and medium-shots motivated by narrative considerations (someone is speaking, cut in for a close-up; someone answers him, cut to a similar reaction shot, and so on). In fact, the camera movement actively subverts the integrity of the scene, distancing the viewer from what's unfolding on screen.

Even before it became the horror genre's favourite and most-mockable cliché (in the wake of the success of John Carpenter's 1979 *Halloween*, which opens with an extended Steadicam shot of the stalking and killing of a teenage girl by a heavy-breathing maniac), the killer's point-of-view shot was a familiar device. From a purely functional standpoint, it made it easy to conceal the killer's face without limiting the range of his actions; stylistically it became genre shorthand for the temporary identification with the murderer that's widely considered a major horror movie attraction. But *Deep Red*'s manipulation of the killer's eye POV provides no easy vicarious thrills - just as one becomes accustomed to seeing through the killer's eyes, the viewpoint shifts; the viewer is kept always at a distance, always on the outside looking in. *Deep Red* is no roller-coaster ride like *Friday the 13th*; it's an altogether more discomfiting experience.

The auditorium scene is followed by still another indicative sequence: after the long shot of Helga and Giordani, Argento cuts to an extreme close-up of an object isolated in the darkness, a doll house cradle. The throbbing theme of the credits sequence fills the soundtrack as the camera begins a swirling, uninterrupted pan over a series of objects, some innocuous, some creepy in and of themselves, all given sinister significance by the camera's relentless gaze. The cradle is tipped over by an unseen hand; its contents spill and the camera wheels away, past a red yarn doll, its torso stuck with pins, a childish drawing of a woman pierced by a huge knife, a metal figurine, wool braids, a naked baby doll (lifted out of frame by the black gloved hand first glimpsed in the preceding sequence, in the bathroom), a red clay demon, marbles and two slender switchblade knives...

There's a cut to an extreme close-up of a vast eye, gazing sightlessly into the lens as it's ringed with black eye make-up, only the tip of the eye-liner brush visible. Still again, the sequence raises more questions than it answers. Is the owner of the vast eye also the possessor of the twisted brain? Once

114

again, is it a man or a woman? Make-up implies a woman (wasn't the warped mind in the men's room - there was a man there, at any rate), but the crudeness of application is distinctly unfeminine. It suggests military camouflage, ritual war paint, rather than cosmetic make-up. What do these objects - idols, fetishes - mean; do they even really exist, or are they symbols, concrete manifestations of the images that crowd the killer's disordered brain?

In four scenes lasting a total of eight and a half minutes, the first four of the film (one of which is nothing more than a tantalizing fragment), *Deep Red* establishes a pattern of deceptive speech that will characterize the entire film. It raises questions on a variety of levels and refuses to answer them, supplanting each question with a new one - rather than with some kind of response - while providing carefully occluded suggestions that may add up to a coherent picture. There are questions about the story (who did what, when, where, and why?), questions about technique (how is it done and why; to what end, if not in conventional narrative service), questions about structure: if the images aren't arranged so that they fit together logically, providing first a general outline then filling in the detail (to use the ever-popular jigsaw puzzle model of filmmaking) of a story, yet are also not at the service of a genuinely abstract vision, then what is the pattern? One often speaks of the imaginary geography of the cinema, but the Rome of *Deep Red* isn't merely the product of imaginary topography: it's imagined by a maniac. Its camera wanders according to compulsions as incomprehensible as those that drive its psychopathic killer; the soundtrack erupts into atavistic syncopation at the slightest hint of violence. This is light years away from the stereotypical "horror music" of creepy chords and dissonant organ wails; likewise there are no shrilly shrieking violins *à la Psycho* or harsh discordant tones like the ones that accompany Michael Myers' depredations in *Halloween* (to use only two of the most familiar modern horror movie soundtracks); *Deep Red*'s score is the backup to an orgiastic dance of death, swelling and quickening with the very hint of on screen aggression. *Deep Red* is the first of Argento's films to function as a true *"fête sanguinaire,"* a bloody spectacle whose high priests and (more importantly) priestesses are themselves lightning rods for violence, and it's the first with a soundtrack to match.

Despite the provocative presence of David Hemmings, *Deep Red* is not *Blow-Up* which (among other things) undertakes an altogether more linear exploration of its thematic underpinnings. Antonioni's warped variation on the conventions of detective fiction plunges its protagonist into a situation in which there are no answers of any kind; in which the ultimate impossibility is that of knowing itself. The very crime is an enigma ("There is no body because there was no murder," recites the hapless witness/investigator of Brian De Palma's *Sisters*, denying everything she's seen and heard at the very moment someone else is finally willing to listen - Thomas is only one step removed from her negation). Thomas is at the scene of the crime but doesn't see it happen, and when he discovers it in an apparently idyllic photograph, the very medium works against his acquisition of knowledge. The images of the body, the gun, the murderer are tiny fragments of a larger picture and as they're blown up to afford a closer look, the very grain that composes those images threatens to overwhelm them. Argento's Marc, by contrast, doesn't receive quite so stern a lesson in the credo that seeing is *not* believing.

His initial view is of a very present body (Helga's), and the next thing he sees is the killer's face reflected in a mirror - he doesn't interpret what he sees correctly at first, but it's most certainly there. *Blow-Up* is overtly about the relationship between "reality" (remember here Nabokov's admonition that the word means nothing without the quotation marks) and image. *Deep Red* has a less conspicuously metaphysical slant, even as it dabbles in notions of fate and the abysmal nature of the world concealed by the safety of surfaces. One thing the two films share, however, is a fascination with the process of representation; a fascination rooted in their mutual lack of faith in the veracity of two-dimensional representation.

Blow-Up's strategy is well known: close examination of a photograph of an innocuous event - apparently a lover's rendez-

Cover for an Italian horror comic *Profundo Russo,* in which Argento
is made to look like his idol, Edgar Allan Poe.

vous - reveals elements that suggest a crime. There's a con-
spiratorial glance, a man with a gun hidden in some bushes,
there is a corpse almost hidden by another mass of foliage. But
as the picture is blown up in hopes that it can be made to yield
up its secrets, the grain that is normally invisible (subsumed by
the hierarchical superiority of the image it composes) becomes
larger and larger, making the images increasingly elusive. The
final blow-ups are virtually abstract, like experiments in ge-
stalt phenomena. Perhaps there is indeed no body; perhaps
there was in fact no murder - perhaps Thomas has imagined it
all and read his imaginings back into the Rorschach test of the
swirling dots.

There's ample reason to doubt Thomas' ability to draw
accurate conclusions from what he sees: in the park he sees only
the tryst - even though if there was murder this is where it was
committed. And when he first examines the blow-ups he sees
the gunman but not the body, leading him to conclude he's
thwarted a killing. When Thomas, at best a witness once
removed, shows the final blow-up to a friend (the wife of Bill, an
abstract painter), she puts a finger squarely on the dilemma.
"That's the body," he says, indicating a chaos of black, grey,and
white specks. "Looks like one of Bill's paintings," she replies.
And Bill's paintings are certainly problematic. "They don't
mean any thing when I do them...just a mess," he tells Thomas
as they look together at one canvas. "Afterward I find something to hang on to..." He points. "Like that leg. Then it all sorts
itself out. It's like finding a clue in a detective story."

A painting of quite another sort is, of course, the catalyst that
sends Marc on his fantastic journey in *Deep Red*. The hallway
of Helga Ulman's apartment is lined with small, mostly round
canvasses: they depict a veritable sea of Munchian faces, pale,
ghastly, and anguished. In a niche is a mirror in a frame, and
in this mirror Marc sees Marta's chalky face, surrounded by
reflections of the painted faces hers so resembles. He takes no
conscious notice - his concern is to find the woman he has just
seen brutally murdered - but when he returns he realizes that
something is different.

Marc assumes erroneously that a painting has been taken

away; with Carlo he comes to the conclusion that it was "made to disappear because it represented something important." However wrong Marc may be (there's a world of difference between representation and reflection), it's this image that initiates the action; it is the clue in the detective story that - in conjunction with Marc's own photo in the newspaper - sets the plot in motion. Marc's photograph appears in the paper (the place where one finds all the news fit to print; what one reads in the paper is supposed to be true), and it's as contradictory as the image of Marta.

In *Image/Music/Text*, theorist Roland Barthes remarks that the newspaper photograph must be considered a special case, apart from other classes of photographs, because it doesn't exist in imagistic isolation: "... it is in communication with at least one other structure, namely the text - title, caption, or article - accompanying every press photograph." Marc's photograph, taken by Gianna at the scene of the crime - is significant only in light of its caption, which identifies him as the eyewitness; the man who saw it all. Like Sam Dalmas in *The Bird With the Crystal Plumage*, Marc is certain of one thing: he *didn't* see it all, he *can't* identify the killer. In one way they're both right: Dalmas didn't see the face of the black-clad man who fled the gallery and left behind the pitifully wounded Monica, and Marc didn't actually see the murderer. But of course they're also both wrong. The man in black wasn't the murderer - that was Monica, and Sam saw her face as clearly as can be. And Marc saw Marta's face in the mirror. The caption beneath Marc's photograph is both accurate and inaccurate, and the supplemental level of meaning it lends to that photograph is inherently paradoxical.

The two lying images provide the structure of *Deep Red*'s first half; the second is defined by yet another. Against all odds, Marc's investigation (which has proceeded by very strange means indeed, not the least of them being a ghost story recalled by one of Helga's psychic associates; the supernatural part of the story seems irrelevant, but it eventually leads Marc to the house to which Helga referred while in her psychic trance) actually *does* turn up some concrete information. After a circuitous search, he locates the "house of the screaming child" and there finds on the wall a child's drawing, all but completely concealed by a layer of plaster.

Every picture tells a story, and the story this one tells is grim: it depicts a screaming man splashed with red, a bloody knife, and a child clutching the weapon, all frozen before a Christmas tree. The relic of a long past act of violence (which naturally recalls for the viewer the vignette that opened the film) confirms Marc's half-formulated notion that the murderer he seeks (and who seeks him) is the grown-up child of Helga's vision. Marc later finds the drawing's three-dimensional equivalent in a sealed room, also hidden behind a plaster facade: the near-mummified corpse of a man collapsed in front of the cobwebbed remains of a Christmas tree, mute witness to a festive party that somehow ended in bloodshed. But this ghastly tableau - even though it's composed of some of the real objects of the tragedy - is even more misleading than the drawing. While the drawing contains an element - a third figure - that though hidden (by a slab of plaster that falls off only after Marc has already gone, secure in his interpretation of matters) points to the correct solution to the puzzle, the sealed room contains only the corpse: all traces of the murderer are long gone.

A fire destroys the room before Marc can show it to anyone, but while he and Gianna (who has saved him from the blaze) telephone the authorities from the caretaker's house its image almost miraculously reasserts itself. In the bedroom of the caretaker's small daughter, Marc discovers a drawing almost identical to the one on the villa wall. Pressed, little Olga admits that she copied it from something she saw in her school's archive, where projects by former students are stored. And at the deserted schoolhouse Marc and Gianna find what they have been looking for all along: the image with name - Carlo's - appended. The image chain concludes with Carlo's appearance, gun in hand, but however logical the route mapped out by this visual game of "telephone" (in which a phrase is whispered from one person in a group to another; the fun lies in seeing how it's distorted) may seem, it contains hidden detours whose sign-posts aren't clearly legible.

Like *Blow-Up*'s Thomas, Marc is misled at every turn by the images that seem to be leading him from the darkness into the light, and if Marc isn't so thoroughly unsettled by the experience as to be reduced to playing mime tennis (with an imaginary ball whose dull thump when struck by an equally imaginary racket is clearly audible on the soundtrack), then he's certainly not unscathed. Crippled and disillusioned, Marc is last seen gazing at his own reflection, a baffled Narcissus whose face gazes back from the viscous pool of Marta's blood.

It's in *Deep Red* that the notion of Barthesian excess first becomes truly relevant to Argento's work. His first three *gialli*, the "animal trilogy" (*Bird, Cat,* and *Flies*) do, to be sure, contain elements that don't lend themselves to resolution within any system of relationships suggested by the rest of the filmic material.

This is particularly true of *Four Flies on Grey Velvet*. One thinks of the series of dreams that trouble Roberto's sleep, in which he's witness to a ritual Middle Eastern execution rendered in bleached colour and heightened sound: silence broken by the thwack of the executioner's sword. This imagery is adumbrated (and given diegetic motivation) by a story told at a party by one of Roberto's friends, but its obsessive recurrence defies explanation, particularly because the sound of the sword provides in each instance an auditory bridge between the dream and some waking disturbance. Its importance to the structure of the film lies not only in the way it contributes to an overall ambience of fear and violence, but in the very dazzling whiteness of its presentation. The dream doesn't contain a clue, nor does it reflect a waking obsession on Roberto's part; there are no Arabic motifs picked up in other parts of the film, the writer whose story suggests it plays no particularly significant part in the action. The Arabian dream exists in a kind of conspicuous non-relationship to the elements that surround it, set off by its washed-out appearance and its rhythmic progression from extreme long-shot to close-up - from a dazzling establishing shot in a low-walled courtyard to the concluding images of the flashing sword and the victim's rolling head - as a self-contained set piece. And what one is to make of it,

Helga Ulman (Macha Meril) reacts in terror: *Deep Red*.

ultimately, is that one does not know quite what to make of it. Also in *Four Flies on Grey Velvet* one finds isolated shots with a similarly disturbing quality: a low angle long shot of the man following Roberto, for example, is dominated by a grotesque cigarette butt that looms in the foreground in a conspicuous use of forced perspective. In a close-up the same man removes a pair of sunglasses to reveal on the inside lens three pieces of confetti - one red, one yellow, one blue - that form a perfect triangle; he blows them away. These shots have narrative function - the former describes a man's sinister passage through the nighttime streets, the latter provides a character touch - but the impression they make is powerful beyond their narrative importance, just as the grotesque sculptures that fill the Ranieri art gallery in *The Bird With the Crystal Plumage* don't need to be so disturbing merely to signify "art gallery." But these are isolated instances; in *Deep Red* the device is a governing principle.

Deep Red is relentlessly theatrical., The parapsychological conference is introduced with a parting of curtains, and couched in terms that suggest a show of prestidigitation. Giordani's description of Helga's fatal vision (for Marc and Gianna's benefit) becomes a literal re-enactment as he gestures to an invisible audience from the empty stage. Even Helga's funeral (surprisingly enough, given her conspicuously Aryan demeanour, a Jewish ceremony) is a spectacle. Yet *Deep Red* isn't about the theatre, or actors, or even "performers" in any overt sense of the term. The visual centre of attention in many scenes is pointedly displaced to no obvious end: a television screen on which an announcer describes the murder of Helga Ulman (the obvious focal point) finds itself gradually crowded out during a track from long shot to close-up by the profile of a woman smoking a cigarette; the two objects eventually share the Panavision screen space equally, though the woman - who doesn't even react to what's being said - has no function within any larger pattern of images in the film. In fact, we never see her again. Another woman (this one fixing her make-up) occupies the foreground of the frame while Marc asks after Carlo at the Blue Bar (Carlo's place of employment) in the rear;

123

and Marc has *already* been displaced from the centre of attention by a man telling a joke about the problem with the
boomerang business (the merchandise always comes back) to
the bartender.[9] In both cases the women are identified by
significant details: the former by the cigarette she holds between her lips (drawing a straight line in space), the latter by
her open compact; the texture of these objects is the most
riveting thing within the frame. A crazy man on a bicycle
waving the Italian flag, fighting dogs, an abrasive singing fruit
vendor, a sadistic little girl who sticks pins through lizards and
giggles when her father strikes her, the morbid maid (who says
conspiratorially of her employer's mynah birds that what with
all their cackling and imitating things, "it's like having a
madman in the house") who finds a mutilated body and can't
wait to tell all her friends about it; the extreme close-up of
Marc's temple as a rivulet of sweat runs down his fevered
cheek, the exploratory pan over the grossly magnified musical
staff on which he is working, Helga's damp lips, Marta's
quivering eyes, Gianna's profile bathed in multicoloured light
whose apparent source (the burning villa) can't account for the
rainbow hues: all are signs from the realm of the third meaning,
the glittering threads that have no obvious function within the
tapestry of the film yet compel the viewer's attention. The
heightened subtext that informs *Deep Red* throughout and
comes to the forefront when the mechanics of the story fail to
hold the mind's restless eye.

Why, when Marta stalks and kills Giordani, must she first
set loose in his study a cackling mechanical doll? There's no
particular logic to the action, but the image of the broken doll
- arms flailing, skull fractured, mechanical laugh still echoing
- is profoundly unnerving. The toy's blank stare, jerky movements, and tireless tinny gibbering are more creepy-crawly
than Giordani's subsequent murder: the mechanical death
throes don't merely adumbrate his own, but overshadow them
in a curious disruption of the normal hierarchical relationship
of live characters and automata. It's in a sense true that all of

[9]Yet another scene not present in the American print.

Argento's characters are ciphers, but they're flesh and blood ciphers nonetheless; their bloody deaths should count for more than the destruction of a wind-up doll. But they don't; reviewers who compare Argento to a puppeteer (a bloody one, they all hasten to add) aren't totally off target.

More even than an increasing level of technical elegance - achieved both through the director's increasing experience in the medium and by way of the judicious application of more money to the situation - *Deep Red* demonstrates the development of an altered sensibility. Its detective story aspects are extreme expressions of the tendencies inherent from the first (dual/divided protagonists, weird logic, enigmatic narrative structure, displaced visual emphases), but its overall lushness is something new. The textured musical score no longer functions in counterpoint to the images, but combines with them into an integral element; in certain extended passages (notably Marc's exploration of the abandoned villa) it completely replaces dialogue as the aural component of the imagery. The colour is richer, more saturated than that of the preceding films; the camera takes on a freer, increasingly mobile role in relation to the action. *Deep Red* is bigger, brighter, more audacious than the animal trilogy, and if the two films that follow it seem to constitute a light divertissement whose essential function is to prepare the mental palate for *Tenebrae*, it isn't because their stylization has no precedent in *Deep Red*. *Suspiria* and *Inferno* abandon the *giallo* format for a hallucinogenic fairytale approach to horror; they're full of witches, sorcerers, and alchemists who cast evil spells over modern naïfs. But their riotous Technicolor stylization (and it's their look that is most impressive) has its roots in *Deep Red*, in the candy colours that play over Gianna's face after she pulls Marc from the villa fire, the neon flickerings that pierce the darkness of the piazza in front of Marc's building, and the backlit windows crawling with Art Nouveau tendrils of the ruined villa.

Even the overtly supernatural concerns of *Suspiria* and *Inferno* aren't unprecedented; *Deep Red* permits supernatural glimmerings while seeking to absorb them back into a context that permits the effect without demanding a paranormal explanation. During her lecture, for example, Helga takes pains to make clear that her psychic gifts have nothing to do with magic; her remarks follow Giordani's extensive lecture on the occurrence of telepathy in the "natural" world - that is, the world of animals and insects. But after she's been irrevocably silenced by Marta's cleaver, it remains for Gianna - in her role as the voice of the press - to comment on Helga's gift for the record. "She was a kind of magician," Gianna says, making a spooky gesture with her hand, "she could read the future."

Bardi's reference to the account of a haunted house he read in Amanda Righetti's *Modern Ghosts and Black Legends of Today* is similarly double-edged. This story of a shunned villa suggests that it's haunted by the spirit of a child who screams and sings and when Marc circuitously makes his way to the site, it is indeed intimately connected with his own investigation. One might infer that the only haunting is done by Marta, perhaps periodically compelled to return to the scene of her crime; once there she skulks out of sight with her tape recorder, listening obsessively to the children's song that was playing that Christmas night. After all, Carlo is the child of the house and he's not dead - generally a prerequisite for being a ghost. And yet the German writer who was the villa's most recent tenant, Marc learns in talking to the caretaker, died under mysterious circumstances. Was he pushed to his death from a window by mad Marta, whom he discovered lurking the otherwise empty house? Or did something genuinely unearthly drive him to suicide? The caretaker's daughter - who seems disturbingly in touch with dark and evil things - pointedly tells Marc to look out for ghosts in there because everybody knows the house is haunted. From *Deep Red*'s sophisticated hedging it's only a step to the grim fairy tale *milieux* of *Suspiria* and *Inferno*, whose nightmare landscapes are alive with all manner of ghosties, ghoulies, and long-leggity beasties. In keeping with the oneiric quality of Argento's work as a whole, it's hard not to find a significance in the fact that the inspiration for these two films can be traced to a dream, a 19th-century opium dream so perfectly in tune with Argento's own obsessions that if it hadn't existed, he would surely have had to invent it.

SUSPIRIA *and* INFERNO

"Bad luck isn't brought by broken mirrors, but by broken minds."
- Franco (*Suspiria*)

"What's that, a riddle? I'm not good at riddles."
- Kazanian (*Inferno*)

When a dream becomes a nightmare, the average dreamer just wants to wake up and shake off the cold grip of night terrors. But the history of horror literature is full of dreamers who carried over their nightmares to the waking hours, then committed them to paper. The three most famous examples gave us *Frankenstein, Dracula* and *Dr. Jekyll and Mr. Hyde.*

Mary Shelley was vacationing in Switzerland with her half sister, lover (later husband) Percy Bysshe Shelley, his friend, the mad-bad-and-dangerous-to-know Lord Byron, and Byron's high-strung companion, Dr. Polidori. Her dream gave her the material with which to rise to a literary challenge: each of them was to write a spooky story with which to amuse the others. *Frankenstein* filled the bill and more.[1] Bram Stoker (who, eminent Victorian that he was, owed his troubled sleep to over-indulging at dinner) found the Lord of the Vampires he called Dracula in a nightmare, while Robert Louis Stevenson reprimanded his wife when she woke him from "dreaming a fine bogey tale," *Dr. Jekyll and Mr. Hyde.* The enduring power of all three works is obvious: each has been adapted dozens of times, and has inspired hundreds of movies, plays, novels and short stories.

Frankenstein is the atypical case, overtly philosophical and ultimately less horrifying than overwhelmingly sad. Its successful ("successful" here meaning appealing to a popular

[1]Whether Polidori's story, *The Vampyre* (often attributed, incorrectly, to Byron), was also inspired by a dream is anyone's guess.

127

audience) adaptation to the popular stage and then to the screen has always demanded radical reworking of the basic material. Shelley's intelligent, literate creature (whose soul is eventually warped by the constant rejection his ugliness inspires) is almost invariably made mute or barely articulate. At best the monster is child-like, as in James Whale's *Frankenstein* (1931) and its sequel, *Bride of Frankenstein* (1935). At worst it becomes - in countless sequels, updatings and variations - a violent brute, little better than a rabid animal.

By contrast, the strength of movie versions of *Dr. Jekyll and Mr. Hyde* and *Dracula* lies precisely in the doctor and the vampire, who've been lifted from the page virtually intact. Even in contexts that couldn't be more foreign from those of outraged Victorian propriety envisioned by Stevenson and Stoker, Dracula and Jekyll/Hyde survive and flourish, monsters from the subconscious whose iconic function can accommodate innumerable superficial changes. Each generation gets the Dracula or Jekyll/Hyde it deserves, because they're not just the products of specific dreams, dreamed by individuals.

The vampire, the manmade monster, and the shape-shifter (*Dr. Jekyll and Mr. Hyde* is a werewolf story in all but name) are the stuff of myth, folklore, and fairy tales, part of the vast collective dreams of the societies from which they sprang. The myth and folklore of the twentieth century, dreamed in the collective darkness of movie theatres, live in the cinema. And the nightmares - dark dreams of blood and death - are horror movies, whose potent images often do not even pretend to mirror waking reality but rather spring directly from an oneiric maelstrom.

Suspiria (1977) and *Inferno* (1980) represent Argento's first and to date only forays into the realm of the purely supernatural horror film. What's most remarkable about both films and particularly about *Suspiria* - perhaps only because it was made first and paved the way for *Inferno* - is their mind-boggling artificiality. Remarked less-than-enthusiastic John Coleman in *The New Criterion*, "Suspiria... is Lewis Carroll meeting Caligari, or fun and maims in a Chinese brothel," referring mostly to the outrageous decor, rather than the plot, while the

Soho Weekly News' Rob Baker, more sympathetically but in the same vein, called it "gorgeously filmed in bright, gaudy primary color, reminiscent of Fassbinder at his most perverse... Everything in the film is slightly cockeyed, both visually and aurally (the voice-overs, for example, have a hollow eeriness - a calculated flatness - that really got to me and that I think was absolutely intentional, like the vocals on a Kraftwerk album). It's sort of like Polanski doing *Alice in Wonderland* just after filming *Repulsion*." The references here are significant: the horror film (*The Cabinet of Dr. Caligari*) laden with references to dreams and hallucinations (*Repulsion*) and the self-conscious, convoluted fairy tale - *Alice in Wonderland*, an artificial and sophisticated word game for adults couched in the terms of a children's story. *Suspiria* and *Inferno* look like big, bright, nightmare fairy tales, but they don't derive their underlying narrative and thematic structures from unadulterated dream imagery or rustic folklore: their antecedents are altogether more studied.

At the time he began working on *Suspiria*, Argento has said he "was supposed to do a film inspired by the stories of (H.P.) Lovecraft for an American production company, but I had to back out; it wasn't easy to get a cohesive story out of them. I mulled over the idea of making a fantasy film. Witches always fascinated me; I don't believe in the devil, in the movies he always makes me laugh... What's more, *Suspiria* is heavily influenced by *Snow White and the Seven Dwarfs*; in an early draft I even planned to have the action take place in a child's school where the witches were teachers who tortured the children." Though the Lovecraft project never came to anything - as with the Agatha Christie novels to which he was offered rights by Dino De Laurentiis, it seems likely that Argento wasn't really interested in adapting another writer's work - it suggests a methodology eventually manifest in *Suspiria* and *Inferno*.

Howard Phillips Lovecraft has been adapted to the screen many times, in such films as: *The Haunted Palace* (1963, based on *The Case of Charles Dexter Ward*), *Die, Monster, Die* (1965, *The Colour Out of Space*), *The Shuttered Room* (1967), *The*

Suzy Banyon (Jessica Harper) in *Suspiria*.

An imperilled heroine (Jessica Harper), an ogre (Flavio Bucci) and a sacrificial victim-to-be (Stefania Casini): *Suspiria*.

Crimson Cult (1968, *The Dreams in the Witch House*), *The Dunwich Horror* (1969), *The Farm* (1987, *The Colour Out of Space*, again), *Re-Animator* (1984, *Herbert West: Reanimator*) and *From Beyond* (1986). A reclusive pulp writer whose sexual retardation, racial prejudices, hypochondria, misogyny (misanthropy, really, but women were clearly the greater of two evils) and affected contempt for all aspects of 20th-century life informed (and often marred) all his writing. But he made an enduring contribution to modern horror fiction in the form of the Cthulu Mythos. A self-contained mythology, complete from creation myth to apocalyptic prophesies, with sacred texts, rituals and a complicated pantheon of gods and semi-divine (or perhaps semi-infernal) individuals, the Cthulu Mythos is a rigorously contrived construct, the kind of artificial structure that results from the application of the peculiar fantasies of a perverse, educated sensibility to a primitive cultural framework. It's hard to see Argento buying in to someone else's artificial mythology as enthusiastically as he created his own for *Suspiria* and *Inferno*. Vladimir Propp's *Morphology of the Folklore* proposes a deconstructive method of analysing traditional folktales, which he rightly recognizes as highly stylized constructions. His system isolates and examines individual elements of action (he calls them "functions") that, in various combinations, comprise all such tales, rather than in light of more traditional concerns (the moral, for example). It's a system that looks as though it might work equally well for *Suspiria* and *Inferno*, but first you need to look at the authentic folk tale, then the more sophisticated fairy tale, to see how they differ. Propp finds the following story typical of the traditional peasant tale in its language, its imagery, and it structure, so it can serve here as an example:

There lived an old man and an old woman; they had a daughter and a little son. "Daughter, daughter," said the mother, "we are going out to work and will bring you back a little bun, sew you a little dress, and buy you a little kerchief. Be wise, take care of your little brother, and do not leave the courtyard." The elders went away, and the daughter forgot what they had ordered her to do. She placed her little brother on the grass under a window and ran into the street and became absorbed in playing and having fun.

The swan-geese flew down, seized the little boy, and carried him away on their wings. The little girl came back, looked, but her little brother wasn't there. She gasped and rushed hither and thither, but he wasn't anywhere. She called out; she burst into tears, wailing that harm would come to her from her father and mother, but her little brother did not answer. She ran out into the open field; the swan-geese sped away into the distance and disappeared beyond the dark wood. The swan-geese had long before acquired ill-fame, caused much mischief, and had stolen away many a little child. The girl guessed that they had carried off her little brother, and she set out to catch up with them... She would have run through the fields and wandered in the forest a long time if she had not by good fortune met a hedgehog. "Little hedgehog, little hedgehog," she asked, "did you not see where the geese have flown?" "Away, over there," he pointed. She ran, and came upon a hut on chicken legs. It was standing and turning around. In the hut sat Baba Jaga, hag-faced and with a leg of clay. The little brother also sat there on a little bench, playing with golden apples...

This story (which ends with the children safe at home) demonstrates in places a dream-like logic that glosses over the dull mechanics of getting from one place to another while emphasizing repetitious, ritualistic elements: "Daughter, daughter"; "little hedgehog, little hedgehog"; "We... will bring you back a little bun, sew you a little dress and buy you a little kerchief"; the almost incantatory repetition of the term "swan-geese" and a series of questions and answers that Propp eliminates in the interest of space because he has already discussed the structure at some length. It contains certain grotesqueries, like the hut on chicken legs (the trope "It was standing and turning around" is particularly dreamlike) and Baba Jaga with her artificial limb, but the overall tone cannot compare with that of, for example, the following excerpt from Hans Christian Andersen:

So the little mermaid left the garden and went into the foaming

132

whirlpool, beyond which dwelt the enchantress. She had never been this way before - neither flowers nor sea-grass bloomed along her path; she had to traverse an extent of bare grey sand until she reached the whirlpool, whose waters were eddying and whizzing like millwheels, tearing everything they could seize along with them into the abyss below. She was obliged to make her way through this horrible place, in order to arrive at the territory of the enchantress. Then she had to pass through a boiling, slimy bog, which the enchantress called her turf-moor: her house stood in a wood beyond this, and a strange abode it was. All the trees and bushes were polypi, looking around hundred-headed serpents shooting up out of the ground; their branches were long slimy arms with fingers of worms, every member, from the root to the uppermost tip, ceaselessly moving and extending on all sides. Whatever they seized they fastened upon so that it could not loose itself from their grasp. The little mermaid stood still for a minute looking at this horrible wood; her heart beat with fear, and she certainly would have returned without attaining her object, had she not remembered the prince - and immortality. The thought gave her new courage, she bound up her long waving hair, that the polypi might not catch hold of it, crossed her delicate arms over her bosom and, swifter than a fish can glide through the water, she passed these unseemly trees, who stretched their eager arms after her in vain. She could not, however, help seeing that every polypus had something in its grasp, held as firmly by a thousand little arms as if enclosed by iron bands. The whitened skeletons of a number of human beings who had drowned in the sea and had sunk into the abyss, grinned horribly from the arms of these polypi; helms, chests, skeletons of land animals were also held in their embrace; among other things might be seen here, even a little mermaid whom they had seized and strangled! What a fearful sight for the unfortunate princess!

Scary stuff! It's a wonder Walt Disney ever managed to whip Andersen's *Little Mermaid* into the frothy 1989 children's cartoon of the same name. This is sophisticated perversion, bizarre sado-erotic imagery couched in the faux-naïf language of the children's tale by an intelligence whose training (formal or informal) can't help but warp the form of the genuine rustic tale. And in Andersen's case we're in all likelihood still talking about a largely unconscious process. For a truly self-aware example of this strategy, take a look at Angela Carter's *The Bloody Chamber and Other Adult Tales*. Carter takes the raw material of fairy tales and weaves it into sophisticated, frankly erotic vignettes awash in blood and spunk. Two of these tales, "Wolf Alice" and "The Company of Wolves," were made in into Neil Jordan's 1984 *The Company of Wolves*, a dream-like, supremely self-conscious horror movie with no pretence to being children's entertainment.

Suspiria and *Inferno*, the first two installments of a projected trilogy, have at their centres the figures of the "Three Mothers." Couched in lurid fairy tale terms, the films were inspired by a literary rendering of an opium dream whose mythological aspect is so convincing that it's led many writers to speak of the Three Mothers as though they were figures of authentic legend. Their origins are, in fact, rather more baroque.

Thomas De Quincey's claim to fame is a small one, almost a footnote to literary history. Born in 1785, dead in 1859, he was the author of *Confessions of an English Opium Eater*, the friend of William Wordsworth and fellow addict Samuel Coleridge, and the quintessential 19th-century visionary writer. Seduced by hallucinatory dreams that dazzled him under the influence of opium, reconciled early in life to the idea that he'd never be free of longing for those glorious visions, De Quincey was both an apologist for drug use and realist enough to recognize its destructive effects. University-educated, bookish as a child, and morbidly romantic as an adult, he had visions of heaven and hell, dreams of classical deities and wholly self-generated wraiths. One such dream (or rather, literary construct that may have been inspired by an actual dream; it's far too elegantly coherent to be the direct transcription of some welling up of subconscious concerns) is recounted in De Quincey's *Suspiria de Profundis* (*Sighs from the Depths*), a collection of essays intended as a follow-up to the *Confessions*. Its title is *Levana and Our Ladies of Sorrow*, and it contains the essential notions that underlie *Suspiria* and *Inferno* and that will equally shape the third film - tentatively referred to as *Mother of Tears* - yet to be made.[2] For this reason, I've quoted this essay almost in its entirety.

Therefore it is that Levana often communes with the powers that shake man's heart; therefore it is that she goes upon grief. "These ladies," said I softly to myself on seeing the ministers with whom Levana was conversing, "these are the Sorrows; and they are three in number, as the Graces are three, who dress man's life with beauty; the Parcae are three, who weave the dark areas of man's life in their mysterious loom always with colours sad in part, sometimes angry with tragic crimson and black; the Furies are three, who visit with retribution called from the other side of the grave offenses that walk upon this; and at once even the Muses were but three, who fit the harp, the trumpet, or the lute to the great burdens of man's impassioned creations. These are the Sorrows, all three of whom I know." For already, in my fervent youth, I saw (dimly relived upon the dark background of my dreams) the imperfect lineaments of the awful sisters - by what name shall we call them?

If I say simply "the Sorrows," there will be a chance of mistaking the term; it might be understood of individual sorrow - separate cases of sorrow - whereas I want a term expressing the mighty abstractions

[2]Something may need to be clarified here. Luigi Cozzi has made a film called *The Black Cat* in the United States in an attempt (on the part of the distributor, 21st-Century) to cash in on the 1989-90 fad for films based on the works of Edgar Allan Poe - including Argento/George Romero's two-part compendium film *Two Evil Eyes*. Argento's segment was based on Poe's *The Black Cat* and other stories, but Cozzi's film - co-written with Argento's ex-, Daria Nicolodi, who *also* co-wrote *Suspiria* (still with me?) - started out as *De Profundis*, the third Three Mothers picture. It concerns a film crew making a movie about a witch, Levana, and the dreadful things the real Levana does to them. By the time the film was done, Cozzi claims, the Three Mothers material was just a homage to his mentor; he felt it was inappropriate for him to complete Argento's trilogy. As far back as 1984 Nicolodi claimed the third Three Mothers picture - co-written by Argento and herself - was practically ready to go. But though she said the script was finished and they were just working out production details, the film is still just a tantalizing notion.

that incarnate themselves in all individual sufferings of man's heart; and I wish to have these abstractions presented as impersonations, that is, as clothed with human attributes of life and with functions pointing to flesh. Let us call them, therefore, Our Ladies of Sorrow. I know them thoroughly and have walked in all their kingdoms. Three sisters they are, of one mysterious household; and their paths are wide apart; but of their dominion there is no end... The eldest of the three is named Mater Lachrymarum, Our Lady of Tears. She it is that night and day raves and moans, calling for vanished faces. She stood in Rama, where a voice was heard of lamentation - Rachel weeping for her children, and refused to be comforted. She it was that stood in Bethlehem on the night when Herod's sword swept its nurseries of Innocents, and the little feet were stiffened forever, which, heard at times as they tottered along floors overhead, woke pulses of love in household hearts that were not unmarked in heaven.

Her eyes are sweet and subtle, wild and sleepy,by turns, oftentimes rising to the clouds, oftentimes challenging by heavens. She wears a diadem around her head... By the power of her keys it is that Our Lady of Tears glides a ghostly intruder into the chambers of sleepless men, sleepless women, sleepless children, from Ganges to the Nile, from Nile to Mississippi. And her, because she is the first-born of her house and has the widest empire, let us honor with the title of "Madonna."

The second sister is called Mater Suspiriorum, Our Lady of Sighs. She never scales the clouds nor walks abroad upon the winds. She wears no diadem. And her eyes, if they were ever seen, would be neither sweet nor subtle; no man could read their story; they would be found filled with perishing dreams and wrecks of forgotten delirium. But she raises not her eyes; her head, on which sits a dilapidated turban, droops forever, forever fastens on the dust. She weeps not. She groans not. But she sighs inaudibly at intervals. Her sister Madonna is oftentimes stormy and frantic, raging in the highest heaven and demanding back her darlings. But Our Lady of Sighs never clamors, never defies, dreams not of rebellious aspirations. She is humble to abjectness... Hers is the meekness that belongs to the hopeless. Murmur she may, but it is in her sleep. Whisper she may, but it is to herself in the twilight. Mutter she does, but it is in solitary places that are as desolate as she is desolate, in

ruined cities, and when the sun has gone down to his rest... all that
are betrayed and all that are rejected; outcasts by traditionary law
and children of hereditary disgrace - all these walk with Our Lady of
Sighs. She also carries a key, but she needs it little. For her kingdom
is chiefly amongst the tents of Shem and the houseless vagrant of
every clime. Yet in the very highest ranks of man she finds chapels
of her own; and even in glorious England there are some that, to the
world, carry their heads as proudly as the reindeer, yet who secretly
have received her mark upon their foreheads.

But the third sister, who is also the youngest! Hush! Whisper
whilst we talk of her! Her kingdom is not large, or else no flesh should
live; but within that kingdom all power is hers. Her head, turreted
like that of Cybele, rises almost beyond the reach of sight. She droops
not, and her eyes rising so high might be hidden by distance. But,
being what they are, they cannot be hidden; through the treble veil
of crepe which she wears, the fierce light of a blazing misery, that
rests not for matins nor for vespers, for noon of day or noon of night,
for ebbing or for flowing tide, may be read from the very ground. She
is the defier of God. She is also the mother of lunacies and the
suggestress of suicides. Deep lie the roots of her power, but narrow
is the nation she rules. For she can approach only those in whom a
profound nature has been unheaved by central convulsions, in whom
the heart trembles and the brain rocks under conspiracies of tempest
from without and tempest from within. Madonna moves with uncertain steps, fast or slow, but still with tragic grace. Our Lady of Sighs
creeps timidly and stealthily. But this youngest sister moves with
incalculable motions, bounding, and with a tiger's leaps; She carries
no key, for though coming rarely amongst men, she storms all doors
at which she is permitted to enter at all. And her name is Mater
Tenebrarum - Our Lady of Darkness.

The essay provides the foundation upon which *Suspiria* and
Inferno rest, though this doesn't become readily apparent
unless you've seen both pictures. Daria Nicolodi's contribution
to shaping *Suspiria* needs to be taken into account. During the
filming of *Deep Red*, she told Argento about her grandmother's
experiences at a finishing school where black magic was prac-
tised after hours. The finishing school became *Suspiria*'s dance

academy, one of the houses of the damned. At first glance *Suspiria* looks as though it will benefit from being read through, for example, a formalist or structuralist system like Propp's, which is doubly appealing because the film plays like nothing more than a particularly nasty fairy tale.

Young Suzy Banyon (Jessica Harper), an aspiring ballet dancer from America, elects to continue her studies at the prestigious *Tanzakademie* in Freiburg, Germany. Her arrival in the country is accompanied by a ferocious storm, and she finds the gargoyle-encrusted academy a daunting place. The first thing she sees there that dark and stormy night is another girl - who's later murdered and mutilated - fleeing the building for the surrounding woods; Suzy can't get in and has to spend the night in town.

The next day she returns and meets the faculty and her fellow students. The other girls are petty and malicious; with the exception of the unpopular Sara (Stefania Casini), whom Suzy befriends, they treat her like a poor relation. The administrators - capricious, treacly Madame Blanc (Joan Bennett) and stern Miss Tanner (Alida Valli) - are off-putting. The instructors are cruel, secretive, and worse, as Suzy learns after Sara disappears one night: they're witches in the service of a centuries-old sorceress named Helena Marcos, and from the academy she and her minions spread evil throughout the region. Guided by the words she heard spoken in the storm by the fleeing student (they're a clue that lead to a secret passageway), Suzy finds the witches' lair - concealed at the centre of a maze of labyrinthine corridors behind the walls of the school - and stabs Helena Marcos to death with a crystal spike. Suzy then flees as the building bursts into flames and is consumed as yet another thunderstorm rages.

A number of the functions delineated by Propp in connection with the traditional fairy tale can be equally applied to *Suspiria*. "A member of a family absents himself from home" (Function I) - Suzy leaves America for Germany, both foreign and distant. Several interdictions, which constitute Propp's Function II, are implicit in Suzy's first encounters with her teachers and classmates: the murdered student was "a busybody," "always arguing and making trouble"; Suzy should mind her own business. She must live at the school rather than boarding in town with Olga, a third-year student ("I had no idea you were so strong-willed," hisses the grotesque Miss Tanner through her too-white teeth when Suzy protests mildly) and, after a suspicious fainting spell, she must adhere to a restricted diet ("bland food for about a week") and drink red wine supplied by the school (to "build up the red corpuscles") on the advice of the curious Professor Verdegast[3] whom the school sends to attend her. As must the protagonist of any fairy tale, Suzy violates these interdictions (Function III); she doesn't remain at school willingly (her things are brought from Olga's after she collapses in class), she noses into all sorts of things (where the teachers go at night; what happened to Sara; what the murdered student meant with her cryptic allusion to "secrets" and "irises"), and throws away her special food and wine. Function VII has the hero tricked into complicity with the villain, as Suzy is when she once eats her special meal and falls into a drugged sleep. This unwitting complicity costs Sara her life; with Suzy asleep she has to go exploring the school by herself and meets with bloody death. Sara's death fulfills Function VIII, in which the villain caused injury to a member of the hero's family - in this instance Sara serves as substitute sister or cousin to Suzy; even their names are similar. The witches pursue Suzy ("She must die, die, die!" shrieks Madame Blanc, the sorceress' right hand) in fulfillment of Function XXI and she is rescued as Function XXII demands: after she stabs the sorceress, the very house begins to fly apart as though it can't hold without its evil centre. Function XXX has the villain punished; the death of Helena Marcos, her witches, and the destruction of the house from which they conduct their evil business certainly fulfills this requirement.

It's all very suggestive, but you have to be careful. Propp's system was devised for application to a very specific form - the primitive Russian folktale - and *Suspiria* is no such thing.

[3]The name recalls the very disturbed Dr. Vitus Verdegast, of Edgar G. Ulmer's *The Black Cat*...it's a small world of influences, after all.

Aspiring ballerina Suzy Banyon (Jessica Harper) is terrorized by one of the minions of Mater Susperiorum in *Suspiria*.

A blind man and his dog, soon to be victims of Mater Susperiorum's wrath. *Suspiria*.

Propp himself notes carefully that such analysis "is complicated... by the fact that the uncorrupted tale construction is peculiar only to the peasantry - to a peasantry, moreover, little touched by civilization. All kinds of foreign influences alter and sometimes corrupt a tale... Complications begin as soon as we leave the boundary of the absolutely authentic tale. In this relation, the Afanas'ev collection [from which Propp draws his examples] is surprisingly gratifying material. But the tales of the Brothers Grimm, presenting the same scheme in general, display a less pure and stable form of it. It is impossible to provide for all the details. One must keep in mind that just as elements are assimilated within a tale, whole genres are also assimilated and intermingled." *Suspiria* and *Inferno* are very corrupt tales indeed, inspired by the literary dream of a classically educated opium addict and incorporating influences as diverse as Walt Disney's *Snow White* (once a peasant folk tale, but now an American pop culture artifact) and various forms of bizarre occultism. Sara's friend Franco, a psychiatrist, contributes the notion that witchcraft is linked to mental disorders, backed up by his friend Dr. Milius, author of *Paranoia or Magic*, "the last word on the subject." Sara is raised from the dead like a traditional voodoo zombie, grotesquely reanimated by Helena Marcos (whose Greek origins invoke the world of classical magic), and the *Tanzakademie* is a house of the damned (destroyed in a Jungian apocalypse of fire and water) behind those doors lurk a very Christian hell. What's explicitly lacking is De Quincey's vicious matriarchal trinity. They're introduced by way of a book, E. Varelli's *The Three Mothers*, in *Inferno*'s prologue.

"I do not know what price I shall have to pay for breaking what we alchemists call *Silentium*," intones a man's voice over shots of a young woman, aided by her Cassell's Latin dictionary, reading a leatherbound volume. "The life experience of our colleague should teach us not to upset laymen by imposing our knowledge upon them. I, Varelli, an architect living in London, met the Three Mothers and designed and built for them three dwelling places. One in Rome, one in New York, and the third in Freiburg, Germany. I failed to discover until

141

too late that from those three locations the Three Mothers rule the world with sorrow, tears, and darkness. Mater Suspiriorum, the Mother of Sighs and the oldest of the three, lives at Freiburg. Mater Lachrymarum, the Mother of Tears and the most beautiful of the sisters, holds rule in Rome. Mater Tenebrarum, the Mother of Darkness, who is the youngest and cruelest of the three, controls New York. And I built their horrible houses, the repositories of all their filthy secrets. Those so called mothers are actually wicked step-mothers, incapable of creating life... these three were sisters as well as mothers, just as there are three muses, three graces, three fates, and three furies. The land upon which the three houses have been constructed will eventually become deathly and plague-ridden, so much so that the area all around will reek horribly. And that is the first key to the mothers' secret, truly the primary key. The second key to the poisonous secret of the three sisters is hidden in the cellar under their houses. There you can find both the picture and the name of the sister living in that house. This is the location of the second key. The third key can be found under the soles of your shoes; there is the third key."

   In retrospect, this twisted rendering of De Quincey's altogether more elegant obsession makes clear precisely what's the matter at the *Tanzakademie*: it's the blighted residence of Mater Suspiriorum, and the witches who live there call on the wicked strength of her avatar - Helena Marcos - to make possible their evil-doing. Like the weird New York apartment building of *Inferno*, the house isn't just a wild, extravagant monument to some spectacular individual bad taste, but the physical evidence of the evil of the Three Mothers, embodied in the writhing Art Nouveau decor and saturated primary colours.
   "[In] *Suspiria*... we were trying to reproduce the colour of Walt Disney's *Snow White*; it has been said from the beginning that Technicolor lacked subdued shades, was without nuances - like cut-out cartoons," Argento said. *Suspiria* certainly isn't shot in subtle shades. As soon as Suzy leaves the fluorescent safety of the Freiburg airport she's adrift in a psychedelic world of swirling red, yellow, and blue jewel-tones. Great washes of

Through a *trompe l'oeil* door, colourfully: *Suspiria*'s internal space breaks up spectacularly.

Defying logic for effect: *Suspiria*'s chamber of barbed wire.

143

colour define the film's interior spaces (indeed, the very names of different rooms in the academy reflect this hierarchy; Miss Tanner calls for class in the Red Room, directs students to rehearsal in the Yellow Room, and so on) like physical dividers. Within individual shots, huge solid areas of single colours abound; the background will be dominated by strips of yellow, the middle ground cool deep blue, while in the foreground a character's face will glow red. Pure, intense red light pulsates behind the odd-shaped panes of glass in the academy's many doors; Sara is pursued through rich blue rooms by the razor-wielding sorcerer's apprentice who eventually cuts her throat in a room improbably full of barbed wire; a yellow haze suffuses the piazza in which the academy's blind pianist - who's run afoul of Madame Blanc and the shrieking Miss Tanner - is attacked and killed by his own guide dog, turned suddenly and inexplicably savage. The occasional scene that takes place in relatively naturalistic light - like the one in which Suzy meets Franco in an anonymous modern piazza outside a high-rise office building, and confides to him her suspicions about the academy - looks strangely surreal after the eye has accustomed itself to the candy-coloured universe. The consistency of *Suspiria*'s colour strategy, in which the riotous dayglo colours embody the hysterical, hypersensitive world of witchcraft and sorcery, is truly marvelous; it was both rigorously planned and meticulously executed. *Suspiria* wasn't just designed and lit according to a complicated visual scheme, but was also manipulated in the laboratory to achieve its final extreme effect. "With [Director of Photography Luciano] Tovoli, we used the same procedures as they did in the fifties with Technicolor, with very vivid colours," Argento remarked. "It's a matter of using three film matrixes for the three base colours: red, green, and blue, and then superimposing them while each time stressing the colour you want to have stand out. Kodak didn't even have more than a few thousand meters of this type of stock." The success of their endeavour is evident in virtually every frame of *Suspiria*. Even if you're thoroughly unimpressed by the simplistic narrative, you can't ignore the systematic and sumptuous colour scheme. *Suspiria* proved to be Argento's greatest ever box office success in the United States, despite the generally ghastly reviews - most were on the order of John Simon's assessment in *New York*: "It is," he wrote, "a horror movie that is a horror of a movie, where no one or nothing makes sense: not one plot element, psychological reaction, minor character, piece of dialogue, or ambience." Well no, it doesn't precisely make sense... not in any conventional way, but then neither does the story of *Little Red Riding Hood*; what kind of stupid little girl can't tell her grandmother from a great hairy wolf? Does the situation call for complicated solutions involving associative mental disorders? No. That isn't the *point*.

Inferno explores much the same territory as its predecessor with - if it's possible - even less concern for the constraints of plausible fiction. Rose Elliot (Irene Miracle), a poet living in a strange New York apartment building, discovers in an old leather-bound book the legend of the Three Mothers who, from their specially constructed houses in Rome, Freiburg, and New York, generate all the misery and misfortune in the world. Convinced that she lives in one of those houses, Rose writes to her brother Mark (Leigh McCloskey) - a music student in Rome - asking him to come to New York and help her investigate. Evil forces intervene; Mark's girlfriend Sara reads the letter and is soon after hideously murdered - all that remains of Rose's missive are some tantalizing fragments. Attempts to reach her by telephone are frustrating - the trans-Atlantic lines are more than usually unclear - and by the time Mark arrives in New York, his sister has vanished. Her friend and neighbour, the neurotic, sickly Countess Elise (Daria Nicolodi), adds to Mark's concern with her own worries about Rose's peculiar behaviour in recent days. Mark's search leads him into the building's grim corridors, hidden passages, and concealed recesses; the staff is weird, the neighbours a curious collection of cripples and miscreants, the atmosphere tense and stifling. He finally finds himself face to face with Mater Tenebrarum, Death incarnate, but manages to escape with his life while the hideous house burns around her. Unlike *Suspiria*, whose fairy tale underpinnings help propel the admittedly weak narrative along at a respectable pace, *Inferno* lacks even that logic. Its flimsy yet convoluted narrative is nothing more than an excuse for Argento to compose still more outrageous images and light them from a lunatic palette. *Inferno*'s appearance is not quite so extreme as *Suspiria*'s in some respects, and though this may be due in some part to the presence of a different Director of Photography - Romano Albani - it is principally because the film is shot in a conventional contemporary Technicolor process; the extreme saturation of colour that marked *Suspiria* is not in evidence, although the flamboyant compositions in colour remain. *Inferno*'s music track, composed by Keith Emerson (of Emerson, Lake, and Palmer), also strikes a less urgent note than *Suspiria*'s "relentless and obvious" (to put the worst possible construction on it, by way of Russell Davies of *The Observer*) score, a Goblin composition with which Argento reportedly frightened his actors into character by having it played over the otherwise empty sound stages on which much of the film was shot.[4] Departing from the repetitive synthesizer sound that dominates *Deep Red*, *Suspiria* (and, later, *Tenebrae*), *Inferno* is informed by a fairly delicate piano composition that periodically bursts into Orffian hysteria, à la perpetual soundtrack favourite *Carmina Burana*. *Inferno*'s strength lies in its set pieces, some of which are exceptional in their dreamlike eeriness.

Perhaps the most elaborate of these set pieces occurs at the very beginning of the film, in the cellar (where the second key is hidden) of Rose's building. Compelled to investigate, Rose finds herself in a dank basement whose very walls are crisscrossed by tiny rivulets of water that pools on the floor, beneath the planks on which she walks. Startled by something, Rose drops her keys into one such puddle; when she reaches down to recover them, her arm plunges into the water up to the elbow:

[4]This was not only a mean thing to do (that wouldn't stop lots of directors), but also one that required having the score composed before the film started shooting. Ordinary filmmaking practice leaves the score for last. Interestingly, Sergio Leone did the same thing with Ennio Morricone's score for *Once Upon a Time in the West*, which may be where Argento got the idea.

Spanish poster art for *Inferno*.

the effect is reminiscent of the mirrors that become watery doors to another world in Jean Cocteau's *Orpheus* (1949). Rose fishes for her keys, but the puddle seems bottomless; eventually she slips into the pool and sinks into a silent, aquatic deep. Beneath the water's placid surface is a vast room, a ballroom whose walls bear the name "Tenebrae." Rose finds the keys caught on a sconce but dislodges them and must dive still deeper to effect their recovery. In the dim watery depths she is attacked by a disintegrating corpse and only barely manages to swim to the surface and escape. This sequence, on which Argento's friend and aesthetic precursor Mario Bava worked, lacks nothing save narrative sense. Rose's experience in the womb-like submerged chamber, beautiful, serene, and desperately ominous, is - for example - the perfect structural adumbration of Mark's climactic encounter with the Mother of Darkness herself. Rose's underground trial is by water; that of her sibling takes place aboveground in a vast chamber alive with flames. Their means of entrance into the arenas are identical: Rose slides into the water between two planks, while Mark pulls up the floorboards in Rose's apartment and lowers himself into the resulting chasm. In each case the space entered is illogical - the pool beneath the basement floor has no business being there (not only shouldn't it exist, but it couldn't; buildings don't stand on foundations of water), anymore than the enormous tunnel beneath Rose's floor does. And within these illegitimate spaces, Rose and Mark meet supernatural foes: she comes face to face with a living corpse, he with Death in all its skeletal glory. The resonance of this structural juxtaposition of fire and water is intellectual; the disturbing spatial dislocations within the two scenes have a powerful emotional impact. While the exploration of the cellar recalls fleetingly Marc Daly's excursion to the flooded basement of *Deep Red*'s "haunted house" (evoking that film's obsession with secret sins and the oppressive past), its real function is to implant the notion that the house of Mater Tenebrarum is an evil fun-house, where nothing can be taken at face value. Voices echo through strange ducts and vents that connect the apartments for no logical reason, service doors open into mazes filled with fiends, windows become guillotines, and the very floors drop away to uncover wells with their origins concealed in some primal darkness; the pool in the cellar is some unfathomable swamp of standing water breeding reptiles of the mind.

Still further, the cellar set piece establishes a visual motif that recurs at intervals throughout the film: *Inferno* - whose very title suggests an entirely different set of images - is awash in images of water. In particular one might mention the death of Kazanian, the crippled, eccentric antique dealer who sells Rose the book of the Three Mothers. While he tries to drown a sack full of cats (creatures who have some supernatural affinity with the house) in a Central Park pond,[5] he slips into the slimy water and thrashes impotently as he is attacked first by rats, then by a snack vendor with a big knife, presumably possessed by some evil connected with the house and/or the eclipse of the moon that's taking place. Kazanian's watery death is utterly gratuitous in a narrative sense (Argento has said so in so many words to interviewers), but reinforces the aqueous matrix. Even stranger is a brief scene involving Mark. After wandering through the passages that follow from the service entrance to Rose's apartment, he suffers some kind of seizure (very like the one that strikes down Suzy during ballet class in *Suspiria*) and collapses in the lobby; there several of the peculiar residents force him to drink some "heart medicine." He faints. The screen ripples to black, and the next image is of golden waves lapping on some faceless shore. The waves dissolve into a medium close-up of the unconscious Mark, and as he awakens the image of the waves vanishes completely. This apparent dream sequence is the only one of its kind in *Inferno* (or, for that matter, *Suspiria*) and it's almost as startling as, say, the waterfall hallucination in Sam Fuller's *Shock Corridor* (1963); it's profoundly out of synch with the images that surround it. In a film whose imagery is all hysterical and dreamlike, what is one to make of a perfectly straightforward shot that's bracketed in such terms

[5]Though the bulk of the film was done on studio sets, Argento did shoot in New York for a week. So that really is Central Park, though it certainly doesn't look it.

(a character is about to faint - narrative - the screen ripples and fades to black - structural) that one can hardly help but read it as a conventional dream? What's interesting here is that Argento has claimed that the underlying psychology of his films isn't Freudian but Jungian, and while this would be impossible to defend on a consistent basis, it does provide an interesting angle on *Suspiria* and *Inferno*. Much of Jung's dream theory (always the relevant system when you want to talk about movies) revolves around his notion of archetypal iconography. Archetypes are images that aren't derived from the specific psychological processes of the individual dreamer, but rather drawn from the vast reserve of images that inform all cultural phenomena, from religious symbolism to the world of legends and fairy tales. The image of water - particularly bodies of water: oceans, pools, lakes - is consistently associated with the first of Jung's major archetypes, that of the Great Mother who embodies the conflicting aspects of the feminine principle, simultaneously nurturing and devouring. The Great Mother can also be personified in dreams by houses, a particularly provocative association in light of the entire notion of the houses of the Three Mothers (repositories of their filthy secrets, etc.) which are a central part of the iconography of *Suspiria* and *Inferno* yet aren't mentioned by De Quincey.[6] *Inferno* easily surpasses *Suspiria* in this respect, adding Jung's notions to a web of allusion that encompasses De Quincey's refined 19th-Century opium dreams and the psychedelic hallucinations of

[6]Freud in his turn remarks on the frequency with which dreams of tunnels, corridors, and passageways allude to the womb, and thus to women; there's an obviously visual metaphor to play here. And if he talks about parts of buildings standing in for parts of bodies, *Inferno* refers directly to the reverse. "This building has become my body," says Varelli of the house of Mater Tenebrarum. "Its bricks my cells, its passageways my veins, its heart my very heart." This equation is later echoed in Michele Soavi's *The Church*, whose architect is literally one with his creation: his body is buried beneath the floor, and the arcane directions that will bring the walls down are hidden in the mouth of his corpse.

sixties pop design, itself a melange of past styles made bigger, brighter, and weirder by turn. And starting with its complimentary images of fire and water, embodying the archetypes of the Great Mother and the Spiritual Father (female and male principles in their broadest definitions) *Inferno* resolves itself into an endlessly reflexive system of allusions and counter allusions. The problem, of course, is that this sort of dazzling interplay can easily degenerate into sophistry; it calls to mind this exchange from G. K. Chesterton's *The Dagger With Wings*, a Father Brown story:

"Don't you feel in your heart that these contradictions do not really contradict; that there is a cosmos that contains them all? The soul goes round upon a wheel of stars and all things return... Good and evil go round in a wheel that is one thing and not many. Do you not realize in your heart, do you not believe behind all your beliefs, that there is but one reality and we are its shadows; and that all things are but aspects of one thing; a centre where men melt into Man and Man into God?"

"No," said Father Brown.

Confronted with *Inferno*, *Variety*'s reviewer (Yung) said "No," at some length.

"A lavish, no-holds-barred witch story whose lack of both logic and technical skill are submerged in the sheer energy of the telling," began the review, which went on to say, "Argento's unmistakable technical style has a kind of cheap vulgarity that borrows heavily from Hollywood classics like Hitchcock [sic], maximizing viewers' emotions through identification and point-of-view shots and directing every minute of screen time to getting an 'effect'. It fails mainly because it lacks restraint in setting up the terrifying moment, using close-ups and fancy camera angles gratuitously and with no relevance to the story. It is also full of clumsy shots that cannot be edited together."

Perhaps they can't be edited together in any manner that makes particularly good linear sense, but in this respect *In-*

Inferno's haunted interiors delineate a distorted architecture of the mind.

Inferno's fun house of horrors: Rose Elliott (Irene Miracle) meets her end on Mater Tenebrarum's improvised guillotine.

ferno hardly differs from *Suspiria*; that didn't keep *Suspiria* from succeeding admirably at the American box office. Twentieth-Century Fox, *Suspiria*'s American distributor (apparently embarrassed to have its name on the film, if not to profit from it, Fox distributed *Suspiria* through an obscure subsidiary corporation, "International Classics, Inc.") was actively involved in *Inferno*'s production. Surprisingly enough, however, Fox chose not to release the film at all in the United States and to abbreviate its run in England. "It's a very long story with Fox and what they did to *Inferno*," Argento told Martin Coxhead in 1984. "Halfway through shooting the picture the management at Fox changed and the new management boycotted all the films that were being produced by the previous board. Not only *Inferno* but several others, they didn't want anything to do with them." This is, of course, typical unhappy director talk, but it also happens that way sometimes; in this case it isn't an implausible explanation. *Inferno is* incoherent, but no more so than *Suspiria*, whose incoherence in no way made it unreleasable. Though he's never said so, it's possible that Argento's troubles with *Inferno* (which didn't extend to the European markets) may have dampened his enthusiasm for concluding the Three Mothers trilogy. Asked by Coxhead whether the killing of a character played by Ania Pieroni - who made a brief but striking appearance as Mater Lachrymarum in *Inferno* - in *Tenebrae* constituted a concealed reference to the state of the film *Mother of Tears*, Argento said he had a virtually completed screenplay for that film ready. Around the same time he claimed to be ready to shoot with Jennifer Connelly - later the star of *Creepers* - in the title role. But *Mother of Tears* remains unmade as of this writing, and in the interim he's written and directed four films - *Tenebrae, Creepers, Opera* and *Two Evil Eyes* - three *gialli*, and one *gialli*-esque adaptation of Edgar Allan Poe.

During the three years between the release of *Suspiria* and that of *Inferno*, Argento involved himself in a project that was something of a change of pace, teaming him with one of the most influential American horror filmmakers of the 1970s: George A. Romero. The New York-born Romero insured his place in the history of the horror cinema with the release of his first film, the 1968 *Night of the Living Dead*. Shot for approximately $114,000 outside Pittsburgh - where Romero owned a commercial production house - in grainy black and white with local talent both in front of and behind the cameras, *Night of the Living Dead* is a relentlessly ugly exploration of a classic nightmare situation: seven people - confused, unarmed, and ill at ease with each other - are trapped in an isolated farmhouse by an apparently unstoppable army of the hungry dead. Called everything from a film which "casts serious aspersions on the integrity and social responsibility of its Pittsburgh based makers, distrib Walter Reade, the film industry as a whole and exhibs who book the pic, as well as raising doubts about the future of the regional cinema movement and about the moral health of filmgoers who cheerfully opt for this unrelieved orgy of sadism," (*Variety*, October 16, 1969) to one which "manages to bring us closer to the question of American involvement in Vietnam and racism than any of the recent documentary-type features which tackle such issues head-on" (David Pirie, *A Heritage of Horror*), *Night of the Living Dead* revolutionized American horror filmmaking and, by extension, horror filmmaking around the world. It brought to the screen a level of explicit violence virtually unprecedented in the commercial cinema[7], untempered by the conventional morality that underlies most earlier horror movies. At its conclusion the order of the world isn't restored; most of the main characters have been eaten by the living dead, and the hero - who survives the ghastly night by dint of such conventional virtues as courage and ingenuity - is shot dead the next morning by a zombie-hunting posse. Despite

[7]There's always Herschell Gordon Lewis, of course. Aimed primarily at the Southern drive-in trade, *Blood Feast* (1963), *2000 Maniacs* (1964) and *Color Me Blood Red* (1965) all preceded *Night of the Living Dead* and were all a lot grosser - they're even in colour. But their jocular tone is worlds away from *Night of the Living Dead*'s dead (excuse the pun) seriousness. While *Night* is still disturbing today, Lewis' pictures are camp entertainment at best. Lewis was an isolated - though indicative - case; Romero defined a trend.

its aggressively open-ended conclusion, the sequel to *Night of the Living Dead* was more than a decade in the making ("I always say I spent five years trying to resist making a sequel, and then an additional five trying to set up a deal to make one") while Romero tried his hand - with varying degrees of success - at a number of projects that didn't involve cannibal zombies. When he returned to them, it was with Dario Argento - whose European connections provided a significant portion of the film's financing - on board as co-producer.

They were brought together by a mutual friend, Italian distributor Alfredo Cuomo, who showed Romero's treatment for *Dawn of the Dead* to Argento. "I saw *Night of the Living Dead* and loved it," Argento told Coxhead, "... I like his work and one day we arranged to meet in New York and talked and talked and talked. We thought that maybe we should make a film together, and from that came *Zombi* [*Dawn of the Dead*'s European release title]. I wrote the screenplay with George [Argento's credit reads "Script Consultant"; the screenplay is credited to Romero alone] and then worked on the music with Goblin. George is a very great friend of mine. We do work differently, but the spirit is no different. Before we wrote I travelled around the Caribbean islands to study the stories of the zombie legends and myths. [This was fairly pointless research since Romero's zombie mythology - such as it is - is self-created, but it betrays an appealing enthusiasm] George works the American way, I the European way, but together we worked very well."

Dawn of the Dead is a very different film from *Night of the Living Dead* on all levels. Technically speaking, *Dawn* is infinitely the superior picture, shot in slick colour and featuring state-of-the-art special effects by Tom Savini, whose contributions to the field of gore effects are almost as extensive as they have been extensively publicized (*Night*'s effects, by contrast, are primitive indeed, though they serve their purpose admirably). Thematically, *Night*'s grim nihilism stands in sharp contrast to *Dawn*'s cynical good humour, predicated on a grim visual joke (cannibal zombies run amok in a vast suburban shopping mall) about consumer societies. You'd be hard put

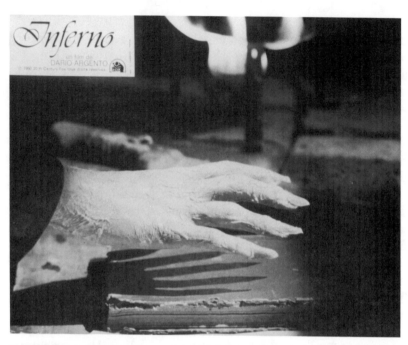

The hand of an alchemist: *Inferno*'s library leads to the sure knowledge of damnation.

Central Park in the dark: an Argento-eye view, on location in *Inferno*.

(and misguided) to attribute any of these elements to Argento's aesthetic influence; they're logical developments reflecting such factors as the relative availability of production money and the substantially different tenors of the times during which the two films were made.

Where Argento's influence is indisputably present is in the soundtrack; while *Night* relied on stock spooky music, *Dawn* features a Goblin-composed extravaganza that incorporates many of the elements associated with the scores of Argento's own post-*Deep Red* films. Even so profoundly unsympathetic a reviewer as the *New York Times*' Janet Maslin made note of his contribution: "Mr. Romero is an acknowledged dean of this sort of thing, and he has been assisted this time by another red-meat magnate, Dario Argento. Mr. Argento, who most recently directed the less stomach-turning "Suspiria," has provided a lot of thumpity-thump music for the sound-track, along with his combo, the Goblins." Talk about damning with faint praise - *Suspiria* is less stomach-turning than *Dawn of the Dead*! In addition, Argento had final cut control over the European version of *Dawn of the Dead*, which opened in Italy in September 1978, a full half-year before its opening in the United States. According to Romero's partner, Richard Rubinstein (quoted by Donald Chase in *Millimeter*), "It went through the roof: in the first five and a half weeks it did a million dollars in box office in the major cities." This was on a reported (hard to confirm because the film was shot non-union) investment of some $500,000. (before advertising costs); an impressive showing that presumably helped persuade potential North American distributors that there was a profit to be made, though concern about ratings was an ever-present problem. *Dawn of the Dead* was eventually released unrated after, according to Rubinstein, the MPAA asserted that it "didn't have a computer large enough to list all the changes that would have to be made to get an R."

While Argento has only said that he used more Goblin music, and mixed it louder (no surprise to anyone who's seen *Suspiria* and *Inferno*), Romero and Rubinstein described at some length (to Chase) their relationship with Argento and the other Italian

157

investors as well as the differences between the two cuts:

[Romero] Part of our deal with our Italian co-financiers was that Dario Argento (a director himself) had final cut for their territories and I had final cut for our territories. Sure, I'd have liked to control it worldwide, but it was a matter of giving something (worldwide final cut rights) to get something (financing) and I was satisfied that, in Dario Argento, I was dealing with a man who would not violate the spirit of my work. Contractually, we had to deliver a rough cut of the picture to the Italians as of a certain date. This rough cut - really my second cut on the film - was two hours and seventeen minutes long. Dario cut it to two hours, one minute; my final cut is two hours, six minutes. So there's a five minute difference, and basically it's humor; he cut jokes that he thought wouldn't work with an Italian audience.

The film I delivered to him had a scratch track of library music on it. We keep a little mix stage in our shop in Pittsburgh. I don't cut on a flatbed or a moviola; I just use a table because I don't like to work at speed when I'm seeing it for the first time and I like to play with the elements, mix it down and put up and put effects in, to see what the overall effect is as I finish each scene... In any case, there was a playable track on the film delivered to Dario. Our deal called for him to produce a music score, which we had the right to use all, part, or none of in our version. And I did use elements of it that I liked. In doing his score he was very respectful of my indicated intentions, following conceptually what I indicated on the scratch track. Where I put in shopping mall Muzak, he put in Muzak - original Muzak with an Italian flavor to it. Muzak in the style of Nino Rota or Ennio Morricone!

[Rubinstein] Argento directed the actors who dubbed the Italian version, taking a kind of care that's unusual. With the Spanish and German versions (which he also controlled), he sent out the tracks and had the voices dubbed in those languages, then had the tracks sent back to him so that he could personally mix the voices and the music. In the U.S. the release version of the film is 100% as George wants it; elsewhere, subject to local censorship restrictions and Argento's alterations, it's 90% as George would have it.

Dawn of the Dead was a tremendous hit in Europe despite certain censorship problems, notably in France, where according to Argento (quoted in *Mad Movies* No.25), "it was brought before the censors four times... but four times they rejected it" before it was finally shown in 1984. It spawned many imitations in Italy (the *filone* principal at work again), including Lucio Fulci's 1980 *Zombie/Zombie Flesh Eaters* ("We are going to eat you!" shrieked the American ads) which was called *Zombi 2* in Europe in an attempt to make it look like a sequel. "That irritated us, George and me," Argento remarked to Robert Schlockoff (in *L'Écran Fantastique*), "because we were in the midst of preparations for the real *Zombi 2* [*Day of the Dead*] and we had to interrupt the project. We stopped for three years, during which *Zombi 2* and *Zombi 3* (*Zombie Holocaust*) came out. But right now they're not making any more *Zombi* pictures; the fad is over, so we have the way cleared, Romero and I, for our film."

At that time Argento also said that he and Romero had written a 40-page treatment for *Day of the Dead* and suggested they intended to work together on it as they had on *Dawn*. Unfortunately, this was not to be, in part because of the abnormal strength of the American dollar against European currencies in 1984/1985, when it went into production. When asked in 1985 (by Caroline Vié and Claude Scasso for *L'Écran Fantastique*) why he hadn't collaborated on the film with Romero, Argento replied: "Because the picture was too expensive. For Europeans it has become impossible to deal in dollars. Two years ago it would have been possible, but today I would have had to assemble half the budget of the film, maybe $5 million.[8] It was impossible. I wasted a month working on that film, but I like the scenario: it will be very mystical and very good." In the end *Day of the Dead* was neither very mystical nor very good. Even Romero himself was reportedly unhappy with the finished film because of the drastic alterations in the screenplay necessitated by a budget that was slashed at the

[8]The final budget for *Day of the Dead* was quoted at $3 million total, but it was originally meant to be a far more expensive film.

eleventh hour. "With the budget cut way down we couldn't do the original script - it was like *Raiders of the Lost Ark* with zombies," said Tom Savini, who created *Day of the Dead*'s special effects. "It was incredibly large scale. George feels - and says - that this isn't the end of [the *Dead* series], because it isn't the film he wanted to make, had in mind to make."

Although Romero has yet to make his final *Dead* film, in 1990 he produced a remake of *Night of the Living Dead*, intending to compensate investors in the original film who never saw any of the profits the film generated over the years. In addition to the usual raw deal first-time filmmakers get when they shop their films for a distributor, the 26 investors in Image Ten (the *ad hoc* company formed to produce *Night*) lost out again when distributor Walter Reade neglected to copyright the film under the title *Night of the Living Dead*; Image Ten's copyright was under the *original* title, *Night of the Flesh Eaters*. Adding insult to injury, the film wound up in the public domain, colourized, marketed on videotape and generally making money for everyone except the original investors. Directed by Savini, it's a competent production that neither shames nor improves upon the memory of the original film, and it's another curious footnote to the convoluted history of the *Dead* films, a history which includes two sort-of sequels: Dan O'Bannon's *Return of the Living Dead* (1985) and Ken Wiederhorn's *Return of the Living Dead Part 2* (1987).

Return of the Living Dead was announced in 1983 by producer Tom Fox as *Tobe Hooper's Return of the Living Dead*, in 3-D. Fox bought the remake rights from John Russo - Romero's co-writer - and the credits for the completed film credit the story to Russo and two other original investors - Russell Streiner (who also played Johnny) and Rudy Ricci. Two months later, Laurel Entertainment (Romero and Rubinstein) filed a protest with the MPAA citing rights problems and a title confusion issue. That issue was cleared up (though it took the better part of a year), Hooper dropped out of the project, the 3-D craze had passed and O'Bannon, originally announced as screenwriter, took over as director as well. *Return II* was both written and directed by Ken (*Shockwaves*) Wiederhorn; Russo,

Ricci and Streiner's names don't appear in the credits at all. The *Return* films mixed thrash metal soundtracks and smart-ass dialogue to produce a pair of pictures about corpses "back from the dead and ready to party;" they couldn't have been less like *Night of the Living Dead*, but the mixture of humour and horror found an audience.

By the time the 1990 remake rolled around, Romero, Russo and Streiner were back on the same side: Romero (re)wrote the screenplay and executive produced with Menahem Golan; Russo and Streiner were credited as producers. The advertising was a little hard to get a handle on; the words "George Romero's *Night of the Living Dead*" and "All New!" looked odd together. But the state-of-the-art zombies continued to chill, and the story retained its power to disconcert, more than 20 years after it all began.

Despite the disappointing conclusion to Argento and Romero's zombie collaboration, the two directors remained in touch socially and kept an eye on one another's work. Ten years later, they worked together again on *Two Evil Eyes*, a project that paired them as directors on two separate but equal segments of a two-part film. Though the result was less than stellar, the experience was smooth for both, as recounted in chapter seven.

Argento's next horror film marked his return after six years to the *giallo* format. *Tenebrae* was in fact inspired by an unnerving incident related to the American release of *Suspiria*, and in many respects it is the finest film that Argento has ever made.

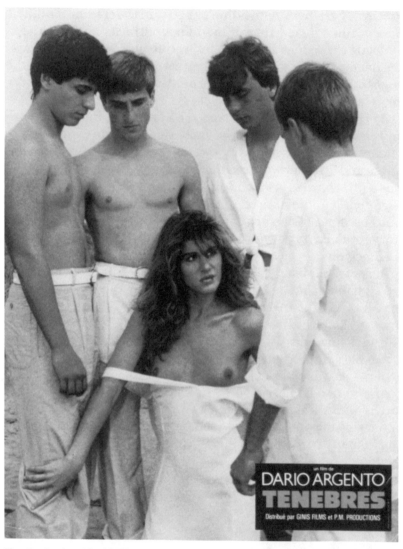

Tenebrae's pivotal flashback sequence, featuring the sexually ambiguous Eva Robins/
Roberto Coatti.

TENEBRAE *and* CREEPERS

"The impulse had become the irresistible. There was only one answer to the fury that tortured him. And so he committed his first act of murder. He had broken the most deep-rooted taboo and found not guilt, not anxiety or fear, but freedom. Every humiliation which stood in his way could be swept away by the simple act of annihilation: murder."
- from the novel *Tenebrae*, by Peter Neal

"What is this association between insects and the human soul?"
- Dr. John MacGregor (*Creepers*)

"The mechanism of *Tenebrae* is like that of a mass, an ancient rite. You sacrifice yourself, and your dark aspect is crucified at the ceremony's conclusion," Argento told *Starfix*'s Christophe Gans. "Tenebrae" means shadows, darkness; *Tenebrae*, a film of cold, clear light, is suffused by a darkness darker still than the night or the patches of shadow in which the cinema's monsters and bogeymen traditionally hide. Argento's invocation of the notion of ritual is not a specious one in this respect. The idea of the horror film as cathartic spectacle or rite of passage (explicated by J.P. Telotte in his essay *"Faith and Idolatry in the Horror Film,"* and subscribed to by Argento himself) is an obvious enough one, but *Tenebrae* is a special case. Within the offices of the Catholic church there is a liturgical service called *Tenebrae*; it takes place on Wednesday of Holy Week (the day associated with Judas Iscariot's betrayal of Jesus) and is thought to be one of the oldest in the organized church, tracing its roots back to monastic ritual. The ceremony is described in these terms in *The New Catholic Encyclopedia*:

The service was thus designated because during the Middle Ages it was celebrated in complete darkness... At the end of each psalm, one of the 15 candles is extinguished on the triangular candlestick

163

placed before the altar. At the conclusion of Psalm 146[1], only one candle, at the top of the triangle, remains lighted. When benedictus is sung, the six altar candles are extinguished one by one after every second verse; and when the antiphon Traditur autem is repeated after the canticle, the one lighted candle is taken from the triangle and hidden behind the altar, where it remains until the end of the service. Medieval liturgists seem to have introduced this custom, and thus their own allegorical interpretation probably accounts for the practice. The gradual extinguishing of all but the last candle was meant to point to the Apostles' desertion of Christ, and the last candle was supposed to depict Christ's burial (in its disappearance behind the altar) and resurrection (its reappearance). The clatter at the end of Tenebrae originally had no significance; it was simply the din occasioned by the closing of the chant books at the end of every hour of Office when the abbot or superior gave the signal to leave. This came to be interpreted as the shaking of the earth at Christ's death.

Though two of *Tenebrae*'s central characters - writer Peter Neal and his dark shadow, television interviewer Christiano Berti - are self-proclaimed "strict Catholics", it would be a mistake to try to read into *Tenebrae* too much of the liturgical Tenebrae's allegorical re-enactment of the story of Christ's betrayal, death, and resurrection. But the liturgical office echoes certain of the film's motifs, particularly its obsessive

[1]Allelujah!/Praise Yahweh, my soul!/I mean to praise Yahweh all my life/I mean to sing to my God as long as I live/Do not put your trust in men of power,/nor in any mortal man -- he cannot save,/he yields his breath and goes back to the earth he came from,/And on that day his schemes perish./Happy the man who has the God of Jacob to help him,/whose hope is fixed on Yahweh his God,/maker of heaven and earth,/and the sea, and all that those hold!/Yahweh, forever faithful,/ gives justice to those who are denied it,/gives food to the hungry,/ gives liberty to prisoners./Yahweh restores sight to the blind,/Yahweh straightens the bent,/Yahweh protects the stranger,/he keeps the orphan and the widow./Yahweh loves the virtuous,/and frustrates the wicked./Yahweh reigns for ever,/Your God, Zion, from ages and ages. *The Jerusalem Bible* (Garden City: Doubleday and Company, 1966) pp.927-928

A DESCENT INTO MADNESS

Unsane

Sleazy American ad slick for *Tenebrae*, extensively edited and retitled *Unsane*.

concern with light and darkness, both literal and metaphorical. For Argento *Tenebrae* was a return to the *giallo*; five years had passed since the release of *Deep Red* and during the intervening years he had submerged himself in the hallucinatory world of the Three Mothers. Writers for the genre magazines - who were quicker than mainstream writers to elevate Argento to the status of *auteur* and afford his work the scrutiny that term implies - were not slow to point this out in print. Some went so far as to call *Tenebrae* a return to the thrillers of the sixties (thinking particularly, no doubt, of Bava's *gialli*) and to Argento's own earliest films. Interestingly Argento has never been more articulate and/or analytical than he was on the subject of *Tenebrae*. In an interview with Alan Jones (*Cinefantastique*, Volume 13, No.8/Volume 14, No.1) he addressed directly this notion that it constituted a return to the past:

> The major difference [between *Tenebrae* and *The Bird With the Crystal Plumage*] is that *Tenebrae* isn't based in the present, but about five or more years in the future. It was never meant to be a story about something that is happening now. It isn't exactly my *Blade Runner*[2] of course, but nevertheless a step in the world of tomorrow. If you watch the film with this perception in mind, it will become very apparent.
>
> *Tenebrae* occurs in a world inhabited by fewer people with the results that the remainder are wealthier and less crowded. Something has happened to make it that way but no one remembers, or wants to remember.

Whether or not it is apparent to the unprepared viewer that *Tenebrae* is set in a Rome of the future (and it is not, to be honest), it undeniably takes place in a Rome that has no past: there are no shots of the Colosseum, the Trevi fountain, classi-

[2]Ridley Scott's neo-*noir* vision of the future through the cinematic past (darkly) is quite another thing; its *mise en scène* is informed by the relentlessly romantic urban darkness of American pulp novelists, most notably Cornell Woolrich, and no-one could take it for contemporary realism.

cal statuary, Renaissance paintings or churches, or any of the architecture of centuries past that define "Rome." *Tenebrae* takes place in a city of dazzling white concrete, high-rise apartment buildings, malls, airports, television studios, and modern private homes; no baroque or rococo influence is permitted to sully the *mise en scène*, no superfluous ornament clutters its clean planes. It's all cool, stark, and slightly remote.

Like so many of Argento's films, *Tenebrae* revolves around a writer. He is Peter Neal (Anthony Franciosa), an American who writes violent suspense thrillers. His latest, *Tenebrae*, is a tremendous hit in Europe and he is in Italy to promote the book. He has an agent, Bullmer (John Saxon); a devoted secretary, Anne (Daria Nicolodi); and an unstable former wife, Jane McKerrow (Veronica Laria). Just before Neal's arrival in Rome, a beautiful woman is murdered by a razor-wielding maniac; pages from *Tenebrae* have been stuffed into her mouth. The killer soon makes contact with Neal, claiming that he finds inspiration in Neal's books. Neal in turn works with the police - represented by chic Detective Giermani (Giuliano Gemma) and his female partner, Inspector Altieri - in an effort to stop the murderer's ghastly homage to his writing. More women die: a lesbian journalist and her lover, and Maria, the young daughter of Neal's landlord. Acting on a hunch, Neal and Gianni - whom Bullmer has assigned to squire Neal around town - stake out the house of Christiano Berti (John Steiner), whose interest in Neal's work has struck the writer as potentially unhealthy. The two split up and Berti is killed with an axe before Gianni's horrified eyes. He doesn't see the killer, and finds Neal unconscious on the lawn, apparently knocked out with a rock. Investigation shows that Berti was indeed obsessed with Neal and his writing, but his death forces the police to continue searching for the killer - Berti didn't, after all, commit suicide. Soon after, Bullmer - who has been conducting a sordid affair with Jane - is murdered, as is Gianni, who had returned to the scene of Berti's murder because he's haunted by the thought that he saw something important that night. He remembers too late: he heard Berti confessing "I killed them all, I killed them all!" to his own killer. Jane dies next amidst a welter of blood; her killer is revealed to be Neal. A few moments later he kills Altieri, mistaking her for Anne, who soon arrives with Giermani. Neal is mad, driven by some inner demons first to write about murder, then to commit it. But he's also cunning, and having learned of Berti's murderous obsession, devised a scheme whereby he could kill his ex-wife and her lover and blame the killings on the depredations of a maniac. Neal appears to commit suicide, but his death is faked and he kills Giermani as soon as the detective's guard is down. Anne is saved from the same fate by a lethal piece of sculpture that she accidentally dislodges while trying to open the door. Neal is impaled on one of its silver spines, and all Anne can do is stand in the doorway, the rain pouring down behind her, and scream and scream and scream...

Tenebrae's narrative is surprisingly strong, given Argento's notorious lack of interest in matters of plot, and the device of transferring guilt from one character to another (to the eminently sympathetic protagonist, no less) in midstream is striking. It suggests strongly, in fact, the most paranoid excesses of *film noir*. One thinks of Fritz Lang's *Beyond a Reasonable Doubt* (1956), in which a man convicted of murder on false evidence (planted as part of a high-minded liberal scheme to discredit the practice of capital punishment) is in fact guilty of the murder; or of *Black Angel* (1946, Roy William Neill), adapted from the novel by Cornell Woolrich, in which the man who tries to clear a murder suspect does so at the cost of learning that he himself is the killer. But *Tenebrae* puts a twist in the equation: Peter Neal is both guilty from the outset and aware of his guilt. Despite his protests, it's clear that his book, *Tenebrae*, has stirred a psychopath to action; it's also true that Neal himself is guilty of murder before he kills Berti and takes over his identity as the razor-killer. The pale, dreamy flashbacks that interrupt *Tenebrae*'s narrative at intervals recall Neal's introduction to the world of violence as a youth in Rhode Island, first as its victim (he is beaten and sexually humiliated by a group of his peers at the behest of a cruel, beautiful woman on a beach) then as its perpetrator (he murders the woman with a knife and steals her shiny red pumps - about which, more

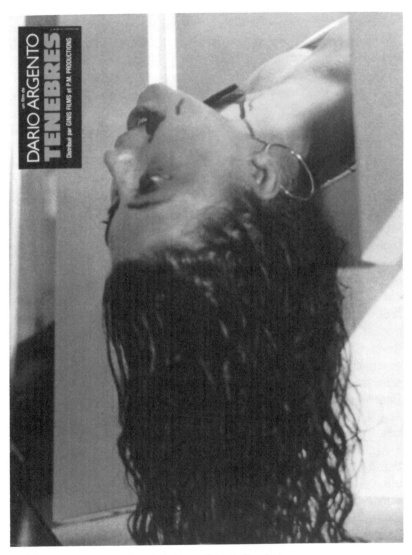

Maria (Lara Wendel) pays the price of loose living in *Tenebrae*.

later). Madness is all around Neal, and he immerses himself willingly in its crimson waters - its red sign may be hidden until after Altieri's death, but it is always there like a caste mark beneath a veil of makeup.

Tenebrae's architectural landscape, a "stunningly beautiful... mad mixture of Antonioni and *House and Garden*" (per *The Observer*'s Philip French, who didn't have anything else good to say) is a key element in the differentiation of *Tenebrae* from Argento's earlier *gialli*; the plot may recall *The Bird With the Crystal Plumage*, in certain respects, but the studied unreality of the *mise en scène*, which the director has referred to as "hyper-realism," is yet another aspect of his post-*Four Flies on Grey Velvet* style. Though shot largely on location - except for the shots in Jane McKerrow's apartment; the special effects bloodbath required a studio set - *Tenebrae*'s fictive space couldn't look less "real." Its imaginary geography is pieced together out of fragments of "Rome" - the Rome of travel brochures and coffee table books, whose landmarks signify a teeming metropolis of trattorias, pavement singers, pickpockets and bicycle thieves, nightclubs and paparazzi - that emphasize vast underpopulated boulevards, piazzas that look like nothing more than suburban American malls, hard-edged Bauhaus apartment buildings, anonymous clubs, and parking garages. Pretty girls turn out to be foul-mouthed shoplifters, lovers argue viciously in public places, and even the sight of a child retrieving his ball from beneath a bench is ominous. "For *Tenebrae* I dreamed an imaginary city in which the most amazing things happen. For this reason I stayed away from anything old. My decor is ultramodern. Extreme..." Argento told Gans *apropos* his Rome of the mind. But as carefully as *Tenebrae*'s locations were chosen, it's the film's lighting that really established the cool, stark aesthetic that shapes the imagery. Its director of photography was Luciano Tovoli, with whom Argento had worked five years earlier on *Suspiria*; the style of the two films couldn't be more superficially different, but they share a highly artificial intensity. Argento further explained to Gans:

... we started from American television series like *Columbo* and

Charlie's Angels in defining a realistic[3] manner of lighting. People spit on this kind of police show, but personally I find in them a very precise aesthetic, produced in all these shows by the quick shooting schedules and the cathode light. This economically imposed standard and the conditions of projection are embedded in the style, which is deranged by way of its directness. I also find this in [Andrzej] Zulawski's *Possession*,[4] a film I adore and which is part of a great spontaneous trend, a new way of looking at things in general... I adopted a modern style of photography, deliberately breaking with the legacy of German Expressionism. Today's light is the light of neon, headlights, streetlamps, and omnipresent flashes, at home and on the streets. Caring about shadows suddenly seemed ridiculous to me and, more than that, reassuring. In the gloom one can hide what one wants to reject, what one doesn't dare show. But we are ill at ease in the harsh glare. We have everything right in front of us.

Paradoxically (but perhaps predictably), this clear cold light illuminates a film whose very title invokes the rejected shadows of the German Expressionist cinema. The darkness with which Argento concerns himself in *Tenebrae* is a darkness of the soul, a blackness all the more stygian for being largely invisible to the human eye. Whenever he's asked about the way he writes his screenplays, Argento falls back on the image of a kind of trance state, claiming that he isolates himself until - out of

[3]"Realistic" is more like it, since he goes on to speak in specific terms of the factors that contribute to the anti-realism of television.
[4]Made in 1981, *Possession* concerns a woman whose husband and lover learn to their mutual dismay that she's deceiving them both with a third lover - a slimy, tentacled monster to which she also gave birth, presumably in some fit of rage and frustration given physical form (a scenario that would do proud Canada's "master of venereal horror," David Cronenberg). It's set in West Berlin, in the bad old days when it was still a city divided. The Polish director described it as a "town, with its wall and various languages [that] is hardly a real town." Quoted by Frederic Albert Levy, *"Possession," Cinefantastique*, October 1981.

Out of the past: Jane McKerrow (Veronica Laria) and the shadow of the axe. *Tenebrae*.

Author Peter Neal (Anthony Franciosa) caught in the act of creation in *Tenebrae*.

172

sheer frustration and boredom - inspiration comes. This almost disassociated state he describes recalls the automatic writing beloved of the surrealists and is, given the dreamlike quality of both the narratives and imagery he favours, additionally eminently plausible. Argento said similar things about the actual composition of *Tenebrae*, but the film's inspiration lay in an altogether more concrete occurrence, something that diverted his attention from another project already in progress. Again, Argento described the situation to Gans:

It all began with a rather alarming thing. About two and a half years ago [in 1980] I was in the process of presenting a project to MGM, a kind of horror story. Courtesy of the American production company, I was staying in a luxury hotel in Los Angeles. And one day somebody called me there to talk about *Suspiria*. We had a harmless discussion, and then the stranger called again the next day to ask if he could meet me. He confessed that *Suspiria* had made a very strong impression on him, like a jolt of electricity, and he wanted to ask me if making the film had given me the same sensations. That put me on my guard. Day after day he called me to confide more and more horrible things and, at the end of the fifteenth call, he told me that he wanted to kill me. He was insane. I spoke to my father and we went to the police. They studied the calls and concluded that it was nothing more than a horrible joke. The stranger called me again to say that he knew the police were near me. He swore he would have my skin. Why? I think a kind of retribution like the one inflicted on John Lennon. *Suspiria* had left its mark on his madness. Obviously, everyone around me advised me to leave town. But this danger, so nearby, inspired me to write something new, and it was *Tenebrae*.

On the surface of it this is simply too good to be true; a dreamer of dark tales haunted suddenly, horribly, by an all-too-real nightmare. Gans has alluded to a curious similarity between Argento's story and the second segment of Mario Bava's 1964 anthology film *Black Sabbath* (*I tre volti della paura* - "*Three faces of fear*"), in which a young woman is driven nearly to madness by a malevolent telephone caller. In fact the resemblance is only superficial; in Bava's tale the caller is a lovesick lesbian trying to frighten the object of her affections into her comforting arms (by making calls purporting to be from the woman's pimp, whom she betrayed and who has escaped from prison), not a faceless psychopath hidden in the urban underbrush. Gans might equally have mentioned the *film noir* ring to the story.

In, for example, *A Double Life* (1948, George Cukor), an actor preparing to undertake the role of Othello absorbs that character's insane jealousy and is destroyed by it. In *The Big Clock* (1948, John Farrow) a crime reporter is implicated in a murder, apparently by a vicious stranger (in fact by his insane publisher, the real murderer) and suddenly finds himself the object of relentless pursuit by his colleagues, using the very investigative methodology that he himself has employed in the past. Though hardly exact analogues, these films forge a link between artists and madmen attracted to their art, as does Fritz Lang's 1945 *Scarlet Street*, in which a gentle painter's work binds him to a sociopathic woman and her vicious lover. Certainly Argento's own films don't lack for examples of artists brought into contact (even collusion) with psychopaths: writers Sam Dalmas and Carlo Giordani and musicians Marc Daly and Roberto Tobias spring immediately to mind. Argento and Daria Nicolodi (who co-wrote *Suspiria*, then co-starred in *Tenebrae*) have both recounted the story of his Los Angeles persecution as true and it very probably is; but if it weren't, then - like De Quincey's fable of the Three Mothers - he would most certainly have been obliged to invent it.

It's been said that *Tenebrae* is the first of Argento's films to have an overtly erotic aspect, and to a large degree it's true. *The Bird With the Crystal Plumage*, *The Cat O'Nine Tails*, *Four Flies on Grey Velvet* and *Deep Red* are full of sex, of course: transvestitism and sexual role-playing are in all four films central factors and none lacks for imagery dealing in diverse forms of sexual behaviour. But *Tenebrae*'s overall sensuality sets it apart from Argento's other *gialli*. They're about madness and spiritual corruption revealed through sexual deviation: Monica Ranieri's transsexual identification with a sadistic murderer makes her one too; the moral bankruptcy of Profes-

Quirky framing in *Tenebrae*, as Tilda (Mirella D'Angelo) prepares to meet a killer.

Sleazy literary agent Bullmer (John Saxon) finds out more than he wanted to know about the connection between Peter Neal and the grisly murders terrorizing Rome in *Tenebrae*.

sors Terzi and Braun and Anna Terzi is embodied in their decadent sexual carryings-on; Nina Tobias' vengeful insanity is manifest in her deadly androgyny; and Marta and Carlo are entangled in a web of incestuous guilt whose origins lie in the murder of Carlo's father.

Tenebrae is fraught with free-floating anxiety that's specifically sexual in nature, but it doesn't spring from a particular act of sexual transgression (Oedipal murder, rape or the like); *Tenebrae*'s uneasy landscape - both physical and metaphorical - is both incessantly sexualized and infinitely voluptuous. Its visual starkness is not ascetic or austere, but simply sleek and streamlined, filled with erotic promise. The clear, intense light that illuminates *Tenebrae*'s interior and exterior spaces does not yield the bleached palette of, say, the Arabian dream sequence in *Four Flies on Grey Velvet*. Instead it produces a range of glowing pastels, limpid blues and greens and pure, glittering reds. The very space itself is seductive, even before it is populated by a veritable army of pliant women with hard, lush smiles and gleaming eyes. Even *Deep Red*, *Tenebrae*'s direct antecedent (both stylistically and chronologically - it was the last *giallo* before *Tenebrae*), is nowhere near so extreme.

The seductiveness of *Tenebrae*'s internal system lies in the overwhelming influence wielded within its diegetic space by a series of oneiric flashbacks. Like the glimpses of the past in *Deep Red*, they have their own theme music - an eerie, tinkling melody that introduces each flashback aurally - while an iris-in on the pupil of a vast grey eye (recalling the killer's eye in *The Cat O'Nine Tails*) serves as a visual cue. Though the physical surroundings are different, the dominant aesthetic of the past images is identical to that of *Tenebrae*'s present-tense imagery. There are two past locales, and two sets of past actions that reach out through time and space to overwhelm the present. First there is a white beach beneath a pale sky; a beautiful young blond woman with a hard, arrogant face is surrounded by four youths dressed in summer white. She wears a pink sundress and wicked red heels; her manner is teasing, seductive. As the boys watch, fascinated, she sinks to her knees on the sand and begins to undress. One boy is disgusted by the display; he slaps the woman and runs, only to be overtaken by the others. They beat him and hold him down as the woman grinds her shoe on his face, the phallic heel trapped in his mouth.

The second flashback takes place near a swimming pool; it's surrounded by terracotta tile and, beyond that, thick well-tended foliage. The woman in the red shoes walks with a young man who leaves her side on some pretext. As she stands alone someone who has been hiding in the bushes (someone whose point of view has been appropriated by the camera) stabs her to death and steals her red shoes.

These images - mostly in fragmentary form - are reintroduced throughout the film, generally (though not exclusively) in conjunction with the blood-spattered set pieces that define *Tenebrae*'s dominant iconography. Together the image clusters - beautiful woman/boys/red shoes, and blood/razor/axe/dead bodies - set the parameters of *Tenebrae*'s fetishistic and fetishized visual vocabulary, couched in terms both ritualistic and orgiastically out-of-control. "In all my films the vision of love is platonic or at least very chastely shown. Furthermore, in *Tenebrae* the hero is puritanical and acts accordingly," Argento observed, again to Gans. Or perhaps more correctly, it - the film - acts accordingly. Peter Neal indulges in sins of the flesh and *Tenebrae* revels in them,[5] inviting the spectator to join in; in fact, it dares the viewer not to do so.

The classical thriller is invoked at every turn; a world of logic, order and fundamental decency embodied in Sir Arthur Conan Doyle's famous dictum and spoken by literature's (the world's, in his own estimation) first consulting detective: "When you

---

[5]Though Argento's films have never drawn much inspiration from mainstream religion, an intensely Catholic sensibility - guilty and driven by voluptuous, sensual oppression - informs *Tenebrae*. Interestingly enough, Catholicism is discussed diegetically as well: "What is aberrant behaviour?" Berti asks Peter Neal. "I was brought up a very strict Catholic. Were you?" "I guess so." "But I believe in abortion...I believe in divorce," Berti says with a flourish. "That makes me aberrant from a strictly Catholic standpoint."

have eliminated the impossible whatever remains, however improbable, must be the truth."[6] Neal appropriates the quote first, speaking with Giermani at the scene of Berti's murder. The timing is significant: Neal has put into motion his plan to get away with murder and Giermani is falling in with the version of matters that Neal wants to put forth. Berti's files make clear that he was obsessed with Neal and Giermani has been proceeding on the assumption that the razor-killer must have just such an unhealthy interest in the writer and his work. Yet Berti has just been found with his head split open; if he has been murdered, logic dictates, then he cannot be the murderer. When Sherlock Holmes' words are next spoken, they issue from Giermani's lips. He has unravelled the mystery and caught Neal - literally red-handed - with the corpses of his two latest victims: his former wife and Giermani's late partner. This timing would seem to suggest that Holmes' motto for a world of sensibly motivated crime (that is to say, crimes committed for profit or some other motive that can be rationally understood, if not condoned) can in fact be adapted profitably to *Tenebrae*'s *noir*-ish landscape of doubles, shadows and guilt shared and displaced. Giermani has, after all, put together the pieces of a difficult puzzle and come up with the right answer. "You, Neal are mad... completely mad," he says in horrified amazement. "No, no, no," Neal asserts frantically, "I didn't kill the other women." "I know. That would have been impossible." And it would have been - in a scene like the one in *Deep Red* (showing Carlo with Marc when Helga is killed) Neal was seen on an airplane while Elsa, the shoplifter, was being murdered. But it is also Giermani who observes, "I read all those books: Agatha Christie, Mickey Spillane, Rex Stout, Ed McBain..." "And you never guess who the murderer is," Neal ripostes. "Right." With this series of names Giermani alludes to the full range of systems of literary detection: Stout and Christie embody the consummately genteel universe of classic crime and punishment; McBain writes of violence explained and restrained by

[6]This is, of course, Occam's razor, but Holmes made it famous.

178

the relentlessness of proper procedure; Spillane delineates a disordered universe of aimless brutality and defensive nihilism. And each system comes up short, providing no answers, no viable way of dealing with the eruption of concealed madness, no structure that can be used to contain the whirlwind of violence that rushes through *Tenebrae*. Even after he has solved the mystery of the razor killings, Giermani is unable to correctly 'read' Neal's false suicide; he accepts the act at face value and dies for his inability to comprehend. Giermani invokes these detectives only to have *Tenebrae* strike them down; its violently sexualized universe resists all attempts at containment.

"... I've made charts, I've tried building a plot the same way you have," Neal tells Giermani when the policeman asks his assistance in solving the chain of killings that is terrorizing Rome. "I've tried to figure it out. But... I just have this hunch that something is missing. A tiny piece of the jigsaw. Somebody who should be dead is alive, or... somebody who should be alive is already dead." "Explain that." "You know, there's a sentence in a Conan Doyle book... 'When you have eliminated the impossible, whatever remains, however improbable, must be the truth'." "*The Hound of the Baskervilles*."[7] "Yes... You know that the impossible in this case is that the chain of killings doesn't make sense. In *The Hound of the Baskervilles* the impossible was a giant ghost mastiff; the improbable in this case, again like the book, is almost certainly weird... unbelievable... but possible. That's what we have to find... truth is always possible." Of course the chain of killings only makes sense if one allows for the existence of the second murderer, who kills the first and takes his place. In a classical mystery this device would be a cheat; in *Tenebrae* it is only one more twist in an endlessly deceptive construct. *Tenebrae* is the *giallo* to end all *gialli*: madness and irrationality inform its inspiration, its subject matter and its method in equal degrees. It is a deranged dream of a thriller in which substructure yields to

[7]Actually, it's *The Sign of the Four*; Giermani may read mysteries, but he doesn't seem to sweat the details.

179

surface, a book that not only can but must be read by its cover.

"*Tenebrae* is a sexist novel," declares Tilda at the impromptu press conference held by Peter Neal in the airport upon his arrival in Rome. "Why do you despise women so much? Women as victims... ciphers. The male heroes with their hairy macho bullshit... how can you say it isn't? Do you write to a fixed pattern, or do your publishers tell you this kind of sexism sells copies?" Neal is taken aback by her vehemence - he thinks that his consciousness has been adequately raised; after all, he offers by way of illustration, he supported the Equal Rights Amendment. Her outburst sets the tone for *Tenebrae*'s sexual mine-field: it bristles with hostility, miscommunication, ugly innuendo and violence, repressed and all-too-unrepressed. "You're not gay, are you?" sneers the beautiful shoplifter (who was trying to steal a copy of *Tenebrae*) to the store detective she is trying to buy off with sexual favours; Inspector Altieri, meanwhile, responding to Giermani's remark that his needs would be better served by a "tough, male assistant who runs fast," snarls "You'd hate it... you'd have nothing to bitch about." Tilda and her lover Maria argue viciously over the man Maria has picked up in a bar for some casual sex; Christiano Berti puts a bloody end to both of them while whispering "Perverts... filthy, slimy perverts," in a tone of fascinated horror. It is also Berti who calls *Tenebrae* a novel about "human perversion and its effects on society," then asks Neal (who is once again rather disingenuously unprepared for this slant on his writing) how he sees "the effects of deviant behaviour on our lives." And it is Berti who writes (anonymously): "I will eliminate those who disgust me... the human perverts. Soon now, the corrupter himself." The corrupter is, of course, Neal, though the news report seen the evening after Berti has claimed his most recent victim (the under-age daughter of Neal's landlord, with whom he had engaged in some harmless flirtation) treats the reference as something of a joke. "The victim was 17 year-old Maria Alboretto; what happened to her between 2:45 and 7:00 this morning still remains a mystery. Meanwhile, we understand our killer has sent another letter to the police. In this message he warned that he'll be striking again - he says his next victim will be someone he refers to as 'the great corrupter.' Well, as a matter of fact, this message is expected to result in several businessmen and politicians leaving the city as..." the newscaster's voice is cut off in mid-sentence when Anne - disgusted - turns off the television. Even the affair between Jane and Bullmer - a fairly acceptable thing on the face of it, since she is Neal's ex-wife - has a hostile, sordid cast, and young Maria Alboretto's date with a boyfriend ends with her shrieking "Go fuck yourself!!! Bastard!!!" as he drives off on his motorcycle, leaving her alone on the deserted Rome streets. Out and out war is raging here; in vain Giermani suggests to the medical examiner that a certain murder victim's lover was not necessarily her killer (and in this case he's right). "No," the pathologist answers, "but they often are." In *Tenebrae* desire is a dangerous business, no matter what form it takes.

The girl on the beach of the obsessive flashback sequence is the matrix of this deadly desire; she defines the film's hard-edged yet dreamlike eroticism, fraught with potential - and often realized - peril. Argento explained to Gans:

Using a hermaphrodite[8], Eva Robbins, in the role of the young woman who haunts the killer's nightmares contributes to this idea of trapping the spectator in his desire. If you put your attraction to her to the test, you get caught in the web. Eva is just a dream, an illusion... she's a strange girl with a hard smile who fits into the dreamy *mise en scène*. In the same way, Gabrielle Lavia's (Carlo's) lover in *Deep Red* is played by a woman. Over and over, false appearances... life is an illusion, a trap, and the cinema must be its image.[9]

The girl on the beach is a dream whose nightmare aspect is never far from view; she is beautiful (perhaps more so because her beauty has some strangeness to it) and her hard smile promises that its allure is not without some price. Her allure is

[8]Transsexual is more to the point.
[9]In an interview with Alberto Farina in *Mad Movies*, Daria Nicolodi claims that this role was originally hers, but at the last minute Argento told her she was to replace the actress cast as Anne. The effect would have been rather different.

embodied in a pair of gleaming red pumps, the nexus of a web of connotation. High-heeled shoes: delicate, impractical, alluring, feminine; yet also aggressive, threatening, phallic and so masculine. They're fetishistic - conjuring up images of footbinding in the way they alter the conformation of the foot and restrict movement - and they're also linked with the sado-erotic iconography of bondage and discipline. They're *red* shoes; in addition to the allusions implied by the colour alone (and discussed at some length in the chapter on *Deep Red*), you have to think of the fairy tale in which a girl is danced to death by her bewitched party pumps, or Michael Powell's film of that title (Argento is a great admirer of Powell's), in which crimson pointe shoes (can we talk about fetish objects here - what does a foot in a pointe shoe look like?) embody the masochistic joys of life in the world of the ballet. They're profoundly out of place on a practical level - who, after all, walks on the beach in high heels? - but in terms of *Tenebrae*'s visual vocabulary, they could be nothing else. The shoes, like the girl/not-girl who wears them, are all surface - shiny, slick, bright. And in that gleaming surface the world is reflected, warped and coloured by the unconventional mirror. These scenes have a diegetic reality that transcends the issue of whether or not they represent something that really (diegetically speaking) happened.

After Neal's false suicide, Giermani and Anne flee to his waiting police car. As she protests tearfully that she cannot believe what has just happened, cannot believe that Peter Neal was really a depraved killer, he commiserates. Giermani declares that he could not believe it either, until he got a Telex from Interpol concerning Neal's past. "When Peter Neal was a teenager in Rhode Island, a girl he knew was killed... brutally. Someone accused him, but there wasn't any real evidence and it was never brought to trial". One is led to believe, then, that the flashbacks have been explained: they are the final key to *Tenebrae*'s puzzle, in the same way that the flashback to the killing of Carlo's father is the key to *Deep Red*, since it reveals that it was Marta - not Carlo - who was the killer. Yet with his next breath Giermani qualifies the story. "If it was Peter Neal, then he committed an act which haunted his life and twisted his

Witness Gianni (Christian Borromeo) remembers the all important detail in Christiano Berti's (John Steiner) murder, but doesn't live to regret it: *Tenebrae*.

Tenebrae's final, unsettling image: Anne (Daria Nicolodi) screams and screams and screams . . .

mind forever..." 'If' is the key word here. For even if Peter Neal did not commit this crime, if the scenes of the girl on the beach represent something other than Neal's haunted memories of a youthful transgression (dreams, hallucinations, scenes from a book or film, a story from a newspaper appropriated by Neal's writer's imagination, someone else's memories) then they still dominate the fictive space, setting the tone of pervasive, dreamy menace. They're the embodiment of *Tenebrae*'s driving imagination, its very image of desire.

Tenebrae is also - despite the allusions to external texts scattered throughout - an unnervingly self-contained work; it establishes its own internal schematic elements and then repeats them obsessively in a series of subtly shifting variations. Neal and Berti, for example, act as mirrors to one another, each twisting the reflection into a warped parody of the other. Berti takes Neal's fiction and duplicates it in reality (his crimes are described by Giermani as a homage to Peter Neal) while Neal makes an elaborate fiction out of real life. "It was like a book... a book!" he screams at Giermani when caught in the gruesome process of creation. Giermani in turn is made to reflect Neal even as Neal appropriates his role as investigator. Neal is, of course - in a grand old mystery tradition - the amateur to Giermani's professional. "Just remember, Mr. Neal... you write about these things, but I turn over real dead bodies." Yet he acquiesces to Neal when the writer responds to his questions about Berti's murder with "I've tried building a plot the same way you have"; first there is the writer as detective, then the detective as writer. Further, the detective/writer and the writer/detective, each belittles his other half, as though by being demeaned this inverted reflection could be made to go away. Having confessed that he is never able to guess the solution to fictitious mysteries, Giermani pointedly tells Neal: "By the way, I finished your book... you know what? I guessed who the killer was on page 30... page 30! Never happened before." Neal, his murderous plan spoiled at the eleventh hour by Giermani, needles: "I realized Christiano Berti was the killer... and it didn't take long to realize that... !" The missing clause is all the more obvious for being left unspoken. As there are pairs, so also there are triangles: Anne/Neal/Gianni (whom Bullmer has assigned to be, in effect, a male Anne; a secretary who will attend to Neal's every whim), Neal/Jane/Bullmer, and - perhaps most importantly - Berti/Neal/Giermani.

This last triad is particularly carefully worked out in the film by the substitution of each element for the others. In plot terms, Neal replaces Berti as the razor-killer, while in visual terms Neal replaces Giermani in a shot that is as schematically logical as it is logically outrageous. Having returned to Jane's apartment to examine Neal's body (which is no longer there), Giermani kneels down to pick up something from the floor; as he sinks gracefully out of frame, Neal is revealed standing directly behind him. The effect is that of a layer of skin being peeled off to reveal the new skin underneath. Beyond supporting the thematic suggestion that beneath the surface of every superficially bourgeois heterosexual patriarchal capitalist (that's Robin Wood's notorious prescription for normative social behaviour) can lurk the soul of a psychopath (perhaps sociopath is in this instance the stronger word), this series of substitutions and equivalences establishes *Tenebrae* as a formal puzzle, a work whose logic is centripetal and supremely self-contained. The trick razor with which Neal stages his 'suicide' (the blade is dull and hollow, and when a concealed button on the handle is pressed fake blood is ejected in thin, perfect streams) may recall the false switchblade of *Four Flies on Grey Velvet*, but ultimately that's not why it's important; it's just another of *Tenebrae*'s very own deadly, elegant illusions.

A two-and-a-half minute long, louma crane tracking shot - which glides up the side of Tilda's house, over the roof, around the windows, and across a second storey ledge - suggests the spatially disorienting pans of *Deep Red*. But the graceful, sinuous wandering of the camera is truly aimless: it does not represent the point-of-view of Christiano Berti climbing all over the facade of the house before he kills the two women within but must instead be read in terms of *Tenebrae*'s own excess. It signifies, and can be neither discounted nor forced into a pre-existing pattern of spatial relations. In this same scene there's also a conspicuous strangeness in the way the

Glossy promotional flyer for *Tenebrae,* given the English language title *Shadow* for the Japanese release.

music track is deployed. *Tenebrae's* throbbing theme music commences with the beginning of the camera track, apparently motivated by nothing more than enthusiastic complicity with the delirious camera movement, yet it ends abruptly when Tilda shouts, "Turn it off!" and her lover obligingly lifts off the stereo needle from a record she is shown to have been playing. The music, automatically read as part of Argento's *"fête-sangui-naire"* is suddenly, disorientingly motivated. The result is simultaneously beautiful and threatening, seductive and deceptive, attention-getting yet opaque. *Tenebrae* is built on contradiction and misdirection, and its methodology encompasses its every element, from story to *mise en scène*.

Tenebrae was the culmination of more than a decade of genre filmmaking. It was followed in 1985 by *Creepers*, a *giallo* with paranormal (if not quite supernatural) underpinnings. *Creepers* is nowhere near as different from *Tenebrae* as *Tenebrae* is from *Suspiria*. In particular the quality of the lighting and the manipulation of locations to produce a fictitious city out of fragments of a real one (in this case, Zurich) is very similar to *Tenebrae*. *Creepers'* soundtrack is another matter, however, constituting a radical departure (if not an altogether successful one, even in the director's own estimation) from the seductive scores of his earlier works. The story is a wild compendium of ideas that have been present in Argento's work from the very beginning, combined - one could argue haphazardly - into a creepy cinematic salmagundi.

Young Jennifer Corvino (Jennifer Connelly) - daughter of an internationally renowned movie star - is sent to study for a year at an exclusive academy in Switzerland while her father is away (conveniently incommunicado) on location in the Philippines. The boarding school is riddled with the usual petty jealousies and back-biting spitefulness one associates with large groups of adolescent schoolgirls, but there is a far more serious problem to be considered: a psychopathic killer is at large, and he has already murdered one of the academy's students. Jennifer isn't popular with her peers. They think she's conceited and strange, an impression lent credence by her sleepwalking and - more alarming by far - her curiously empa-

187

thetic relationship with the insect world: bees crawl placidly on her palm, flies buzz contentedly in her presence, fireflies guide her through the darkness. The somnabulent Jennifer wanders off the school grounds one night and is befriended by local entomologist Dr. MacGregor (Donald Pleasence), who's confined to a wheelchair and attended by a trained chimpanzee. MacGregor also knew the psychopath's last victim, and has been using his knowledge of insects (carrion flies and the like) to assist the police in their investigations. Though the school officials - especially strange, repressed Mrs. Bruckner (Daria Nicolodi) - are disturbed by Jennifer's unusual gifts, MacGregor encourages her to use them to try to track down the killer. Jennifer and a fly (the *grand sarcophagus*) find his lair, but in the meantime MacGregor is killed and his chimpanzee left to wander. Jennifer falls into the clutches of Mrs. Bruckner, whom nobody realizes is both dangerously insane and the mother of the deformed killer. The insects rally to save Jennifer from Mrs. Bruckner's monstrous child; while Bruckner is killed by MacGregor's bereft chimpanzee who - in the course of its wanderings - has found both a straight razor and the wherewithal to use it. Jennifer survives, but is left alone in the darkness.

Creepers' excess of plot elements is a little difficult to deal with. There is telepathic communication and - further - telepathic communication with insects. There are both a psychopathic killer and a mutated monster, conflated into one all-purpose bogeyman. There is the academy full of vicious schoolgirls and the terminally weird staff: Mrs. Bruckner - who was raped by a deformed lunatic and bore his dreadful child - and the chic headmistress, who is improbably convinced that Jennifer's sleepwalking is a sign of incipient insanity or demonic possession. A crippled doctor and his simian companion, a chamber of horrors and a policeman in chains, a lunatic asylum located somewhere in the ninth circle of hell and a boarding school in the "Swiss Transylvania"... the effect is that of spiralling into some skewed tunnel of a fun-house. *Creepers'* guiding principle is neither the hyper-reality of *Tenebrae* nor the phantasmagoria of *Suspiria* and *Inferno* but an odd melange of influences, mostly from within the body of Argento's own work.

Even *Creepers'* most superficially problematic conceit - mental communication with insects - is adumbrated in *Deep Red* when Professor Giordani addresses the European Congress on Parapsychology ("... butterflies, termites... all these animals and many, many others use telepathy to transmit orders and relay information..."), as well as - perhaps coincidentally - in a remark made by the wife of the unstable entomologist in Bava's *Twitch of the Death Nerve*. "My poor husband," she purrs, "he thinks that even insects have souls." The boarding school setting recalls the isolated, artificially confined milieux of *Suspiria*'s ballet school, *Inferno*'s weird apartment building, and even the insular Terzi Institute; Mrs. Bruckner's deformed child is the product of a genetic quirk as bizarre (and as scientifically conceived) as the one that produced *The Cat O'Nine Tails'* XYY killer. *Creepers* seems to be engaged in some synthetic enterprise, bringing together the warped hyperrealism of the late *gialli* (*Deep Red* and *Tenebrae*) and the fantastic dementia of the Three Mothers films. But rather than weaving together these two strands of Argento's work, *Creepers* is schizophrenic, and this dual orientation is reflected - as is so much in Argento's films - in the soundtrack. Much of *Creepers'* musical sphere consists of abrasive hard rock by bands like Motorhead and Iron Maiden, but these songs are interspersed with hypnotic compositions by Claudio Simonetti and Fabio Pignatelli (two former members of Goblin) and Rolling Stone Bill Wyman; there's no common ground between the two styles.

Creepers is ultimately more than just a little silly, and the full panoply of Argento's directorial mannerisms (and here they really do seem mannered, inadequately integrated into any overall vision) cannot conceal this deficiency. "... Dario Argento is the rock Toscanini of the hack-em-up; people are carved up to the accompaniment of synthesized guitars... maggots do the twist on severed limbs; and, for the grand finale, heads burst through windows in slo-mo...," wrote *Village Voice* reviewer David Edelstein, capturing much of the tone of aimless hysteria that propels *Creepers* forward. For all its graceful use of landscape (it may well be an obvious device to infuse the cloyingly serene and pretty Swiss countryside and its gingerbread architecture with menace by means of ominous camera movements and eerie, glowing red/blue lighting, but it is nonetheless effective) there is something seriously lacking in *Creepers*. Like *Tenebrae*, *Creepers* takes place in a never-never land defined by intense, hard-edged lighting and dotted with architectural oddities that conspire to define a city of the mind. But *Creepers'* coldness is more than ironic detachment: there is something distant about the film as a whole; something uncommitted and almost conventional. *"Tenebrae* was a personal, interior story," the director told *Starfix*'s Vincent Ostria on *Creepers'* set. *"Creepers* is a story that I look at from the outside, slightly fantastic." Perhaps it is this very sense of being on the outside - of not being sucked into its disordered diegesis - that accounts for *Creepers'* shallowness; whatever the reason, it is a film that simply marks time, rather than constituting an advance over its predecessor.

Following *Creepers*, which was the first film produced by Argento's own DAC (later ADC) Film company (formed after his father withdrew from the business because of ill health and Argento and his brother Claudio decided to pursue different artistic avenues), Argento took a breather from directing to produce, giving his seal of approval (financial and artistic) to Lamberto Bava's *Demons/Demoni* (1985). *Demons*, which has already spawned a less-than-distinguished sequel[10], incorporates many elements characteristic of Argento's own recent work. The original idea for the screenplay - actually one segment of a projected three-segment anthology, expanded to feature length - came from Dardano Sacchetti, who co-wrote *The Cat O'Nine Tails*. The script was a collaborative effort between Argento, Bava and Franco Ferrini, who co-wrote *Creepers*. *Demons* revolves around two girls, music students, who are given tickets to a special screening in an isolated movie theatre. The film, a violent horror movie, exerts a malevolent

[10]*Demons 2*, also directed by Bava and starring Argento's younger daughter, Asia, was released in 1986.

190

An unwary tourist (Argento's daughter Fiore) comes to a bad end in *Creepers*.

Jennifer Corvino (Jennifer Connelly) falls into a vat of slimy maggots in *Creepers*.

influence over the theatre patrons who are transformed - one by bloody one - into a slavering horde of zombie-demons (an idea that owes more than a little to Romero's zombies). The cast includes Argento's daughter Fiore (who also appeared in *Creepers*, as a tourist decapitated by the monster/killer during the film's first few minutes), and the special effects were created by *Creepers'* Sergio Stivaletti; cinematographer Gianlorenzo Battaglia photographed *Creepers'* underwater sequences.

Originally scheduled to be shot in England, *Demons'* production was moved to Berlin because Argento and Bava both liked that city's "coldness" and "fakeness." Additional shooting took place at the De Paolis studios; the singularly menacing Metropol movie theatre, just the sort of place where patrons are likely to be possessed by the legions of hell, was right around the corner. *Demons'* soundtrack is another compilation of heavy metal mania (Argento has commented on the "Nazi-like" quality of heavy metal music and found it appropriate to contemporary attitudes) combined with Simonetti interludes. In the music video made to Simonetti's "Phenomena" (part of the film's soundtrack), Argento even makes an appearance, ushering theatre-goers into *Demons'* cinema of the damned. Alan Jones (*Cinefantastique*, Volume 16, No.1) asked the inevitable question: why didn't he direct *Demons* himself? Argento replied:

Mainly because it was Bava's idea, and as it was such an obvious commercial idea from the start, I didn't think it mattered who directed it. Bava and I have been close friends for many years. We know each other like brothers. We share ideas. In all honesty I don't think the film would have been as good if I had decided to direct, mainly because I tend to hold back when I shoot my own films. My role as producer meant I was wilder with my imagination and more willing to let Bava do the things I would usually be reticent about.

That's fine as far as it goes. Certainly far more than in the case of *Dawn of the Dead*, Argento's role as producer on *Demons* wasn't an abdication of the creative role in filmmaking, but rather an extension of it.

For all his contention that he can let other filmmakers do

They will make cemeteries
their cathedrals
and the cities will be
your tombs.

DARIO ARGENTO

presents

"It may be one of the best horror films of the last decade!"
—Philip Nutman,
Fangoria Magazine

DEMONS

"DEMONS"

A Film By **Lamberto Bava**

Music Performed By:
Billy Idol · Motley Crue · Pretty Maids · Rick Springfield
Go West · The Adventures · Accept · Saxon

Produced By DARIO ARGENTO For DACFILM

American ad slick for Lamberto Bava's *Demons*, produced by Argento.

Jennifer Corvino (Jennifer Connelly), Dr. MacGregor (Donald Pleasence) and the soon-to-be razor wielding chimpanzee: *Creepers*.

Argento and protégé Lamberto Bava on the set of *Demons*, making Argento's daughter Fiore slide down a nasty chute.

what he himself would hesitate to, Argento's protégés have done little more than make films that look an awful lot like his own films. They duplicate his strengths (particularly his visual *élan*) and his faults equally, as even a cursory examination of their shaky narrative structures demonstrates. Once again, the image of the puppet master comes to mind. All in all, it's a surprisingly rich image, one that works on multiple levels. There's Argento pulling the strings of his two-dimensional characters, setting them up to be killed in bizarre and brutal ways. Argento manipulating the responses of his audiences, seducing them with his technical wizardry, then gut-punching them with scenes of vicious violence. And, finally, Argento controlling the careers of his protégés, encouraging them to produce films so like his that they're almost indistinguishable from his own.

In addition to Lamberto Bava, Luigi Cozzi and Michele Soavi have also made films under the master's spell. Cozzi's *The Black Cat*, already discussed in a note to chapter five, is his out-and-out homage to Argento, with its self-referential structure and overt allusions to the Three Mothers films. Cozzi's co-writer on *Paganini Horror* (filmed under the title *De Profundis/ Out of the Depths*) was Daria Nicolodi, but by all reports the results were nowhere near as impressive as her collaborative contributions to *Suspiria* might lead one to hope.

Michele Soavi[11] may be the most accomplished of the acolytes, though it's still a little early to tell. Like Bava and Cozzi, he's done time directing second unit for Argento, and graduated to a better-than-competent documentary about Argento, *Dario Argento's World of Horror*, interspersing clips from Argento's films with interview and behind-the-scenes footage. Soavi also directed the video-clips for Bill Wyman and Terry Taylor's *Valley*, from the *Creepers* soundtrack. His first feature was

[11]The handsome Soavi started his career as an actor, and has continued to make appearances in movies with which he's involved. He can be spotted in *Creepers*, in *Demons* as the masked man dispensing tickets to attend the deadly screening, and as a police officer in *Bloody Bird*.

195

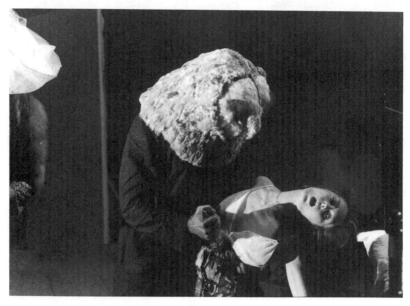

Michele Soavi's *Bloody Bird*. Argento's stylistic and thematic influence is clearly apparent.

produced by Joe D'Amato (renowned director of *Anthropopha-gus* and sundry other disgusting pictures), but Soavi's stylistic and thematic debt to Argento is inscribed in virtually of every frame of *Bloody Bird* (1988, also called *Stagefright* and *Aquar-ius*), a polished piece of work by any standards. Revolving around a theatre group performing an Edgar Wallace-style murder mystery in an isolated theatre, it quickly becomes a body count movie, with the addition to the picture of homicidal lunatic escaped from a nearby insane asylum. The killer's identity is little more than an aside; the point of the exercise is to set him loose in an ersatz old dark house and throw various nubile young people in his way. From the insistent soundtrack to the primary colour palette and the carefully staged murder tableaux, *Bloody Bird* does Argento in spades with a self-conscious twist: you can hardly look at the chainsaw-wielding killer in his oversized owl head mask without smiling that this is what two decades of taboo-busting in horror movies has come to.

Soavi's second film, *The Church/La Chiesa* (1990), is equally Argento-bound and in its earliest incarnations was called *Demons 3*; the title then became *Cathedral of Demons*, suggesting the direction the film was taking - away from the *Demons* series. The screenplay, by Argento, Franco Ferrini and Soavi, takes off from one of the ideas that drives *Suspiria* and *Inferno*: the notion of a damned house built by an architect/alchemist, from which a pestilential malevolence radiates and taints everything with which it comes into contact. But *The Church* goes one step further - the house of the damned isn't a spooky dance school or a macabre apartment building; it's the very house of God, a glorious Gothic cathedral, perverted and made evil. Argento shrugs off the implications - "It's just a haunted church, and why shouldn't a church be one of the houses of the damned?"[12] - but they lend *The Church* an extra blasphemous punch.

Again weak on the narrative front, *The Church* opens with a medieval prologue in which a band of Templar Knights (referred to later as "Teutonic" Knights, but clearly Templars[13] in their white cross-emblazoned mantles) massacres a village of witches. Their bodies are thrown into a pit, and the order given to build a church on the spot. Flash forward to the present, where the church is the centre of a flurry of attention: the

[12]Argento speaks with great enthusiasm of his love of Gothic aesthetics (unsurprising, in light of their glorious excesses), and his infatuation with Pittsburgh - where *Two Evil Eyes* was shot - seems to spring in part from its pervasive gothic and neo-Gothic architecture. The most famous example is probably the neo-Gothic ice castle of plate glass.
[13]Formed in Jerusalem during the 12th century, the Order of Poor Knights of the Temple of Solomon was a Christian Knighthood whose members were pledged to protect pilgrims travelling to the Holy Land; they later took up the fight against unbelievers and heretics everywhere. In time the Templars were suppressed and persecuted, and popular mythology transformed them into magicians and idolaters. They are the subject of Armando de Ossorio's "Blind Dead" films: *The Blind Dead* (1972), *Return of the Blind Dead* (1973), *Horror of the Zombies* (1974) and *Night of the Seagulls* (1975).

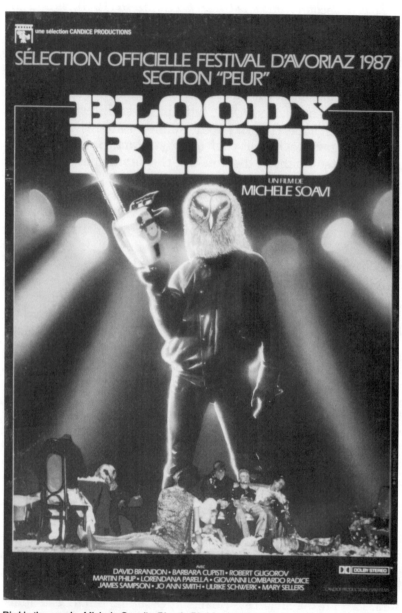

SÉLECTION OFFICIELLE FESTIVAL D'AVORIAZ 1987
SECTION "PEUR"

BLOODY BIRD

UN FILM DE
MICHELE SOAVI

AVEC
DAVID BRANDON • BARBARA CUPISTI • ROBERT GLIGOROV
MARTIN PHILIP • LORENDANA PARELLA • GIOVANNI LOMBARDO RADICE
JAMES SAMPSON • JO ANN SMITH • ULRIKE SCHWERK • MARY SELLERS

DOLBY STEREO

Bird is the word... Michele Soavi's *Bloody Bird*, imagery out of Argento by way of *The Texas Chain Saw Massacre*.

198

Promotional art for the US video release of Michele Soavi's *The Church*.

library is being catalogued by handsome Evan, lovely Lisa is retouching its hellfire and brimstone frescos, workmen are drilling in the basement with an eye to restoration, a fashion photographer is staging wedding photos in the nave and school children are taking a guided tour. Is it any surprise that the evil past comes flooding back?

Once Evan has found (with the help of a manuscript Lisa discovered) and unsealed the pit, *The Church* bears more than a passing resemblance to *Demons*, brought to mind early by the sermon revolving around the man whose name is Legion, because he is possessed by many demons. Evan is possessed first, and passes the demonic contagion along like a communicable disease. As the contagion spreads, the church's single door grinds shut, trapping everyone (including Argento's younger daughter, Asia) inside. Priests fume and blaspheme, women copulate with demons, ordinary tourists turn murderous and the very stones ooze wickedness; Soavi's fun-house of horrors is open for business.

Where *The Church* is at its strongest is in its set pieces. Richly coloured tableaux depicting the torture of the architect who built the church vibrate with the sensuality of torture, and the scene in which the basement floor drops away in the shape of a vast cross is simply breathtaking. Though not consistent, Soavi occasionally demonstrates a gift for imbuing superficially innocuous images with dreadful undertones. In particular, a shot of the possessed Evan, his back to the camera, typing in the church library is dread-inspiring; the visual punchline - that he's typing "666" over and over and over - should be funny, but isn't. The film's weaknesses are Argento's, laid bare(r) by Soavi's less consistently extravagant vision: at best perfunctory characterization and indifferent plotting.

For better and worse, Soavi shows no sign of abandoning the path Argento blazed for him. *The Sect* (1991) pays still more homage and by all reports offers further evidence that Soavi has thoroughly absorbed Argento's aesthetics and mastered the craft of filmmaking far more completely than Cozzi and Bava. It will be interesting to see him develop as he moves away from Argento-style subject matter.

OPERA *and* TWO EVIL EYES

"I think it's unwise to use movies as a guide for reality. Don't you, Inspector?"
- Marco (*Opera*)

"Perversity is one of the prime impulses of the heart. Who hasn't done something wrong just because it was forbidden?"
- Roderick Usher (*Two Evil Eyes*)

Opera - also called *Terror at the Opera* - is more than the subject of Argento's tenth film: it's also the key to its stylistic conceits. Beginning with *Deep Red*, Argento's films followed a clear arc of ever-increasing visual extravagance and stylization. Even *Creepers*, whose icy *mise-en-scène* lacked the lushness of the films leading up to it, represented a logical step: it's visually cold, but it's extreme in every respect: extremely violent, extremely dumb, extremely weird. But *Opera*... well, *Opera* is operatic; in Argento's hyperbolic words an "aria of violence beyond imagination." It's not so much that the violence is *so* extreme - it's excessive in the way of all Argento films, but dozens of lesser filmmakers have devised more horrible acts. What distinguishes Argento's nasty imagination is his relentless emphasis on looking long and hard. *Opera* revolves around an image that says it all: a woman with her eyes open wide because there's a row of straight pins taped under her eyelids. Argento has complained that he's annoyed when people shut their eyes at the gory parts of his films, and *Opera* is his taunting response to the squeamish.

Opera is the most lavish (and expensive, with a budget of $8 million) production Argento has ever undertaken, exceeding even the glorious excesses of *Suspiria* and *Inferno* (though not quite so aggressively stylized, particularly in terms of colour). And it's a spectacle in the purest sense: whatever the other thematic resonances of eyes - seen repeatedly in ghastly close-

201

up - they suggest first and foremost that *Opera* is designed to knock your eyes out; metaphorically speaking, of course. The film's first, surprisingly witty image is of a bird's eye that fills the screen, a theatre reflected in an anamorphic curve on its convex surface. Never mind reflections in a golden eye - Argento's reflections in a raven's eye are seductive enough.

No horror film called *Opera* can escape the suggestion that it's somehow inspired by the classic *Phantom of the Opera*, and there is some connection here. In addition to recalling the film (the 1943 Claude Rains version) from his childhood, Argento has said that there were only two classic horror films he was ever really interested in remaking, and *Phantom of the Opera* is one of them (the other, *Frankenstein*, got to the script stage during the '70s[1]). But *Opera* seems to have been more directly inspired by Argento's abortive attempt to direct a version of Giuseppe Verdi's *Rigoletto* for the Sferisterio Theatre in Macerata. Even though Franco Zeffirelli and Ken Russell have staged operas with some success, the idea of Argento tackling *Rigoletto* sounds out of left field. On the other hand, the story (adapted from Victor Hugo's 1932 play *Le roi s'amuse* and considered quite scandalous in its day) is pretty horrific. The debauched Duke of Mantua corrupts an innocent girl whose father then hires a professional killer to exact vengeance; the girl learns of the plan and kills herself to save her seducer. Argento's notion was to take the character of the Duke, who taints and defiles everything he touches, one step further and make him into a literal vampire. Argento's *Rigoletto* never made it past the concept stage (the Italians take their opera seriously; a more

---

[1] Luigi Cozzi, who co-wrote the screenplay with Argento, says: "He wanted to take a very classical approach, but to set the story in pre-Nazi Germany, during the Weimar Republic. The Frankenstein monster would have been a kind of symbol of the birth of Nazism. We had trouble with the Americans there [specifically Universal Pictures] - they said *Frankenstein* was dead, and anyway, no-one who wanted to see a horror movie cared about politics." Packaged with Timothy Dalton (now James Bond) in the lead, the project was also offered to Hammer with no luck.

Captive audience: young diva Betty (Cristina Marsillach) on the other side of the footlights in *Opera*.

conventional version was produced), but his glimpse of the hothouse world of the opera proved inspiring.

Opera's plot is equal parts *42nd Street*, *The Fan* and *Phantom of the Opera*, which is to say Argento added a dash of each to a plot of his own feverish devising. Young Betty (Cristina Marsillach), a second generation opera singer, inherits the lead in an avant-garde staging of Giuseppe Verdi's *Macbeth* when diva Mara Cecova ("The great Mara Cecova," as her name seems to be) breaks her leg after a fight with the sadistic director. "The great Mara Cecova has been knocked down by a car," the theatre manager announces dramatically, setting the film's overwrought tone. Director Marco (Ian Charleson) is noted for his horror movies, and his opera work has been badly received by the press; he's dictatorial, mean, has an axe to grind with the world and wants to seduce Betty. Between Marco, his temperamental collaborators (including a raven handler and his cackling flock), *and* the fact that *Macbeth* has a reputation for being bad luck to produce, the atmosphere backstage is highly charged. Though nervous and psychologically troubled, Betty tackles the difficult role with great success.

But her triumph is undermined by the discovery that she has a secret admirer, someone far more threatening than the average eccentric opera buff. Betty's fan is a psychopathic murderer, and he wants her to share his preoccupations. Kidnapped, bound, her eyes taped open (the vicious needles), Betty is forced to watch as he murders first her boyfriend Stefan, then generous wardrobe mistress Julia and finally her agent and mentor, Mira (Daria Nicolodi). No-one and nothing is safe from his vicious attentions: he creeps into the theatre by night and mutilates Betty's elaborate costume, killing three ravens for good measure. Sinister Inspector Alan Santini (Urbano Barberini)[2] frightens Betty almost as much as the killer, and she's haunted by a recurring dream that dates back to her childhood and seems to presage the bloody events unfolding in her real life. "I can't decide whether it's just a dream, or the

[2]Barberini had coincidentally just finished shooting a small role in Franco Zeffirelli's *Otello* before starting *Opera*.

memory of something that really happened," she confesses to Marco.

Between the murders and the investigation, the entire opera troupe is in an uproar, and Marco hits upon a far-fetched scheme to unmask the killer, whom he's convinced will attend the next presentation of *Macbeth*. Knowing the ravens saw the killer, and aware that they're said (by their handler, at least) to be intelligent and vengeful, he sets the birds loose in the middle of the performance. And he's right: they seek out the killer - Inspector Santini - and attack him viciously, pecking out one of his eyes (and eating it for good measure). Half blind, Santini kidnaps Betty and escapes to an isolated room in the opera house, which he saturates with gasoline as she sits helpless, bound and blindfolded. As he prepares to set the room on fire, Santini rants. Betty's mother was his lover, he explains, and their relationship was intensely sadomasochistic. Before strangling her, Santini murdered and tortured others at her command, and her death left him bereft. When he saw Betty as Lady Macbeth, it was as though his prayers had been answered; she looked and sounded exactly like her mother, and Santini hoped she would prove as debauched. But having failed to awake her blood lust by forcing her to watch his murders, Santini has decided they must die together. Betty escapes the blaze, and Santini is burned to death. Or so it seems.

Betty and Marco go to the Swiss Alps to rest and decide what to do next. As she walks on a tranquil hillside, he learns from a newscast that Santini's "death" was a brilliant *coup de théâtre* involving a mannequin. He has followed them to the Alps, and kills Marco. Betty escapes one last time before the local police arrive and take him away.

Unlike *Creepers*, whose ludicrous inventions utterly overwhelm the plot, *Opera*'s flamboyant *mise en scène* manages to absorb such outrageous conceits as the vengeful ravens. It's far closer in tone to *Tenebrae*, taking place in a world of relentless shared guilt and all-encompassing anxiety, a world in which artists and their fans combine to form an unholy - and lethal - hybrid. Betty isn't quite Peter Neal; she's not a killer, even though she inspires one. "I'm not like my mother - I'm nothing

Betty (Cristina Marsillach) sings the lead in *Opera*'s avant-garde production of *Macbeth*.

like her," she tells Santini emphatically, but that doesn't stop the visitation of her mother's sins on her head. And come to think of it, isn't it a little odd that though Betty's relationship with the sweet-natured Stefan is troubled, she gravitates towards the twisted Marco as though it were the most natural thing in the world? Even more, the role of Lady Macbeth inflects her character. Never mind, as another character points out, that Verdi's first Lady Macbeth was 17 years old; Betty is really too young to take on the role of a woman driven by an all-consuming lust for power to manipulate her weak-willed husband into the betrayal and murder of his friends and allies. Yet she's brilliant (the reviews all say so), despite her youth and lack of professional experience - no amount of rocking back and forth and muttering "I shouldn't have sung that role, I shouldn't have sung it..." can erase its implications.

In all, *Opera*'s characters are a sorry lot. Marco's a petty tyrant - his own girlfriend calls him a sadist and adds for good measure that everyone who knows him says so. Santini is a psychopathic killer and Betty is frigid and neurotic. The theatre manager is a venal snob, the great Mara Cecova a temperamental termagant and Betty's closest neighbour is a hard-faced bitch who beats her sweet little daughter, Alma. Niceness, in *Opera*'s milieu, is a one-way ticket to bloody oblivion. Concerned young officer Daniele Soavi[3] is summarily dispatched as he tries to guard Betty in her apartment - the first time we even see his face is when he collapses in death. Gentle Stefan dies in a welter of gore, good-natured Julia is gutted with a pair of scissors and Mira, a substitute mother figure to the orphaned singer, is shot through the eye at point blank range. Even the amiable house keeper in the Alps - who's on screen all of a minute - pays the ultimate price for her cheery "*Guten Tag.*"

Also like *Tenebrae*, *Opera*'s mode of articulation is discourse, located specifically in the interplay between present-time action and a series of stylized flashbacks, again introduced to the

---

[3] The name is an affectionate nod to Michele Soavi, who was - as he has been on several other Argento films - *Opera*'s second unit director.

sounds of water and set off by their own unique score. While the main action takes place to Verdi - with the exception of the murder set pieces, underscored by speed metal - the flashbacks (lit cool blue and designed like some divinely decadent fashion spread[4]) unfold to eerie synthesizer music. *Tenebrae*'s world, a few years into the future or wherever, is a world of pervasive, quotidian violence, and *Opera* is much the same, *con brio*.

Argento's relentless search for the outer limits of style has produced images as diverse and arresting as *Deep Red*'s floating pans and the saturated palettes of *Suspiria* and *Inferno*. *Opera*'s signature flourish is a series of shots of the killer's pulsating brain, as literal and audacious a picture of madness as the cinema can generate. In and of itself it's not absolutely unique, of course. In Nicolas Roeg's and Donald Cammell's *Performance* (1970), the camera follows a bullet through a man's skull, into his brain and out the other side into a new world shaped, we infer, by his obsessive and introspective madness. And in the much underrated *Brain Damage* (1988) - a warped fantasy in which an ordinary young man develops a symbiotic relationship with a mutant slug whose saliva produced hallucinations - director Frank Henenlotter's camera exposes not only the protagonist's brain, but a light show of sparks as he experiences altered states through chemistry. But Argento, ever dependable, goes that extra step: not only does the killer's brain throb, but the entire screen throbs along with it. Odd, perhaps, that Paramount's pre-credit sequence for *Suspiria* - the film's title spelled out in pulsating brain-letters - should have adumbrated one of Argento's most grotesquely apt images.

Opera is relentlessly self-referential, what with the produc-

[4]In 1986, Alan Jones reported in *Cinefantastique* (Volume 18, No.2/3, March 1988) on a fashion show Argento directed. "On a catwalk, to the music of Pino Donaggio's *Body Double*, Argento recreated the opening moments of *Suspiria*, complete with rainstorm, and had the glamorous models stabbed to death, then elegantly carted off in see-through body bags. The half-hour video caused a storm of controversy when aired on a prime-time television news program."

The spectator as sacrificial icon: Betty (Cristina Marsillach) in *Opera*.

Argento directing *Opera*'s controversial closing scene.

tion of *Macbeth* on stage, televised live and reproduced on an apparently endless series of video monitors. The larger-than-life quality of the performers' offstage escapades is a thematic equivalent: lust, murder and secret sins of the past make their 'real' lives as melodramatic as the opera itself. Such an oppressive motif demands notice, and suggests a film whose gaze is directed inward. *Opera* also abounds in images linking it to earlier films, almost as though it were intended as a summation to date of characteristic visuals and themes. The emphasis on eyes, in addition to signalling the spectacular nature of the opera-within-a-film experience, recalls not just *Tenebrae*, but *Deep Red* and *The Bird With the Crystal Plumage* as well. Argento also returns to his familiar image of drapery parting to admit the protagonist to a private (and dangerous) world; in *Deep Red* and *Inferno* a heavy curtain leads to, respectively, a conference where telepaths reach out and touch the minds of secret psychopaths, and the lair of an evil alchemist. In *Four Flies on Grey Velvet*, three sets of red drapes separate Roberto Tobias from his fateful encounter in a not-quite-empty-enough theatre; *Opera*'s Betty passes through virtually identical drapes to keep her date with destiny at the opera house. Additionally, *Four Flies* comes to mind when *Opera*'s anonymous killer makes his way to an isolated box in the theatre, the better to watch Betty sing. Opera glasses in hand, he recalls the anonymous puppet figure watching Roberto play a particularly tricky scene in the tragedy of his life.

With *Opera*, music pulls ahead as the clear favourite among professions pursued by Argento protagonists: Betty joins *Four Flies*' Roberto (a drummer in a rock band), pianist Marc Daly in *Deep Red* and music student Mark Elliot of *Inferno*. Even allowing for the exoticism that makes the music world (worlds, rather) a natural for the screen (colourful personalities, nifty trade secrets, behind-the-scenes glamour and lots of sequins) this clearly means something. Argento's identification with writers, tellers of dark stories, is obvious; it's no surprise that three of his movies revolve around them: Sam Dalmas (*The Bird With the Crystal Plumage*), Carlo Giordani (*The Cat*

O'Nine Tails) and most spectacularly, Peter Neal (*Tenebrae*).[5]
But Argento clearly values the directness of affect that charac-
terizes music... all music, from Verdi's *Va Pensiero* to Dokken's
thrash metal noise-making and Goblin's hypnotic synthesizer
scores.

In light of Argento's Theatro Sferistero experience, you can't
help but take notice when reference is made in passing to
Marco's last opera production: *Rigoletto*. And it got devastating
reviews ("Advice to the director: go back to horror films. Forget
opera."); Marco's girlfriend remarks that he was really pissed
off. The Great Mara Cecova has a few choice words for his
Macbeth as well. "It's ridiculous! This is *Macbeth* by Giuseppe
Verdi... this isn't one of your crummy movies. Birds on stage,
back projection, laser beams! What is this? An opera or an
amusement park!"

Sure, it's cheap armchair psychoanalysis, but Marco is clearly
a more literal stand-in for Argento than any other character
he's ever committed to film, and the backstage world of *Opera*'s
Macbeth - hysterical cast and crew and all - reflects the reality
of Argento's shoots. His sets are notoriously volatile; his reputation as a harsh and moody task-master whose sets seethe
with intrigue, discontent and psychodrama precedes him. The
Argento/Marco equation is more than after-the-fact theorizing;
Alan Jones reported the following exchange from *Opera*'s set (in
Cinefantastique, Volume 18, Numbers 2/3):

"He hasn't realized this yet but I'm basing Marco on my observa-
tions while watching Dario at work and his characteristic movements," said [Ian] Charleson. "He'd better not be," cried Argento.
"This film is not a celebration of the director... I wish I hadn't learnt

[5]All other professions tie for third and last. Suzy Banyon is studying
ballet (*Suspiria*). Jennifer Corvino (*Creepers*) is still in high school
and Roderick Usher (*Two Evil Eyes*) is a photographer.

that as it now gives the film a resonance beyond what I'm trying to achieve."

A celebration it's not. Marco is a petty dictator who jokes that he jerks off before shooting a scene and delights in degrading his colleagues. But he's the fulcrum of the film's reflexive structure. When Betty gets the big role because of the Great Mara Cecova's accident, it's Mark who brings the obvious out into the open: "It usually only happens to people in the movies, eh?" he says to her. And it's Mark who reminds Inspector Santini that there's reality and then there's fiction. "I've seen a lot of your movies, and you're really an expert in this field," says Santini after Stefan's death, hoping to goad Marco into saying something rash. "I'd be very interested to hear your opinion." "I think it's unwise to use movies as a guide for reality. Don't you, Inspector?" Marco replies in his iciest voice. The Inspector's reply, something to do with it depending on your definition of reality, ought to be a tip-off. It is, after all, a far cry from the no-nonsense, "Just the facts, Ma'am," attitude we associate with ratiocination, which reflects badly on a policeman. And though Peter Neal is crazy enough to think real-life murder is just like writing a book (and further, crazy enough to *act* on that belief), Marco knows it's not like making a movie.

On some level *Opera* is a response to the critics and detractors who seem to suggest that Argento's aesthetics aren't restricted to the screen; he has been denounced with such virulence one can only assume they believe he encourages murder and brutality in real life. *Opera* is all about the distance between reality and spectacle, and Argento hammers home the message with almost neurotic thoroughness. In costume Betty is a grandiose vision in pearls and feathers and velvet; her voice is awe-inspiring and her demeanour haughty and dismissive. Offstage she's meek and almost plain, everybody's victim; even the little child next door - Alma, who helps her escape the killer through the ventilation shafts - turns out to be more capable than she is. In the theatre, while *Macbeth* is being rehearsed and performed, Marco is a dictator with the power to make the entire cast and crew bend to his will; in Switzerland with Betty

- far from the opera house - he's reduced to torturing flies. The Great Mara Cecova, whose powerful voice[6] rings out from the stage during *Opera*'s opening credits - has no existence at all offstage; once she's out of the action, she's glimpsed only through synecdoche - a leg in a cast and a bottle of suspicious perfume delivered to Betty. Far from encouraging the viewer to translate fantasy into reality, it suggests that this way lies foolishness at the very least, and perhaps madness and destruction as well. In fact, in *Opera*'s closing scene - widely dismissed as cloying and out of sync with the rest of the film - we see Betty on her hands and knees, declaring her solidarity with all nature. Though the soundtrack is angelic and the imagery bucolic, it's all a little too good to be true; the inevitable conclusion is that Betty has let go her tenuous grip on reality and surrendered to madness. Coming on the heels of *Creepers*, *Opera* offered refreshing evidence that Argento was still capable of accomplished and provocative filmmaking.

Two Evil Eyes, first called *Due occhi diabolici*, then *Due occhi malocchio*[7], by contrast, is curiously unpolished. It's a peculiar film, a hybrid inspired by Argento's love of the writing of Edgar Allan Poe. *Two Evil Eyes* - "I think it's supposed to suggest our two visions, Dario's and mine," George Romero joked on set when quizzed about the title. "But you'd better ask him" - is a truncated version of the portmanteau films that proliferated during the '60s and '70s, compilations of short stories strung around a connecting theme, like *Dr. Terror's House of Horrors* and *Torture Garden* (1965 and 1967, Freddie Francis), *The House that Dripped Blood* (1971, Peter Duffell), *Asylum* (1972,

[6]Some last-minute improvisation turned the diva's role into an unseen vocal cameo. Mara Cecova was to have been played by English actress Vanessa Redgrave (coincidentally, David Hemmings' *Blow-Up* co-star), who reportedly arrived demanding that her salary be raised. Argento decided instead to cut the role to its bare bones, and realized no-one really had to see Cecova at all.
[7]An awkward title - could it be a subconscious tribute to Mario Bava's first *giallo*, *La ragazza che sapeva troppo*, called in English *The Evil Eye*?

Roy Ward Baker), and *From Beyond the Grave* (1974, Kevin Connor). Examples as recent as *The Twilight Zone* (1984, John Landis, Steven Spielberg, Joe Dante and George Miller) exist, but the form now seems strained and artificial. With no framing story and only two segments, Romero's adaptation of *The Facts in the Case of M. Valdemar* and Argento's *The Black Cat*, *Two Evil Eyes* never comes together. Though capably directed, Romero's segment was little more than an episode of *Night Gallery* with feature film production values, while Argento's almost completely lacks the stylistic *brio* of his other films. One might argue that Argento toned down his usual excesses out of deference to Poe, preferring to let the writer's work take centre stage, but this won't wash (particularly in light of how freely Argento adapted Poe) - *Two Evil Eyes* is just an idea that didn't quite work out. Highly anticipated on several counts - including as the reunion of Argento and Romero, who had last worked together 10 years earlier on *Dawn of the Dead* - the film was a box office disappointment (despite the presumably double appeal of two celebrity directors) and, like *Opera*, was never distributed theatrically in the United States.

With his domed forehead, narrow chin, high cheekbones and deep-set eyes, Argento bears more than a passing physical resemblance to the ill-fated Poe (whose fame as an alcoholic and drug addict who lived miserably and died young keeps him a member in good standing in the pantheon of doomed Romantics), and is a longtime devotee of his work. His relationship with Poe's writing is a passionate one, and for Argento *Two Evil Eyes* was a project with intense personal implications. Having first read Poe's complete works as an adolescent, he returned to them again and again, fascinated not only by the stories themselves but by the notion that in exploring the darkest recesses of the human mind, Poe may have blighted his own life. In the introduction to *The Tales of Edgar Allan Poe*, a 1985 Italian edition of Poe's writing, Argento wrote eloquently of the connection he feels with the father of the American horror story:

When I began to make films, I recognized that my themes had some

214

affinity with the events told by Poe in his stories; his hallucinatory worlds, his bloody visions. I asked myself: Have I opened my Pandora's box? Would I be invaded by my mad and perverse characters? Can a mind exist in peace that takes its inspiration from hell?... In my solitary moments when some frightening idea strikes me and I think: "With this I will make a film," Poe's handsome and intense face watches me, warns me to pay heed, to be careful.

The tragedy is that Poe wasn't careful. He wandered the streets and was lost. He walked down the paths of arcane secrets written in the monster within us all. And died for it.[8]

Before *Two Evil Eyes*, Argento had never made a film that wasn't based on his own original material, though opportunities (some quite attractive) had presented themselves. Even though the script for *The Black Cat* was his (with Franco Ferrini), it still marks a major departure from his normal way of working. On location in Pittsburgh, Argento reiterated his identification with Poe's life and vision.

Edgar Allan Poe is the origin of all horror. I re-read all his works while I was on holiday - the short stories, the poetry, the essays. I understand his pain; I think it's important to make a picture that is different from the memory people have of the Corman Poe pictures, of all the other adaptations of his work. I think today we can make a picture that more accurately represents the spirit of Poe's work than was possible before, even though we changed many things in the specifics of the stories - both Romero and I. I think it's true to the spirit of Poe to set his stories in the present, because when Poe wrote he wrote about the present; he didn't set his stories on some safe, distant past. I feel Poe would have understood the world today very well.[9]

If not the most adapted author of all time, Poe must come close. His short stories are often little more than macabre sketches, but movie-makers have been bringing them (some-

[8]English translation from the production notes for *Two Evil Eyes*.
[9]Interview with the author; this material also appeared in *Gorezone* No.14.

times kicking and screaming, it's true) to the screen since the silent years, cobbling stories together or attenuating them with extraneous narrative invention and setting them everywhere in the world and in every period from Poe's to the present, with only occasional success. No work is too slight, no connection too tenuous: witness obscuriana like *The System of Dr. Tarr and Prof. Fether* - nobody's ever even heard of it, and it's been filmed *twice*: in 1908 by the Edison film company and again in 1914 by Maurice Tourneur (father of Jacques Tourneur, director of the original *Cat People*). Such poems as *The Raven*, *The City Beneath the Sea* and *The Conqueror Worm* have found their titles associated with pictures whose relation to Poe were tangential at best, and the man himself makes occasional appearances: consider Antonio Margheriti's *Web of the Spider*, which billed itself as based on Poe's non-existent *Night of the Living Dead* and featured the writer wagering on the life of a man who spends the night in a haunted castle.

The last great wave of Poe films was in the '60s, many of them by Roger Corman, who put his name on *House of Usher*, *The Pit and the Pendulum*, *The Premature Burial*, *Tales of Terror* (*Morella, The Black Cat,The Cask of Amontillado* and *The Facts in the Case of M. Valdemar*), *The Raven*, *The Haunted Palace*, (title by Poe, story - *The Case of Charles Dexter Ward* - by H.P. Lovecraft), *The Masque of the Red Death* and *The Tomb of Ligeia* in a mere four years. 1990 promised a major revival of interest: Corman released a remake of *Masque of the Red Death*, directed by Larry Brand (*The Hitcher*), while Stuart Gordon (*Re-Animator*) shot his version (released the following year) of *The Pit and the Pendulum* for Charles Band's Full Moon Productions. Rumours of several other Poe projects created a full-fledged buzz: Menahem Golan's 21st-Century Films announced *The House of Usher* with Oliver Reed and Donald Pleasence, yet another *Masque of the Red Death* (a story whose metaphorical implications in the age of AIDS appear irresistible) and Cozzi's *The Black Cat*, which it tried to pass off as Poe. Veteran exploitation producer Harry Alan Towers also announced his intention to film *Conversations with a Mummy* (a little known satirical essay) with Anthony Perkins

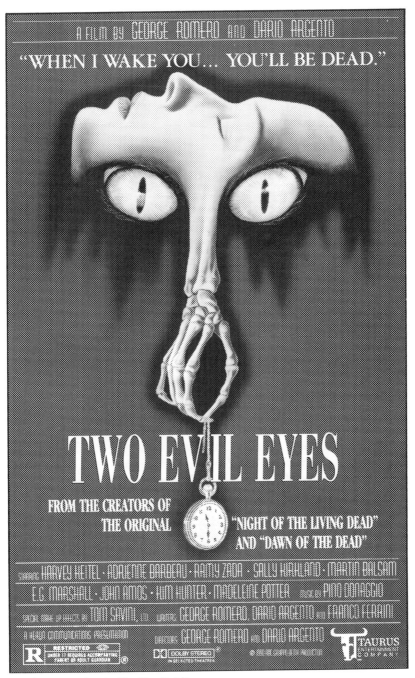

American promotional art for *Two Evil Eyes*.

in the lead. But almost none of these projects came to fruition, leaving *Two Evil Eyes* to stand almost alone.

Argento originally envisioned a project not unlike the 1968 *Spirits of the Dead*: the three-part film featured Louis Malle's fairly straightforward adaptation of *William Wilson*, Roger Vadim's smutty reworking of *Metzengerstein* and Federico Fellini's hallucinatory *Toby Dammit*. Argento had in mind four directors: George Romero, John Carpenter (*Halloween*), Wes Craven (*The Hills Have Eyes, A Nightmare on Elm Street*) and himself. Persistent scheduling conflicts made it seem as though the whole thing was an impossible dream until Argento narrowed down the field, deciding to make the film in two parts. Romero would direct one, he would do the other, and there would be no framing story. There's an argument to be made against framing stories, and anyone who's had enough of motley groups of people telling tales while trapped in elevators, old dark houses and compartments on trains to hell can make it. But *Two Evil Eyes* could have used one.[10]

Despite the fact that they worked together successfully on *Dawn of the Dead*, Romero and Argento could not possibly be more different, personally and aesthetically. There are superficial parallels between their careers: roughly the same age (Argento is the younger by four years) both writer/directors who've made their careers largely outside the studio system, neither afraid of graphic violence. They made their first films within two years of one another - *Night of the Living Dead* was released in 1968, *The Bird With the Crystal Plumage* in 1970 - and both attracted critical attention on a major scale, divided between acclaim and disgust.

But even in the early stages there were conspicuous differ-

[10]Tom Savini suggested a clever and thematically resonant one during filming: "I thought a neat wraparound would be to have Harvey Keitel [the forensic photographer protagonist of *The Black Cat*] come in at the end of George Romero's segment and photograph the body. And then, at the end of Dario's segment, George could come in as the police photographer and tie the stories all together." Argento didn't go for it.

ences. Romero tried - unsuccessfully, it turned out - to avoid being typed as a genre director by following *Night* with two little-seen pictures: the youth-oriented comedy called *There's Always Vanilla* (this from the man who had a problem with the title *"Two Evil Eyes"*) and *Jack's Wife* (aka *Hungry Wives* and *Season of the Witch*), a psychological thriller with feminist overtones. Argento went boldly from thriller to thriller, exploring ever more thoroughly the particulars of violence and madness, digressing only once with *Le cinque giorante,* a violent, black comedy period piece. And while Romero - a big teddy bear of a man - has always been a strong contender for the title "Nicest, most normal guy in the horror business," Argento has cultivated his reputation as an obsessive, spooky, *grand guignol* aesthete. You only have to look at the *Dawn* publicity shots of them together to see that they're cut from different cloth: Romero, tall, broad and beaming, and Argento, rail-thin and smiling, his eyes haunted.

Argento's hallucinogenic revelry in the power of the image at the total expense of narrative stands in stark contrast to Romero's solid practicality; Romero gets the job done and his movies have a beginning, a middle and an end - in that order.

Ten years and many films later, their reunion reflected a decided change in the balance of power. *Dawn of the Dead* was Romero's movie, and Argento's contribution was minimal even in the European cut. *Two Evil Eyes* was Argento's: the concept was his, he co-produced with Achille Manzotti and his brother Claudio executive produced[11]; it was *Dario Argento's Two Evil*

[11]This marked the first time the brothers had worked together since *Tenebrae* in 1982. As mentioned in the introduction, just prior to *Two Evil Eyes*, Claudio produced and co-wrote *Santa Sangre*, the first film in more than a decade by Alejandro Jodorowsky, of *El Topo* and *The Holy Mountain* fame. Interestingly, *Santa Sangre*, which tells the story of a young man driven to madness and murder by the horrors of his grotesque childhood, contains several murderous set pieces. The killing of a tattooed madame in her shanty, and that of prostitute posed on a knife-thrower's wheel are elaborate, bizarre and erotic in their detail in a way that's not much like Jodorowsky's earlier work - which tended to the grotesquely surreal - but strongly recall Argento's.

Eyes in all but name. In addition, Romero's career was going through a rough patch. He was no longer associated with Laurel Entertainment, *Monkey Shines* - an ambitious effort to expand the ever-more confining boundaries of the horror film ghetto - had done badly at the box office, and the long-awaited *Pet Sematary* wound up being directed by Mary Lambert.

During production Argento emphasized the notion that the film was a close collaboration, but Romero was a little more candid, saying (with a slightly defensive edge):

We worked together to some extent; Dario came down to Florida and we talked about the stories and what to do with them. But we're really making our own films. He's the producer of the whole thing, but he's been very good about leaving me alone to follow my own visions and make my own film.

I don't know that we could ever really work together on the same film; first of all, I don't know what we'd do. And second, we're very different - stylistically, temperamentally... in just about every way. Working this way we can have a great time. We get together socially and talk about theory, politics, books, whatever, and then when it comes to work we mostly go our own ways.[12]

Romero chose to adapt *Valdemar* after learning that his first choice, *Masque of the Red Death* was already being made under Corman's auspices. A vignette about a man who dies under hypnosis and is suspended in a state between life and death, *Valdemar* needed expanding, and Romero devised a story about Valdemar's wife and doctor and their plan to get his money. "The story is mostly about the scheme cooked up by the wife and the doctor," Romero said during production, and aptly observed, "I almost feel as though I'm shooting an episode of *Columbo*." The completed segment plays as a television piece; efficient, smoothly constructed and almost completely without character. The same can't be said for Argento's *The Black Cat*. He, too, had originally thought of doing another story, *The Pit*

[12]Interview with the author; this material appeared in *Fangoria* No.95.

and the Pendulum, but changed his mind. He explained,

"I heard it was being redone by Stuart Gordon, but that's not why I changed - I read the story again and found it too šimple. A man is in the dark, terrified - everything happens inside his head, nothing you can see. *The Black Cat* is a real story, and I knew I could work with it.

The leading character in my story is similar to Edgar Allan Poe in the way he is haunted by the things he sees and imagines. He's an artist who's tormented by the morality of the things he creates. He's also based on the figure of the American photographer, Weegee. Weegee had a strange take on the world - he loved humanity at its strangest and most desperate; he saw the beauty in horror and extremity.

The Black Cat is a short segment, but there are many things in it. I use things from many of Poe's stories, and also I was very influenced by Dostoyevsky's *Crime and Punishment*. I'm interested in the possibility of committing a terrible crime and trying to remain silent, only to have what you have done follow you, persecute you.[13]

Poe's *Black Cat* tells the story of a ·man descending into alcoholic madness and murder; he kills his wife with an axe and conceals her corpse in the cellar only to be betrayed by the inopportune howling of his cat, inadvertently walled-up with the body. Grim and grisly stuff indeed. But this piece served as a springboard for Argento, an opportunity for him to weave allusions to a slew of his favorite Poe works into story that revolves around a photographer - Rod Usher, played by Harvey Keitel - obsessed with capturing scenes of violence through his lens. The script's three most obvious homages were murder *tableaux* drawn from *The Pit and the Pendulum*, *Berenice* and *The Murders in the Rue Morgue* (the *Rue Morgue* scene was deleted from the final print). *The Black Cat* also contains references to no fewer than ten other stories, ranging from

[13]Interview with the author; this material also appeared in *Fangoria* No.95.

character names to major plot points: in addition to those already mentioned, there are nods to *The Fall of the House of Usher*, *The Narrative of Arthur Gordon Pym*, *The Cask of Amontillado*, *Eleanor*, *Annabelle Lee*, *The Tell-Tale Heart* and *The Premature Burial*. The allusiveness borders on the obsessive; Romero put the best face on things when he referred to Argento's script as a "love poem to Poe."

The Black Cat opens with photographer Roderick Usher (Harvey Keitel), who specializes in pictures of violence and death, arriving at a crime scene. A woman's body lies on a table, neatly bisected by an elaborate pendulum; even the police are horrified - with the exception of Inspector Legrand (John Amos) - but Usher coolly snaps pictures, even releasing the pendulum to improve the shots.

Despite his macabre interests, Usher's life is in pretty good shape. He lives with Annabel (Madeleine Potter), an attractive violinist, and his new book - *Metropolitan Horrors* - is about to be published. Everything changes, however, when Annabel acquires a cat. Usher takes an instant dislike to the creature, and when Annabel is away he strangles it, simultaneously taking photos. The cat's disappearance poisons their relationship, and when Annabel sees *Metropolitan Horrors*, which includes photographs of the dying cat, she decides to leave him. Usher comes home with another black cat, given to him by a mysterious woman in a bar. He confronts Annabel; they struggle and he accidentally kills her. Usher hides the body behind a false wall, inadvertently walling up the cat, which later claws its way out. Usher kills the cat and disposes of its body as well.

Despite Usher's assurances that Annabel has gone away on tour, the neighbours are suspicious and call the police. Legrand and his assistant arrive to question Usher and are convinced there's nothing amiss until the yowls of a cat draw them upstairs. They find Annabel's corpse, partly eaten by mutant kittens, the offspring of the imprisoned cat. Usher kills both policemen and is accidentally hanged while trying to escape through a window.

Argento's obsession with eyes made it into the title this time, and *The Black Cat* is haunted by images of voyeurism. Usher's

222

profession is the starting point[14], and by patterning Usher on American photographer Weegee (1899-1968, real name: Arthur Fellig), Argento gives the character studied (and chic) resonance. Weegee's photographs are, as Argento says, celebrations of desperation and extremity. Working the urban police beat like an angel of darkness, Weegee defied notions of reticence and propriety. His photographs of corpses and criminals are shocking enough; more shocking still are photographs of lovers at Coney Island or gawkers at a Hollywood premiere. Somehow tainted by Weegee's blunt, sordid eye, they all look squalid and mean - his photographs delineate a world that's nothing short of Hellish.

The scene in which Usher terrorizes Annabel's cat by framing it between his fingers and whispering "Click," plays off the implicit violation in taking a photograph - it's no accident that pictures are *shot*. The cat is explicitly linked to the act of photographic creation from its very first scene: it invades Usher's darkroom and leaves paw tracks on his developing prints. Later, Usher complains the cat is staring at him, saying it could tear his eyes out; its own huge yellow eyes are often shot in eerie close-up.[15]

[14]Movie photographers tend to be a bad lot: forget the occasional debonair lensman like Dick Avery (Fred Astaire) in *Funny Face* and think instead of murderous Mark Lewis (Carl Boehm) in Michael Powell's *Peeping Tom*, voyeur L.B. Jeffries (James Stewart) in Alfred Hitchcock's *Rear Window* and Thomas (David Hemmings) in Michelangelo Antonioni's *Blow-Up*, discussed at some length in chapter 4. And they're just the stars: once you get to pathetic, perverted George (John Ventantonio) in Paul Bartel's *Private Parts* or the cannibal photographer Laurence Harvey plays in his own *Welcome to Arrow Beach*, things have become very sleazy indeed.

[15]Argento originally intended to shoot a number of sequences from the cat's POV, though no such material exists in the finished film. Nicola Pecorini, his regular steadicam operator, described some of their ideas while the film was being shot: "Dario's idea is that because the iris of the cat's eye is not round but vertical, we might use an anamorphic lens without printing anamorphically, so everything will be squeezed. We're also thinking about different colours, or different colour values within the shot."

Usher watches Annabel surreptitiously, staking out a diner near the house and catching sight of nothing more than Annabel and one of her students walking innocently down the street; Mr. Pym (Martin Balsam), the neighbour from next door, is framed grotesquely in the peephole when he comes over to complain about the noise. Following Annabel's death, Usher spies on the neighbours, framed by the windows, and watching with horror as they mouth the word "murder". But even this familiar theme is rendered in a perfunctory fashion. The script mentions a final shot in which a passer-by takes a snapshot of Usher's dangling body ("Rod has become one of his own 'Metropolitan Horrors'," it reads), but even this obvious exercise in circular imagery didn't make it into the film.

While most of the segment is shot in a cool, naturalistic fashion, *The Black Cat* comes to life in a medieval nightmare sequence precipitated by Usher and Annabel's argument about the missing cat. Locked out of the bedroom, Usher falls asleep on the couch and is awakened (it seems) by the sound of laughter: a dwarf and a woman in a phallic mask beckon from the door. He follows, the stairs made unfamiliar by a swirling, blue-tinged mist. When he opens the door of the house, the present is gone and he steps into a medieval festival.

Usher makes his way through the laughing crowd. There is a woman in a long dress, her hair wild; she looks like Annabel. She drinks from a ceremonial goblet and falls to the flagstones; the dwarf appears, singing and holding a stick at the end of which a hanged cat is suspended. The woman cradles it; she twitches and writhes, then points out Rod in the crowd: she tells him cryptically that his destiny is written in the spot on the cat's chest. The villagers seize him and he is killed, suspended with ropes then dropped and impaled on a pointed rod. He wakes, sweating, as his beer bottle crashes to the floor.

Lush and sensuous, the dream interlude is everything the contemporary footage is not; it would be nice to see more of it. The soundtrack that accompanies the medieval sequence - a simple, traditional melody - is heard prior to Usher's dream, subtly prefiguring the scene. This strategy, vaguely suggestive of the use of dreamy flashbacks in *Tenebrae*, hints at a more complex structure than *The Black Cat* ultimately achieves. It's possible that *The Black Cat* would have been more successful had it been played out at feature length; though the story is slight, its details are interesting and could have been more compelling had they been more thoroughly developed.

Though Argento's last work to date, it's doubtless far from his last word. He has averaged a film every two years since 1970, and at 50 - after a full two decades as a director - remains full of enthusiasm for filmmaking. There's every reason to expect Argento will continue to make movies into the next century, and no reason to think his dreams will grow any less dark.

EPILOGUE

In the final analysis films are films and dreams are dreams: no-one can reasonably deny that they're the end results of different processes, with different life-spans, frames of reference, and spheres of influence. And yet there are respects in which they resemble one another, and horror films - more than any other genre - flirt with the patterns of enunciation associated with dreams. In this respect you can hardly resist the temptation to speak of Dario Argento's films as dark dreams of death and night and blood, to borrow Yukio Mishima's rapturously apt phrase.

Argento can be fairly articulate about his work, particularly in interviews given after the making of *Suspiria*. He's spoken persuasively about the ritualistic aspect of *Tenebrae* and about the way in which that film generates a network of deceptive, disquieting erotic signals that entangle the unwary viewer in a web of contradictory seductive messages. He's alluded to his use of images that defamiliarize the process of seeing as far back as *The Bird With the Crystal Plumage*, and about the systematic construction of an artificial mythology based on De Quincey's ideas for the Three Mothers films. There's no question but that Argento is highly self-aware and has - particularly since a substantial segment of the European (particularly French) press began according his films serious consideration - engaged in a conscious critical discourse through his films. Nevertheless, he prefers to write in an aggressively unanalytical way. Argento has spoken often about his extensive use of storyboards, usually the sign of an intensely control-oriented filmmaker, but he admits at the same time that he regards the script as a blueprint from which he feels free to deviate. Even as he refers to the structure of *Tenebrae* (in a 1983 interview with Angelo Nicolini, Fabrizio Bettelli and Antonello Grimaldi in *Mad Movies*) as "mathematical and geometrical," he also stresses that during the actual process of writing his screenplays he's generally in one altered state or another. "Little by little, I work myself into a frenzy; in New York writing *Inferno* I was truly frenzied," he told the same writers, later explaining to Alan Jones (*Cinefantastique*, Volume 13, No.6): "I lock myself away for months on end. Nothing usually happens at first, and I just end up staring at a blank wall and waiting for inspiration from imaginary ghosts or shafts of moonlight. If I don't come up with something, I punish myself and deny myself everything. Eventually my second soul gives in and I come up with something." In fact, he told Vincent Ostria (in *Starfix*), his method of working is "a little like that of the surrealists, using automatic writing." The language is melodramatic, but the sense is clear: Argento's screenplays boil up from the subconscious and are brought to the screen with a minimum of dramatic shaping; he's said that his primary concern is to preserve the images that come to him in these states, rather than to construct plausible narratives. It's certainly easy enough to see why the plots of Argento's films often leave so much to be desired, and equally easy to see why the quality of their imagery is often so arresting: it's tough to fake dreaminess, to produce its disturbing effects through logical, rational processes.

This isn't to say Argento's work is interesting only because it represents an especially unrefined look at the goings-on of a fairly lurid subconscious mind. Fortified by his years as a film critic and, later, as a screenwriter, Argento's sensibilities are sophisticated; but he's managed to retain an open line into the realm of the subconscious and through it material seems to pour out at an alarming rate. Argento has also taken advantage of the fact that the horror genre, because of its guaranteed box office appeal, has always leant itself to freedom of formal experimentation denied to less economically stable genres. You often read of the "stylization" of the horror film... what exactly does this mean? At its worst, "stylization" describes the formulaic repetition of grossly cliched elements demonstrated in many of the stalk-and-slash pictures made in the wake of *Friday the 13th* (1980, Sean S. Cunningham): a group of nubiles proceeds to an isolated location and, one by one, they are slaughtered by a monster/mutant/maniac. This is stylized in the sense that it adheres to a rigid and pre-acknowledged pattern, but it's not particularly interesting. At its best, the stylized nature of expectations in the horror film permits a certain poetry of cinematic expression to shine through minimalist story lines unencumbered by complex considerations of characterization and/or plotting. Look at films ranging from *I Walked With a Zombie* (1943, Jacques Tourneur), *Eyes Without a Face/Les yeux sans visage/The Horror Chamber of Dr. Faustus* (1959, Georges Franju) and *Black Sunday/La maschera del demonio* (1960, Mario Bava) to *Manhunter* (1986, Michael Mann), *The Hitcher* (1986, Robert Harmon), *Near Dark* (1987, Kathryn Bigelow) and *The Drifter* (1988, Larry Brand). Argento's exploitation of the freedom to experiment formally is very much of this kind.

One might well ask why it's worth expending the considerable effort needed to decode a film like *Deep Red* or *Tenebrae*, whose conventionally intellectual concerns are threaded in among elements generated by crassly commercial considerations; why not - if they are to be undertaken at all - confine such efforts to "important" films rather than to the detritus of popular genre cinema? The answer to this question can be very complicated indeed, touching on a wealth of ideas having to do with the sociological value of mass-culture artifacts, the relationship between high and low art, the overall usefulness of *auteur* criticism as a way of containing the commercial cinema or the comparative value of exploitation films as a cultural barometer. The answer can also be a relatively simple "Why not?," if a why not by way of Barthes. The very process of reading films as complex as *Deep Red* or *Tenebrae* - with their multi-levelled systems of allusion to influences as diverse as American television *policiers* and liturgical ritual - is an engaging enterprise: dense, subtle and infinitely rewarding on its own terms. To choose all too obvious an example, *The Color Purple* (1985, Steven Spielberg) may well be about "big" things - racism, the tyranny of the family unit, and one woman's search for her own identity - but as a film it's devoid of intrinsic interest; it's seamlessly pretty, technically well-crafted and utterly vacuous - the message is the medium. Returning to

229

Stephen Heath's allusion to an "obviousness of systems," Argento's films offer an apparently endless number of points of entry into the fiction. You can look at lighting patterns (from naturalistic to stylized in a variety of ways), use of colour, styles of editing (ranging from the obtrusive cutting of *Four Flies on Grey Velvet* to the nearly seamless style of *Tenebrae*); talk about the obtrusive foregrounding of the mechanical means of production, systematic subversion of the narrative codes of traditional mysteries/thrillers, hieratic use of actors, obsessive encoding of allusions to perverse sexuality, tension between the use of certain avant-garde devices and the commercial narrative orientation of all Argento's films, or the shifting relationship between soundtrack and image, to name only a few of the possibilities. You could even make an argument for Argento's use of post-dubbed sound as a stylistic statement, stressing the aesthetic distanciation it produces. It wouldn't be a great argument, given that wholesale dubbing is Italian industry practice; Argento himself has said that having grown up with the practice, he pays no attention to its formal implications. But the argument could be made.

It's been said that if commercial art is always in danger of becoming a whore, then high art is equally in danger of becoming an old maid - the remark's too glib by half, but that doesn't make it untrue. By opting decisively for the low road, Argento has insured that when he errs it's always on the side of exuberant bad taste, rather than high-minded pretension. From *The Bird With the Crystal Plumage* to *Two Evil Eyes*, his films have been many things - some good, some not - but they've never been dull. And that, perhaps, is the final argument for the cinema of Dario Argento.

AFTERWORD TO THE AMERICAN EDITION

"You don't know what a killer looks
like. Anyone can be a killer."
—David Parson (*Trauma*)

Since the UK publication of *Broken Mirrors/Broken Minds*, the
body of writing about Argento has grown steadily, his films
examined and analyzed from every conceivable standpoint. He's
been called, in all seriousness, "The Visconti of Violence," and
with a touch of affectionate mockery, the "De Sica of Sickness,"
"Capra of Carnage" and "Godard of Gore."[1] Actor Frederic
Forrest, featured in Argento's most recent film, *Trauma,* ranked
him alongside Tony Richardson, Costa-Gavras and Francis Ford
Coppola,[2] while co-star James Russo was moved to declare: "Dario
is simply the best there is in this genre. John Ford made westerns,
Dario makes horror movies." High praise indeed; to be the John
Ford of horror film is nothing to sneer at.

But more and more, Argento enthusiasts must wonder about the
direction his work is taking, must wonder what direction it can
possibly take. His films could hardly be more elegantly bloody or
visually baroque, more perversely vicious or less narratively
coherent, more seductively beautiful or intertextually convoluted.
Nevertheless, times have changed since the early '70s, when
Argento made his first films, and, in particular, the motion picture
market has changed. Horror films are a tough sell in today's U.S.
theatrical marketplace. Prevailing wisdom holds that horror fans
are a committed but relatively small segment of the moviegoing
public, and more and more they're being catered to by direct-to-
video releases. It's hard to remember a time when horror movies
were released regularly by major studios; the shock when *Silence
of the Lambs* dominated the Academy Awards for 1991 was a

---

[1]By *The Daily News*' "Phantom of the Movies," in "Hi-ho the Dario, the
filmer & his hell," September 25, 1991.

[2]Forrest has worked with all of them, in *Shadow on the Sun* (1988),
Music Box (1989), and *The Conversation* (1974) and *Apocalypse Now*
(1979), respectively.

reminder, and *Silence* could—and did—take refuge behind the term "psychological thriller." No one would ever call Jonathan Demme a director of horror movies.

Argento hasn't had a theatrical hit in America since *Suspiria*. *Opera* was never released here, and *Two Evil Eyes* made only the briefest, pro-forma stopover in theaters on its way to video. In light of this trend, *Trauma* (or *Dario Argento's Trauma*, as the production materials had it) is disturbing. *Trauma*, Argento's twelfth feature and the second shot entirely in the United States (or maybe the first, depending on how you count his half of *Two Evil Eyes*), has been a disappointment to those who've caught up to it abroad or on bootleg tape.

Argento repeatedly denied commercial motives when asked about *Trauma*'s American cast and locations. "I make my pictures for myself, from what I see and imagine," he claimed. "I cannot make a picture for anyone but myself. That's why it seems to me so terrible when they try to censor my pictures, to cut them. I believe always that the filmmaker must speak with his own voice and hope that when the people come to his movie, they see something they can recognize.

"I think also that the expectations of American and European audiences used to be different, say twenty years ago, but now they are very much the same. The world gets smaller all the time, and we all become more and more alike; video brings my pictures all over the world and different kinds of people can see them and enjoy them. Anyway, I hope they enjoy them!" Plausible denials notwithstanding, the whole business smacks of an attempt to capture an audience outside Europe and hardcore Euro-horror buffs by shooting in the States, with familiar faces: from Piper Laurie and Frederic Forrest to James Russo, Chris Rydell (actor son of pretentious director Mark Rydell) and Brad Dourif. Argento's daughter, Asia, is the only exotic entry on the all-American roster. Shot in Minneapolis and St. Paul, Minnesota (Pittsburgh was a strong contender until very late in the game; local financing reportedly gave Minneapolis the edge), *Trauma*'s physical landscape is resolutely bland and characterless. It could be argued that it resembles superficially the cold, brightly lit Rome of *Tenebrae*, but it really looks like nothing more nor less than a featureless midwestern burg. Argento even had his first American co-writer on the screenplay, horror novelist T.E.D. Klein (*The Ceremonies*), and though *Trauma*'s dialogue does sound less than usual like an awkward translation from the Italian, the net gain is negligible.

Completed in 1992 and released in Italy to lukewarm response, *Trauma* still has neither a U.S. theatrical nor video distributor; the closest it has come to the U.S. is Toronto, by way of a screening at the 1993 Festival of Festivals. And it's no wonder. It's not that *Trauma* is an overwhelmingly bad film; it's just that it's a thoroughly undistinguished one, lacking precisely those simultaneously troubling and beguiling flourishes that differentiate Argento from scores of competent American genre directors. It's driven by a horribly wrong notion, the idea that if Argento's films have failed to seduce a broad-based American audience, then it must be because Americans want to see something more conventional. Judged on considerations of narrative plausibility and linear development (the cornerstones of classical narrative construction, taught to aspiring American screenwriters like the ten commandments), Argento's films have always failed miserably. Enthusiasts treasure his films for their weirdness and their overwhelming visual beauty, precisely those things *Trauma* lacks.

Argento can't make a relentlessly efficient American thriller (neither can most Americans, but that's another issue); it's neither his nature nor his inclination. But *Trauma* feels dumbed down, blanded out; it's neither one thing nor another. Visually, it does indeed look, for the most part, like a not particularly interesting American thriller, set in an anonymous city with little past and no particular future. But the usual Argento narrative deficiencies— incoherence and minimal characterization—are foregrounded without the distinctively lush decor, web of decorative detail and choreography for camera that make up for them in films from *Deep Red* to *Opera*. Reassuringly bizarre Argento touches are scattered throughout: the peculiar paper puppet theater set piece[3] that opens the film, a severed head that mouths a few last words, a psychotropic berry that induces hallucinatory dreams. But overall the film is dull, flat, and eminently forgettable. *Trauma* is certainly of a piece with Argento's previous work, but it doesn't build on its predecessors; at best, he's marking time.

---

[3]The scene is a French Revolutionary tableaux, complete with guillotine; it all has nothing to do with the rest of the film on a story level, though the thematic connections are obvious.

Physically and mentally fragile Aura Petrescu (Argento) is the anoretic daughter of two professional spiritualists, Romanians who have settled in America. She's also a patient at the Farraday Clinic, where the intimidating Dr. Judd (Forrest) supervises her care. She escapes and tries to commit suicide by leaping off a bridge. David Parson (Rydell), a reformed drug addict who works at a local television station, rescues her, but at a nearby diner, she steals his wallet and runs away. She's caught and returned to her parents.

That night, her mother (Laurie) holds a seance that goes very, very wrong: possessed by the spirit of a woman recently murdered by the local serial killer local media have dubbed the Headhunter (the victims are decapitated with a handheld, electric wire noose), Mrs. Petrescu flees into the blinding storm. Aura and her father follow separately; through the sheets of rain, Aura, to her horror, glimpses a shadowy figure holding the heads of her parents aloft.

She enlists David's help in tracking down the murderer, with predictably disastrous results. David's girlfriend leaves him, the police and Dr. Judd pursue Aura, and the killer strikes again and again. Aura is briefly brought back to the clinic, where her nurse is murdered; David rescues her, and they find a key belonging to the dead woman. It leads to a storage space, where they find an old photograph of a doctor and a group of nurses; three of them are dead. They track down one of the remaining nurses, who escapes and is subsequently murdered in an airport motel; Dr. Lloyd (Dourif), now a junkie, claims to know nothing and is decapitated as well. Judd makes a last, unsuccessful attempt to get Aura away from David; he then flees and the police give chase. Judd smashes up his car and dies; the trunk is full of severed heads, and the case is closed.

Aura disappears, and in despair, David returns to drugs and loses his job. After a humiliating experience at a pharmacy, where he tries to get drugs with a fake prescription, David sees a woman wearing a distinctive bracelet, a bracelet that belonged to Aura. He tracks her to her home and finds Aura alive, imprisoned in the basement by her vengeful mother. In a flashback, we see the traumatic delivery of her son Nicholas, born during a raging storm and decapitated by the attending doctor—Lloyd—when the lights failed. Lloyd and the delivery room nurses attempted to cover up the horrifying incident, using shock therapy to make Mrs. Petrescu forget; instead, she was driven insane. She has systematically killed everyone involved, and staged her own death to divert suspicion. When Aura thought she saw two heads, she was really seeing only one, held beside her mother's face. Mr. Petrescu is killed with her own portable guillotine, and Aura and David escape to an uncertain future.

More than anything, *Trauma* recalls *Deep Red* (and *Deep Red* recalls *The Bird With the Crystal Plumage,* in its turn inspired by the novel *Screaming Mimi*), which takes off from a similar premise: a witness sees something that holds the key to a string of killings, but misinterprets what he (Mark in *Deep Red*) or she (Aura) has observed. "I didn't see anything," Aura gasps when Judd confronts her in the downpour; "You must have seen something," he insists, encapsulating the movie's central dilemma. In addition, in both *Deep Red* and *Trauma,* the murders have their origin in long-repressed traumas, and children play a pivotal role in understanding the killer's warped motivations, which revolve around a mother's twisted love for her son. Even *Trauma*'s murder weapon seems inspired by *Deep Red*'s final scene, in which mad Marta is decapitated when her necklace is caught in an ascending elevator[4]; it acts like the portable guillotine wire and slices through her flesh, cutting off her head.

But *Trauma* is full of references to other Argento films as well. A lizard, seen in a cage during *Trauma*'s first murder, becomes a recurring image and recalls the lizard Betty releases at the end of *Opera*; Aura herself—the script was originally called, awkwardly, *Aura's Enigma*—recalls the young heroine of *Creepers,* the last of Argento's films to get a substantial U.S. release and Argento's personal favorite among his own films. Like *Creepers'* Jennifer Corvino, played by then-fourteen-year-old Jennifer Connelly, Aura is a girl on the brink of womanhood, whose adolescent angst manifests itself in bizarre and frightening ways. Again like Jennifer, Aura establishes a close relationship with a damaged older man—in *Creepers* he's paralyzed, in *Trauma,* a former drug addict—who helps her recognize and accept her inner strength.

---

[4]And, of course, there's a murder by elevator in *Trauma*. The portable guillotine wire gets tangled up in Lloyd's gold chain and snaps, so he's dragged to an elevator shaft, where the descending car severs his head.

The image of Aura standing in the rain, screaming and screaming as water pours down her face, evokes the final shot of *Tenebrae* (eerily so, in that *Tenebrae*'s Anne is played by Asia's own mother, Daria Nicoldi) and *Trauma*'s use of hospitals to suggest the ruthless repression of non-conformity recalls *Four Flies on Grey Velvet*, *Deep Red*, and *Creepers*. Mrs. Petrescu is one of a series of maternal monsters, following Marta and Betty's sadistic mother in *Opera*. Argento has said in interviews that his estrangement from his own mother was a milestone in his own life; he has certainly created some of the scariest mothers since Hitchcock. Overall, Argento seems to be reaching back with *Trauma*, trying to rework elements that have succeeded in the past and give them a contemporary gloss. But he's treading water, rehashing material without revitalizing it.

On an encouraging note, Argento's commitment to the genre remains steadfast. It's sobering to look at the careers of Argento's contemporaries, the horror/thriller stars of the '70s. Of David Cronenberg, John Carpenter, Larry Cohen, George Romero, Tobe Hooper, William Friedkin, Wes Craven...what are they doing now? Friedkin, whose *The Exorcist* (1973) catapulted horror films to near-respectability, abandoned the genre entirely, with the exception of the minor and all-but-forgotten *The Guardian* (1990). Romero, the father of the modern zombie movie (with *Night of the Living Dead,* 1969), declares regularly that he'd rather be doing something else, and his most recent film, *The Dark Half* (1993), came and went almost unnoticed, after its release was delayed by the bankruptcy of producer Orion. Hooper, whose brutal *Texas Chainsaw Massacre* (1976) upped the violence ante in genre pictures, is reduced to low budget potboilers—his most recent picture, *Spontaneous Combustion* (1989), went straight-to-video— while Carpenter, whose *Halloween* (1978) is still the standard to which slasher films with aspirations are judged, is working on cable, with the series *John Carpenter's Body Bags.* After several forgettable films, Craven has returned, reluctantly, to the *Nightmare on Elm Street* series he originated a decade ago and has since criticized roundly as debased, gimmicky, and cheap. Cohen, the fertile imagination behind *It's Alive* (1974), *Demon* (1976), and *O* (1982) continues to write and direct. Inauspiciously, the best of his recent efforts, *Best Seller* (1987) and *Guilty as Sin* (1993), have been directed by others—John Flynn and Sydney Lumet (!), respectively—and his directing has been largely confined to low budget sequels. Cronenberg has fared best, continuing to deal with the sexual paranoia and monstrous imagery that first erupted in such films as *They Came from Within* (1975) and *Videodrome* (1983) on ever-larger budgets. But *Naked Lunch* (1991) and *M. Butterfly* (1993), for all their surface peculiarities, are fundamentally mainstream motion pictures.

Argento remains committed to genre filmmaking, and in no uncertain terms. "People often ask me, why do I want to stay with this kind of picture, why do I want to continue to make movies about marginal people and terrible things? Other directors change, they stop making horror pictures and do films about 'serious' subjects. But I think many of them have lost their way. They become concerned about appearances, what other people think of what they're doing. Films have to be the most important thing; they're strong, like dreams or madness, but you have to remain open to the images, or else you lose your touch." *Trauma* isn't evidence that Argento has remained open to the dreams and madness that infuse his best films with a mesmerizing allure, one that supersedes the revultion one normally feels at images of brutal death and baroque torment; perhaps his next film will be the proof. In the meantime, Argento's loyal devotees can only echo early enthusiast David Soren's plea: "Bring us more flies on grey velvet.[5]"

---

[5] "More Flies on Grey Velvet: A Further Look at the Cinema of Dario Argento," *Photon* Number 27 (February, 1975), p. 19.

AN INTERVIEW WITH DARIO ARGENTO[1]

Before becoming a filmmaker, you were a film critic. Very few Americans make that transition...

But many Europeans do - in France especially. I think sometimes that *all* French directors are former film critics. Truffaut, Godard, Chabrol, Rohmer... and the same is true in Italy. Bertolucci, Pasolini, me; you can name many people who have gone from writing about movies to making them.

Writing about film is like being a student, like University. It's a good way to start - you examine pictures closely, you learn the work of different directors. Then after a certain number of years you finish your studies and you're ready to make films yourself.

In America it's totally different, because of your studio system. In Europe there's nothing like them, just producers and financiers. The best thing about it is that your principal relationship is with the bank that gives you the money you need to make your film. Because the bank is nobody, no face, nobody saying, 'But wait, you have to change this in the screenplay.' When you're done, the bank doesn't come in and say, 'You need to cut this and that.' It's a beautiful relationship. Impersonal, and I like it that way. When you work with a studio, everyone is an artist, everybody has a suggestion for some way to change your work. I don't want to have a discussion with *anyone* about these things. I want to make *my* picture.

I've worked with American studios two times, on *Suspiria* and *Inferno*, and on *Inferno* especially, it was a very bad situation.

Though you've directed thrillers and horror films almost

exclusively, you've written in a wide range of genres - war films, Westerns...

One love story, also...

Why, as a director, do you feel you're always drawn to violence and terror?

I don't know... maybe it's destiny. I write my pictures and during shooting I discover they're always this way. I enjoy making this particular kind of film, although when I go to the cinema, I like to watch all different kinds of pictures. When I turn on the television and I'll watch *anything*. Films in black and white and in colour; fiction and documentaries; serious pictures and stupid ones. I love historical epics, spectacles with thousands of horses and extras with spears. *Spartacus*, but also the Maciste films made here in Italy. I'm hypnotized by space, colour, movement, bodies... anything.
I read an interview once with Stanley Kubrick, one of the greatest directors ever, and he said he hated to travel. But he loved Greece - the islands were beautiful, the food delicious, the water, the people, the landscape... all wonderful. The interviewer asked how many times he had been to Greece. Kubrick said, never. But he has seen many documentaries about Greece and that was even better than going there. I feel the same way about it - movies are a way of experiencing many different worlds.

*One of your early screen credits was for Sergio Leone's **Once Upon a Time in the West**.*

Yes, Bernardo Bertolucci and I wrote the story for that film. I remember it was very long, it came out to something like 150 pages. We worked for six months on it, and we watched all the famous Westerns; I remember we saw *Johnny Guitar* three times. And the John Ford film with John Wayne and Natalie Wood - *The Searchers*. Beautiful film.

An Interview With Dario Argento

Once Upon a Time in the West is spoken of as an encyclopedia of Western themes and images...

Because at the time we were writing we were also watching all the Westerns ever made; at least, that's the way it seemed then. Every day, from morning until night, we sat watching films, one after the other. And Sergio Leone would come by sometimes and say, 'What, you've seen this but you haven't seen...' I don't know, something else, so we would see that as well.

Bernardo and I both went on from that experience to direct our own pictures - Bernardo with *The Conformist*, me with *The Bird With the Crystal Plumage*.

What does the term "giallo" mean?

It's a long story. Maybe 60 years ago, mysteries were first published in Italy in editions with yellow covers. And "yellow" is *"giallo"* in Italian. The colour yellow became associated with mysteries in Italy, like black in France. All mysteries aren't *gialli*; Raymond Chandler isn't *giallo* - he's dark, *noir*. Neither is Dashiell Hammett. Agatha Christie, S.S. van Dine, John Dickson Carr, Cornell Woolrich - they're *gialli*. Classic mysteries.

Your casts are always an international mix. Do you find it difficult to direct when there's a language barrier?

No. I don't speak English well, but language doesn't matter to me at all in my films. Also, English is a common ground for almost everyone; the Germans, the French, the Spanish, the Italians... everybody speaks and understands some English. It's like Esperanto.

It's been said that your films bear the same relationship to classical American thrillers as Leone's do to classical American Westerns.

There is a difference, though. With Westerns, we had *only* American Westerns to look at, no others. With mysteries, we saw many traditions: English, German, French... movies and literature. The French writers Pierre Boileau and Thomas Narcejac, for example, are very fine. Many different influences.

I've read you were interested in obtaining the rights to an Agatha Christie novel - is that true?

Not one - many. After one of my films, Dino De Laurentiis sent me a telegram listing all the titles that were available, 27 of them. I studied several of them, but ultimately I prefer to direct pictures I've written myself.

English thrillers are noted for their rational conventions...

Yes, they're very Cartesian in their approach, particularly the older ones. But you know, life has changed a great deal in the last 30, 40, 50 years, and I think they are changing too. I recently saw the English film *The Company of Wolves*, a very beautiful work, like a fairy tale and *strange*... not Cartesian at all. It operates on an entirely different kind of logic, like *Blood Simple*, which I also admire.
The French also are very Cartesian in their thinking, but of course, that's obvious.

You say the French are Cartesian, but look at writers like Boileau and Narcejac, in **Diabolique** *or* **Vertigo** *- they envision a world that's completely mad, where merest chance protects people... or doesn't. The same atmosphere you see in* **The Bird With the Crystal Plumage,** *when Sam Dalmas is trapped between the glass doors. It's as though they're the only thing keeping out the madness.*

Exactly... sometimes I think the director of any picture is insane, at least while he's making it. The process of writing and directing drives you to such extremes that it's natural to feel an affinity with insanity. Or maybe in your everyday life you are normal, then something happens that shows you the madness that's just beyond the façade. I approach that madness as

242

something dangerous and I'm afraid, but also I want to go to it, to see what's there... to embrace it. I don't know why, but I'm drawn.

You're described as the Italian Hitchcock, though your work is far more directly indebted to that of Mario Bava.

It's difficult to isolate your influences. You don't live on an island, you see many things, hear many things and they all stay in your head and become part of the way you think. I'm very influenced by certain painters, surrealists like Magritte and Delvaux, for example... and of course, Hieronymus Bosch made a profound impression on me. The same is true for certain writers like Edgar Allan Poe, Cornell Woolrich, Raymond Chandler. Some directors do particular things very well and you have to admire them, the way they handle actors, perhaps. But for my own vision I think the most important cinematic influence is German Expressionism, the work of directors like Fritz Lang and Murnau. As a child, the look of these films made a very strong impression on me.

Mario Bava, you know, was a friend of mine; he even did some special effects for me on *Inferno*. And his son, Lamberto, has worked for me. I produced his film, *Demons*, as well as the sequel.

You've produced films for a number of your friends, most recently **The Church**, *for Michele Soavi.*

Yes, that's a very nice piece of work, I think. It was shown at the London Film Festival. It starts in the Middle Ages and concerns a church haunted by the devil. The church is a huge, Gothic church; I love the look of Gothic architecture, the vaults and the sculpture and the stained glass. It's like the Cathedral at Chârtres, but it was built by an alchemist, and inside are hidden references to the story of alchemy and the power it can bestow.

It sounds like one of the houses of the Three Mothers...

But it's not - it's just a haunted church, and why shouldn't a church be one of the houses of the damned?

Suspiria *and* **Inferno** *are two thirds of the Three Mothers trilogy; will you ever make the final film?*

Suspiria and *Inferno* came from the fact that I loved the Thomas De Quincey essay *Levana and Our Ladies of Sorrow*, and I wanted to develop the idea of the Three Mothers, the origin of all sorrow and pain. *Suspiria* is about the Mother of Sighs, and *Inferno* about the Mother of Darkness. But *Mother of Tears...* I don't know. I have an idea, but I have to develop it more before I can think about making it.

Inferno *has never been released at all in the United States.*

And I don't know why. It's a mystery. It's incredible, working with the studios. Every stupid person arrives with an opinion; they start every sentence with, "For me..." And I don't care what they think, I don't care about "For you..." That's not the way I work.

Tenebrae *sounds as though it should have been part of the Three Mothers trilogy...*

But of course, it isn't. It's a *giallo*, inspired by something that happened to me in America. *Tenebrae* is about a very modern kind of horror; not monsters, not witches, but the horror of a twisted mind.

Your own films fall into two groups - the naturalistic thrillers and the supernatural horror films.

I think that's an artificial distinction; I don't see a great difference between them. The realistic pictures are not very realistic, even though they're about psychopaths rather than witches.

*In your **gialli** many traditional mystery values are ignored. Solving the crime, for example, usually isn't very important.*

No, it's not very important to me. We don't solve mysteries in real life, why should we do it in films? Motivation doesn't matter to me very much. Yes, there's some motivation for what the characters do, but mostly I'm interested in seeing what goes on in people's minds... the psychology.

And the psychology in your films is very weird psychology. More like magic.

It's just not Freudian psychology, that's all. It's Jungian. For Jung, the border between psychology and magic is very easy to cross. When the psychiatrist in *Suspiria* says that bad luck doesn't come from broken mirrors, but from broken minds, I was thinking of Jung.

Your films are often spoken of as nightmarish, which becomes very appropriate.

Yes, like a dream. Or like a seance. Or like psychoanalysis. The key to everything lies in the past.

The notion of the past seems very important in your films.

Yes, family and children, things from the past come back and haunt the present.

*In **Four Flies on Grey Velvet**, for example, you never know what went on that made Nina Tobias so twisted with hatred, but in the final scene with her husband Roberto, when she shoots him and he's writhing on the floor, the feeling of the past coming back through her is so powerful it's like a physical blow.*

It's powerful because I love her. I love all my killers.

Is that why you stand in for the hands of the killers in so many of your films?

Yes.

You know what people say about that, don't you?

That it's sick. It's also a joke, though. It's difficult for me to talk about my work. I really don't like to talk about it very much, because it's good to maintain some sense of mystery. The origins, the sources of ideas should remain a secret.

Like Sherlock Holmes telling Watson it's a mistake to explain to people how you arrive at your conclusions, but once you've explained it all seems so simple. They're much more impressed if you just present them with the answer.

I like Sherlock Holmes very much. People think he's all about rationality, but his methods aren't rational at all. They're like hyper-realism in paintings... beyond rationality, almost magic. The story with Moriarty, *The Final Problem*, is beautiful because it's *insane*. I also love *The Hound of the Baskervilles*. In movies Sherlock Holmes is always in control, but that's wrong. He's someone with real problems. For this reason I prefer Peter Cushing to Basil Rathbone; physically Rathbone is closer to the description in the stories, but Cushing brings more complexity to the character.

You seem to love film technology; you never miss an opportunity to use it to create incredible pans and tilts and slow motion effects.

I love it, I love the poetry of technology. For me, technological advances are inspiring. I'll hear of a new camera and it will suggest a story to me.

If you were forced to make the choice between an amazing visual effect and a plot point, I imagine you'd always go for the visual.

You're right.

Phenomena, for example, opens with that incredible crane shot that sweeps up over the trees, over the valley - it's breathtaking.

And I knew from the beginning that I had to have that shot, just as I always wanted that shot in *Tenebrae*... the long pan over the house where the girls are going to be killed.

Phenomena was inspired by something I heard about insects being used to solve crimes, and because insects have always fascinated me I began to make a story around this idea. You know, it's a terrible thing, but there are many insects that are disappearing. Becoming extinct. But most people only want to kill them. You know, insects have souls, too; they're telepathic... amazing. People want to save the whales and dolphins, but nobody wants to save the insects. I'm a vegetarian, because I don't want to kill things to eat.

It must have been very difficult making a film with insects - they don't take direction.

No, they don't. In one scene in *Suspiria* we used maggots, but it was nothing like what we did with *Phenomena*. They're almost impossible to work with - they don't hear, they don't speak, they don't see the way we do. We had two entomologists on the production working with us, helping us figure out ways to manipulate them. They taught us, for example, that insects hate the smell of gasoline, so you can use gasoline to keep them away from places you don't want them to go. We spent two months on the insect shots, for only minutes in the film.

I understand that part of the inspiration for **Opera** *was that you were actually supposed to direct an opera on stage...*

Yes, but that didn't work out. The opera we used in the film was *Macbeth* which has a tradition - also in the theatre - of being bad luck. People all warned against using it, suggested using *La*

Traviata or *La Bohème*, and I said, "This is just a story, don't be foolish," but maybe they were right. With *Opera* I had a lot of English crew - that was something new for me - and I learned many things from them. Overall, though, it was a terrible experience.

You know, many cuts were made after I was finished, even though I protested. Many things happened. Vanessa Redgrave was scheduled to be in the film, and she pulled out. One of the actors was crushed by a car. I was engaged to be married, but by the end of the picture that was finished. My father died during the shooting... all kinds of things. But I felt I had started with *Macbeth,* so I had to finish. And anyway, there could be no ravens in *Così Fan Tutte.*

Opera also hasn't been released in the United States, and it doesn't look as though it will be anytime soon.

I know... it's a terrible thing. Some people have told me the end is too sad for American audiences, but I love it. Although the production is very rich and elaborate, *Opera* tells a very simple story, and I think the ending is correct, so I wish audiences in America could see it.

One good thing recently is that *Suspiria* has just been released on videocassette, in a very complete version, letter boxed to preserve the frame. That took almost ten years, so if *Opera* comes to video in a year or two, or even three, I'll be happy. If something is worth seeing, it won't hurt it that people can't see it immediately.

*You've always directed original screenplays, but with **Two Evil Eyes** the raw material came from the writings of Edgar Allan Poe.*

I feel a great affinity with Poe; I understand his pain. I thought it was important to make a picture that would differ from the memory people have of the Corman Poe pictures, of all the other adaptations of Poe's work. We've made a picture that accurately represents the spirit of Poe's work, even though we changed many things in the specifics of the stories - both Romero and I. I think it's true to Poe to set his stories in the present, because when Poe wrote he wrote about the present; he didn't set his stories on some safe, distant past. When he wrote *The Pit and the Pendulum*, he was inspired by things that had happened within his lifetime, and early on I thought about taking that story and setting it in Chile, five or ten years ago - during the Pinochet regime. This is a perfectly valid approach to the story, which isn't abstract and philosophical, like some of his writing. It's very concrete and specific, and I felt it would translate very well into a completely specific, modern day situation. I feel Poe would have understood the world today very well.

*Rather than adapting the story of **The Black Cat** directly, you used it as a starting point for a meditation on recurring themes and images in Poe.*

Exactly. You can't look at my segment and call it "The Black Cat," not really, because it's *The Black Cat* and many other stories. I decided against *The Pit and the Pendulum* as my main text because it was so simple; I wanted something more baroque to be the basis of my picture. Ultimately I can't even really tell you why *The Black Cat*. There are many arguments that sound reasonable, but the truth is one day I was just thinking *The Black Cat*.

I held over the image of *The Pit and the Pendulum* because even though I had decided not to do the story, that picture stayed with me. *The Murders in the Rue Morgue* and *Berenice* are among my favourites, and I couldn't make a Poe movie without including them. I think all three stories are similar in a way, all about the way the mind is when it is very narrow in its focus. In *Pit and the Pendulum* there is nothing but fear; it's a man thinking and thinking and the more he thinks the more fear breeds in his mind. In *Berenice* the man is obsessed with the teeth of a woman - this is incredible, so true! And in *Murders in the Rue Morgue* we read about a man who is always thinking about the way things fit together, a detective in the purest form. There are many other stories I love, and I made mention of them in whatever way I could. I'm also concerned with the personal story of Edgar Allan Poe, and the way it's reflected in his stories. The central character, Rod Usher, is in many ways very similar to Poe himself...

In the way that he's haunted by his art, the way that it drives him insane?

That's right. He's also tormented by the question of morality. Is it right to be obsessed with looking at terrible things and sharing them with other people, especially when many people are perturbed by them?

I think the story, *The Black Cat*, is similar in some ways to Dostoyevsky's *Crime and Punishment*, in that it deals with the psychology of someone who commits a crime and believes he can remain silent. But of course he's wrong, because a crime follows you, persecutes you; it's like something burrowed deep into your brain. I find the resemblance to Dostoyevsky remarkable... the obsessiveness, the glimpse into the darkness of the human soul.

You also based the character in very specific terms on the American photographer...

Weegee, yes... I made Usher into a photographer, and Weegee was an inspiration. I like his work because his interest in humanity was a very strange one. He loved people when they were desperate or dead or drugged; he loved humanity in extreme and dire states. The pictures he made were very strong, and I believe completely in the power of the image.
For this reason I also incorporated many pictures into the set design of the film; they add some more layers to what you see. I chose all the paintings you see in the movie. There's one

painting of the wife of Edgar Allan Poe... no-one will know that's who she is, but I had to put in this picture of a beautiful, dying woman. There's also a picture of Baudelaire; most people will see the picture and think he's just someone's grandfather, but no, it's Baudelaire, and it's important to me that he is there.

Only Dario Argento could take the stories of Edgar Allan Poe and make a movie that's about murdering women in grisly ways.

Do you have a problem with that? I don't think so, and I don't either. There are always people who do, but I don't care about them. Edgar Allan Poe had a terrible imagination. He drank, he took drugs, and he saw many horrible things in his mind. Nice people don't see such things. But he made them into stories we still read today, all over the world. In Europe we discovered Poe through the translations of Baudelaire, who loved him and treated him as a major literary influence. Also through the surrealists, for whom he was very important. I think we have an image of him almost as an angel, as someone who suffered in pursuit of his visions.

*Your last few films have been crawling with animals. Insects and the chimpanzee in **Phenomena**. Ravens in **Opera**. The black cat in **Two Evil Eyes**... does this mean something?*

I love to work with animals; their souls are very special. They're difficult on the set, but so are all actors.

I have two black cats of my own - Dic and Lieb; they're father and son - with a little white patch, just like the cat in the story. I studied them when I was writing, watching the way they move, they way they watch things, the way they sit perfectly still... it's destiny, that I'm making a film with cats.

You know that for centuries cats, and especially black cats, were treated as incarnations of witches. Black cats have been haunted by these beliefs; for centuries they were hanged and burned and drowned. So they're different from other cats. They're more secretive, they keep to themselves. You look at them and you know something goes on in there.

*You originally wanted to have four directors on **Two Evil Eyes**, but couldn't work it out in terms of scheduling. Would you consider producing another film with the other two?*

It's true, I wanted to have John Carpenter and Wes Craven. You never know what might happen in the future - recently I heard that Carpenter and Stephen King are going to be working on an Edgar Allan Poe picture together. Obviously many people have thought about Poe and see the same things I do in his work, so maybe we'll be seeing many, many Poe pictures in the coming years.

I also have a contract to make a new film of my own, but I don't know yet what I'm going to do. Each film I make changes me in some way. When I start the picture I'm one person, and by the time I finish I'm another. I'm not yet finished with *Two Evil Eyes*, so I don't know what person I'll be when it's over.

What other directors do you admire?

Many... Joe Dante, John Landis for *An American Werewolf in London*, John Carpenter. David Lynch; *Eraserhead* is a beautiful film. And *Wild at Heart*... so beautiful. These two young people, they are so much in love. Sam Raimi; I love *The Evil Dead*. George Romero, both as a filmmaker and a friend. The Coen brothers. Stanley Kubrick... amazing filmmaker.

Do you lie on the beach thinking of disgusting ways to kill people in your films?

Yes. I like when people are disgusted, because it means you've made an impression on them. A *deep* impression. Why don't you just make up a reason for me?

An Interview With Dario Argento

I don't make things up.

You ask difficult questions. I really don't like to expose too much of what's behind my films. I work in a surrealistic way, like being in a trance. Sometimes I wake up and begin writing when I'm still almost asleep. When I finish a picture I'm always surprised by the things I see. It's like automatic writing, as though someone else suggested ideas. Like a schizophrenic. As though I have a second soul.

253

THE FILMS OF DARIO ARGENTO

The Bird With the Crystal Plumage *(1970)*

(Originally L'uccello dalle piume di cristallo; *also* The Phantom of Terror, The Gallery Murders, Le sadique aux gants noirs, L'oiseau au plumage de cristal*)*

A Sidney Glazier Presentation of a UMC Pictures Release of a Seda Spettacoli (Rome) and C.C.C. Film (Berlin) Production. Also released as: The Phantom of Terror

Director: Dario Argento. Producer: Salvatore Argento. Screenwriter: Dario Argento. Cinematographer: Vittorio Storaro. Editor: Franco Fraticelli. Music: Ennio Morricone. Art Director (Set Dressing and Costumes): Dario Micheli. Sound: Carlo Diotavelli. Assistant Director: Roberto Pariente. Dialogue Director: Roberto Pietti. Production Managers: Umberto Sambuco and Camillo Teti. Camera Operators: Enrico Umtelli and Arturo Zavattini. First Assistant Editor: Cesarina Casini. Second Assistant Editor: Sergio Fraticelli. Script Girl: Lida Chitarrini. Makeup Artist: Pino Ferrante. Hairdresser: Lidia Puglia. Boom Man: Eugenio Fiore. Administrator: Angelo Tavazza. Stills: Muova Dial. Music Conductor: Bruno Nicolai. Music Editor: Bixio-Sam (Milan). Studios: De Paolis-IN.CI.R (Rome)

With: Tony Musante (Sam Dalmas), Suzy Kendall (Julia), Eva Renzi (Monica Ranieri), Enrico Maria Salerno (Inspector Morrosini), Mario Adorf (Berto Castaldi), Renato Romano (Dover), Umberto Raho (Alberto Ranieri), Raf Valenti, Giuseppe Castellano, Pino Patti, Rosa Toros, Fulvio Mingozzi, Karen Valenti, Gildo di Marco, Omar Bonnaro, Werner Peters, Carla Mancini, Bruno Erba.

Colour/Techniscope/98 minutes/MPAA Rating: GP

The Cat O'Nine Tails *(1971)*

(Originally Il gatto a nove code; *also* Le chat à neuf queues)

A National-General Pictures Release of a Seda Spettacoli/ Mondial Films (Rome), Terra Filmkunst (Munich) and Labrador Films (France) Production.

Director: Dario Argento. Producer: Salvatore Argento. Screenwriter: Dario Argento, from a story by Dario Argento, Luigi Collo and Dardano Sacchetti. Cinematographer: Enrico Menczer. Music: Ennio Morricone. Editor: Franco Fraticelli. Art Direction and Wardrobe: Carlo Leva. Miss Spaak's Gowns: Luca Sabatelli. Titles and Optical Effects: Luciano Vittori. Music Conductor: Bruno Nicolai. Sound Effects: Luciano Anzelotti. Production Manager: Angelo Jacono. Assistant Director: Roberto Pariente. Production Assistants: Carlo de Marchis and Giuseppe Mangogna. Camera Operator: Roberto Brega. Assistant Camera Operators: Roberto Mabcagni and Antonio de Castel Terlago. Second Assistant Camera Operator: Maurizio La Monica. Script Girl: Renata Franceschi. Mixer: Mario Ronchetti. Boom Operator: Eugenio Fiore. Assistant Art Director: Franco Pedacchia. Assistant Set Dresser: Romeo Castantina. Assistant Editor: Cesarina Casini. Second Assistant Editor: Sergio Fraticelli. Stills: Firmino Palmieri. Chief Makeup Artists: Giuseppe Ferranti and Piero Mecacci. Chief Hairstylist: Maura Terchi. Assistant Makeup Artist: Vincenzo Marchetti. Studios: Cinicetta.

With: Karl Malden (Franco Arno), James Franciscus (Carlo Giordani), Catherine Spaak (Anna Terzi), Cinzia de Carolis (Lori), Carlo Alighiero (Doctor Calabresi), Vittorio Congia (Cameraman Righetto), Pier Paolo Capponi (Police Superintendent Spimi), Corrando Olmi (Morsella), Tino Carraro (Terzi), Aldo Reggiani (Doctor Casoni), Horst Frank (Doctor Braun), Emilio Marchesini (Doctor Mombelli), Tom Felleghy

(Doctor Essen), Rada Rassimov (Manuel).

Colour/Techniscope/112 minutes/MPAA Rating: GP

Four Flies on Grey Velvet *(1972)*

(Originally Quattro mosche di velluto grigio; *also* Quatre mouches de velours gris*)*

A Paramount Pictures Release of a Seda Spettacoli (Rome) and Universal Productions (Paris) Production

Director: Dario Argento. Producer: Salvatore Argento. Screenwriter: Dario Argento, from a story by Dario Argento, Luigi Cozzi, and Mario Foglietti. Cinematographer: Franco di Giacomo. Editor: Françoise Bonnot. Music: Ennio Morricone. Production Designer: Enrico Sabbatini. Production Manager: Angelo Jacono. Assistant Director: Roberto Pariente. Assistant to the Director: Luigi Cozzi. Sound: Nick Alexander. Unit Manager: Giuseppe Mangogna. Production Coordinator: Carlo Cucchi. Camera Operator: Giuseppe Lallci. Assistant Camera Operators: Gianfranco Transunto and Mauro Marchetti. Sound Engineer: Mario Ronchetti. Boom Operator: Eugenio Fiore. Script Girl: Patrizia Zulini. Assistants to the Director: Piero Bozza, Alessandro Gabriele, and Catherine Bernard. Cutting Room Assistants: Sergio Fraticelli and Bruno Bianchi. Stills: Roberto Carnivale. Sound Effects: Luciano Anzelotti. Special Effects: Cataldo Gaiiano. Orchestra Conductor: Bruno Nicolai. Set Dresser: Franco Pedacchia. Wardrobe Assistant: Giovanni Viti. Makeup Artist: Giuliano Laurenti. Makeup Assistant: Giovanni Morosi. Hairstylist: Paolo Borselli. Titles and Photographic Effects: Studio 4. Studios: De Paolis-IN.CI.R (Rome)

With: Michael Brandon (Roberto Tobias), Mimsy Farmer (Nina Tobias), Jean-Pierre Marielle (Arrosio), Francine Racette (Dalia), Bud Spencer [Carlo Pedersoli] (Godfrey), Calisto Calisti (Carlo

Marosi), Marisa Fabbri (Hilda), Oreste Lionello (the Professor), Fabrizio Moroni (Mirko), Stefano Sattaflores (Andrew), Constanza Spada (Marial), Dante Cleri, Guerrino Crivello, Gildo di Marco, Tom Felleghy, Leopoldo Migliori, Fulvio Mingozzi, Stefano Oppedisano, Pino Patti, Ada Pometti, Jacques Stani.

Technicolor/Techniscope/101 minutes/MPAA Rating: PG

Le cinque giornate *(1973)*

A Euro International Films and Salvatore Argento Presentation of a Seda Spettacoli Production.

Director: Dario Argento. Producer: Salvatore Argento. Executive Producer: Claudio Argento. Screenplay: Dario Argento and Vanni Balustrini, from a story by Vincenzo Ungari, Luigi Cozzi and Dario Argento. Art Director: Giuseppe Bassan. Director of Photography: Luigi Kuveiller. Editing: Franco Fraticelli. Costumes: Elena Mannini. Story Supervision: Professor Franco Catalano. Music: Giorgio Gaslini.

With: Adriano Celentano (Cainazzo), Enzo Cerusico (Romolo Marcelli), Marilù Tolo (the Countess), Sergio Graziani (Baron Tranzunto), Carla Tatò (la vedova), Luisa DeSantis, Glauco Onorato, Ivana Monti.

Technicolor/Techniscope/100 minutes

Deep Red *(1976)*

(Originally Profondo rosso; *also* The Hatchet Murders, Les frissons de l'angoisse, Suspiria 2)

A Lea J. Marks and Radcliffe Associates Presentation of a

Howard Mahler Films and TriStar Distributors Release of a Seda Spettacoli (Salvatore Argento) Production. Director: Dario Argento. Producer: Claudio Argento. Screen-writers: Dario Argento and Bernardino Zapponi. Art Director: Giuseppe Bassan. Cinematographer: Luigi Kuveiller. Editor: Franco Fraticelli. Costumes: Elena Mannini. Music: Giorgio Gaslini and the Goblins. Special Effects: Germane Natali and Carol Rambaldi. Unit Manager: Carlo Cucchi. Script Continuity: Cesare Jacolucci. Camera Operator: Ubaldo Terzano. Assistant Camera Operators: Antonio Annunziato and Antonio Taoli. Assistant Editors: Piero Bozza and Ernesto Triumverni. Sound Recordist: Mario Farrami. Production Secretary: Vivalda Vigorelli. Boom Operator: Eugenio Fiore. Assistant Set Dresser: Massimo Garrone. Assistant Art Director: Maurizio Garrone. Seamstress: Angelo Viglino.

With: David Hemmings (Marcus Daly), Daria Nicolodi (Gianna Brezzi), Gabriele Lavia (Carlo), Macha Meril (Helga Ulman), Clara Calamai (Marta), Glauco Mauri (Professor Giordani), Eros Pagni (Calcabrini), Giuliana Calandra (Amanda Righetti), Nicoletta Elmi (Olga), Piero Mazzinghi (Bardi), Fulvio Mingozzi, Vittorio Fanloni, Dante Fioretti, Geraldine Hooper, Iacopo Mariani, Fucio Meniconi, Lorenzo Piano, Salvatori Pulzillo, Piero Vida, Aldo Bonamano, Liana del Balzo.

Eastmancolor/Techniscope/115 minutes/MPAA Rating: R

Suspiria *(1977)*

A Twentieth-Century Fox Release of a Seda Spettacoli Production.

Director: Dario Argento. Executive Producer: Salvatore Argento. Producer: Claudio Argento. Screenplay: Dario Argento and Daria Nicolodi. Cinematography: Luciano Tovoli. Editor: Franco Fraticelli. Art Director: Giuseppe Bassan. Costumes: Pierangelo Cicoletti. Music: The Goblins, with the collaboration of Dario Argento. Production Manager: Lucio Trentini. Recorded in

English at International Recording (Rome). Dubbing Editor: Nick Alexander. Unit Manager: Federico Tocci. Production Coordinators: Federico Starace and Massimo Brandimarte. Assistant Director: Antonio Gabrielli. Script Continuity: Francesca Roberti. Camera Operator: Idelmo Simonelli. Assistant Camera Operators: Giuseppe Tinelli, Enrico Fontana and Riccardo Dolci. Action Stills: Francesco Bellamo. First Assistant Editor: Piero Bozza. Second Assistant Editor: Roberto Olivieri. Boom Operator: Corrando Uolpicelli. Sound Recordist: Mario Dallimonte. Re-recording Engineer: Federico Savina. Makeup Supervisor: Pierantonio Meccaci. Hair Stylist: Maria Teresa Corridoni. Assistant Art Directors: Maurizio Garrone and Davide Bassan. Set Dresser: Enrico Fiorentini. Assistant Set Dresser: Massimo Garrone. Wardrobe Mistress: Tiziana Mancini. Seamstress: Bertilla Silvestrin. Special Effects: Germano Natali.

With: Jessica Harper (Suzy Banyon), Stefania Casini (Sara), Joan Bennett (Madame Blanc), Alida Valli (Miss Tanner), Flavio Bucci (Daniel), Udo Kier (Franco), Allessandra Capozzi, Salvatore Capozzi, Diana Ferrara, Christina Latini, Alfredo Raino, Claudia Zaccari (Dancers), Margherita Horowitz, Jacopo Mariani, Fulvio Mingozzi, Franca Scaghetti, Renato Scarpa, Serafina Scorcelletti, Giuseppe Transocchi, Renata Zamengo.

Eastmancolor-Technicolor/Techniscope/100 minutes/MPAA Rating: R

Inferno *(1980)*

(Also Infierno*)*

A Twentieth-Century Fox Release (Unreleased in U.S.) of an Intersound Production.

Director: Dario Argento. Producer: Claudio Argento. Screenplay: Dario Argento. Cinematography: Romano Albani. Art Director: Giuseppe Bassan. Editor: Franco Fraticelli. Music: Keith Emerson. Assistant Director: Lamberto Bava. Unit Manager:

Cesare Jacolucci. Production Assistants: Anna Maria Calvineli, Michela Prodan and Saverio Mancogna. Second Assistant Director: Andrea Piazzes. Script Supervisor: Maria Serena Canevari. Camera Operator: Idelm Simonelli. Still Photographer: Francesco Bellomo. Sound: Francesco Groppioni. Boom Man: Giancarlo Laurenzi. Makeup: Pierantonio Mecacci. Hairstylists: Luciana Maria Costanzi and Giancarlo di Leonardis. Set Decorators: Francesco Cuppini and Maurizio Garrone. Special Effects: Germano Natali. Underwater Sequence: Laurenzo Battaglia. Studios: DePaolis-IN.CI.R (Rome) and Elias (Rome). U.S. Production Services: CINEREX Associates (New York). Executive Producer: William Garroni. Production Manager: Andrew W. Garroni. Sound Effects: Luciano and Massimo Anzellotti. Sound Effects Editor: Attilo Gizzi. Sound Recording Studio: International Recording (Rome). Orchestra: Unione Musicisti (Rome). "Va pensiero..." from Giuseppe Verdi's "Nabucco" performed by the Symphonic Orchestra and Chorus of Rome Radio Televisione Italiana. Chorus conducted by Gaetano Ricitelli, Director: Fernando Previtali, Courtesy of Fonit Cetra.

With: Irene Miracle (Rose Elliot), Leigh McCloskey (Mark Elliot), Eleonora Giorgi (Sara), Daria Nicolodi (Countess Elise), Sacha Pitoeff (Kazanian), Alida Valli (Carol), Veronica Lazar (Nurse), Gabrielle Lavia (Carlo), Feodor Chaliapin (Varelli), Leopoldo Mastelloni (Butler), Ania Pieroni (Musical Student), James Fleetwood (Cook), Rosario Rigutini (Man), Ryan Hilliard (Shadow), Paolo Pauloni (Music Teacher), Fulvio Mingozzi (Taxi Driver), Luigi Lodoli (Bookbinder), Rudolfo Lodi (Old Man).
Technicolor/Techniscope/107 minutes/Dolby Sound

Tenebrae *(1982)*

(Originally Tenebre, *also* Sotto gli occhi dell'assassino, Unsane, Ténèbres*)*

Filmography

A Salvatore Argento Presentation of a Sigma Cinematografia (Rome) Production.
Director: Dario Argento. Producer: Claudio Argento. Screenplay: Dario Argento and George Kemp, based on a story by Dario Argento. Cinematography: Luciano Tovoli. Editor: Franco Fraticelli. Assistant Editors: Pietro Bozza and Roberto Piori. Special Effects:Giovanni Corridori. Music: Simonetti, Pignatelli, Morante. Art Director: Giuseppe Bassan. Sound: Mario Dallimonti. Costumes: Pierangelo Cicoletti. Set Decorator: Maurizio Garrone. Sound Effects: Luciano and Massimo Anzellotti. Assistant Director: Lamberto Bava. Second Assistant Director: Michele Soavi. Script Continuity: Francesa Roberti. Unit Manager: Cesare Jacolucci. Ispettore di Produzione: Giuseppe Mangogna. Production Manager: Saverio Mangogna. Camera Operator: Giuseppe Tinelli. Assistant Camera Operators: Maurizia Piano and Roberto Marsigli. Still Photographer: Francesco Bellomo. Wardrobe Assistant: Barbara Canevari. Sound Recordist: Mario Dallimonti. Boom Man: Giancarlo Laurenzi. Assistant Art Director: Maurizio Garrone. Assistant Set Decorator: Massimo Garrone. Administrators: Carlo du Bois and Ferdinando Caputo. Special Effects: Giovanni Corridori. Costumes: Annamode 68. Mr. Franciosa's Wardrobe: Carlo Palazzi. Mr. Saxon's Wardrobe: Franco Tomei.

With: Anthony Franciosa (Peter Neal), Daria Nicolodi (Anne), John Saxon (Bullmer), Giuliano Gemma (Detective Giermani), Eva Robins/Roberto Coatti (Girl on Beach), Mirella D'Angelo (Tilda), John Steiner (Christiano Berti), Veronica Laria (Jane McKerrow), Ania Pieroni (Elsa), Lara Wendel (Maria), Carola Stagnaro (Inspector Altieri), Christian Borromeo (Gianni), Enio Girotami, Monica Maisani, Marino Mase, Fulvio Mingozzi, Gianpaulo Saccarola, Ippolita Santarelli, Francesca Viscardi, Isabella Amadeo, Mirella Banti.

Technicolor/Techniscope/105 minutes/

Creepers *(1985)*

(Originally Phenomena*)*

A New Line Cinema Release of a Dacfilm (Rome) Production.

Director: Dario Argento. Producer: Dario Argento. Screenplay: Dario Argento and Franco Ferrini. Cinematography: Romano Albani. Editor: Franco Fraticelli. Special Effects: Sergio Stivaletti and the Corridori Brothers. Music: Bill Wyman ("Valley," "Valley Bolero," with Terry Taylor), Iron Maiden ("Flash of the Blade"), Motorhead ("Locomotive"), Andy Sex Gang ("The Naked and the Dead," "You Don't Know Me"), Simon Boswell ("The Maggots"), Claudio Simonetti ("Phenomena"), Fabio Pignatelli ("The Insects"). Production Designers: Maurizio Garrone, Nello Giorgetti, Luciano Spadoni, and Umberto Turco. Costumes: Giorgio Armani. Production Executive: Angelo Jacono. First Assistant Director: Michele Soavi. Second Assistant Director: Bettina Graebe. Supervising Sound Editor: Franco Fraticelli. Music Editor: Piero Bozza. Sound Editor: Nick Alexander. Dialogue Coach: Sheila Goldberg. Script Continuity: Vivalda Vigoretti. Production Manager: Cesare Iacolucci. Production Executives: Serenella Severini and Fabrizio Diaz. Camera Operator: Stefano Ricciotti. Assistant Camera Operator: Aldo Bergamini. Steadicam Supplied and Operated: Nicola Pecorini and Co. Stills: Franco Bellamo. Underwater Photography: Gianlorenzo Battaglia. First Assistant Editor: Piero Bozza. Second Assistant Editor: Roberto Priori. Wardrobe Assistants: Marine Malavasi and Patrizia Massaia. Set Dressers: Rina Villani and Renato Lori. Makeup Artist: Pierantonio Mecacci. Makeup and Special Effects: Sergio Stivaletti. Hairstylist: Patrizia Corridori. Sound Mixer: Giancarlo Lorenzi. Special Stage Effects: Tonino Corridori. Entomology Consultant: Enrico Stella. Assistant Entomologist: Fabio Dell'Uomo. Animals and Insects Supplied by Maurizio Garrone. Special Entomological Photography: Fernando Armati. Special Optical Effects: Luigi Cozzi. Studio Sound Effects: Studio Anzelotti. Chimpanzee "Tanga" owned and trained by Daniel Berguiny. Music Soundtrack Producer: Vincent Messina for Bixio C.E.M.S.A.

Filmography

Titles: Moviecam 2000. Rerecording Engineer: Danilo Sterbini. Shot on Location in Switzerland and at De Paolis-IN.CI.R. (Rome) Studios.

With: Jennifer Connelly (Jennifer Corvino), Daria Nicolodi (Mrs. Bruckner), Dalila di Lazzaro (Headmistress), Donald Pleasence (John MacGregor), Patrick Bauchau (Inspector Geiger), Fiore Argento (Tourist), Fausta Avelli, Marta Biuso, Sophie Bourchier, Paolo Gropper, Ninke Hielkema, Mitzy Orsini and Geraldine Thomas (the Schoolgirls), Federica Mastroianni, Fiorenza Tessari, Mario Donatone, Francescha Ottaviani, Michele Soavi, Franco Trevisi.

Technicolor/Panavision/ Dolby Sound/ 109 minutes/MPAA Rating: R

Opera *(1987)*

(Also Terror at the Opera*)*

A Cecchi Gori Group-Tiger Cinematografica-A.D.C. Production, in collaboration with RAI Radio Televisione Italiana.Director: Dario Argento. Producer: Dario Argento. Screenplay: Dario Argento and Franco Ferrini, based on an original idea by Dario Argento. Executive Producer: Ferdinando Caputo. Director of Photography: Ronnie Taylor. Production Designer: Davide Bassan. Art Director (Regio Teatro, Parma): Gianmaurizio Fercioni. Costume Designer: Francesca Lia Morandini. Editor: Franco Fraticelli. Production Supervisors: Alessandro Calosci and Verena Baldio. First Assistant Directors: Paulo Zenatello and Antonio Gabriella. Second Assistant Director: Alessandro Engamgiola. Script Supervisor: Cinzia Malatesta. Unit Managers: Oliver Gerard and Fabrizio Diaz. Camera Operator: Antonio Scaramuzza. Steadicam Operator: Nicola Pecorini. Assistant Film Editors: Piero Bozza and Alessandro Gabriele. Makeup Artist: Franco Casagni. Hair Dresser: Ferdinando Menolia. Second Unit Director: Michele Soavi. Special Effects:

Renato Agostini, Sergio Stivaletti, Barbara Morosetti. Special Effects Supplied By: Antonio and Giovanni Corridori and Germano Natale. Sound Effects: I.M. Anzelotti. Birds and Animals Supplied By: Luigi Pano. Studio: DePaolis-IN.C.I.R. (Rome). Music: "White Darkness," "Balance" and "From the Beginning" by Brian Eno and Roger Eno. "Opera," "Crows" and "Confusion" by Claudio Simonetti. "Opera Theme" and "Black Notes" by Bill Wyman and Terry Taylor. "Knights of the Night" and "Steel Grave" by The Group Steel Grave. "No Escape" by The Group Northern Light. "Macbeth" by Giuseppe Verdi. "Casta Diva," from Vincenzo Bellini's "Norma." "Amami Alfredo" and "Sempre Libera," from Verdi's "La Traviata," sung by Maria Callas. "Un Bel di Vedremo," from Giacomo Puccini's "Madame Butterfly," sung by Mirella Freni. "Macbeth" arias sung by Elisabetta Norberg Schulz (soprano), Paula Leolini (soprano), Andrea Piccini (baritone) and Michele Perlusi (tenor). Music Performed by the Arturo Toscanini Symphonic Orchestra.

With: Cristina Marsillach (Betty), Ian Charleson (Marco), Urbano Barberini (Inspector Alan Santini), Antonella Vitale (Marion), Barbara Cupisti (Albertini), Coralina Cataldi Tassoni (Julia), Daria Nicolodi (Mira), Francesca Cassola (Alma), William McNamara (Urbano), Antonio Juorio, Carola Stagnaro, Maurizio Carbone, Cristina Glachino, Cyorivani Cyorgy, Bjorn Hammer, Peter Pitsch, Sebastiano Somma.

Technicolor/Panavision/Dolby Sound/100 minutes

Two Evil Eyes *(1990)*

(Originally Due occhi diabolici *and* Due occhi malocchio*)*

Directors: Dario Argento and George Romero. Co-Producers: Dario Argento and Achille Manzotti. Executive Producer: Claudio Argento. Director of Photography: Peter Reniers. Editor: Pat Buba. Production Manager: Fernando Franchi. Production Designer: Cletus Anderson. Camera Operator: Frank Perl.

Lighting Director: Marcello Gabriele. Steadicam Operator: Nicola Pecorini. Special Makeup Effects: Tom Savini. Assistants to Savini: Everett Burrell, John Vulich, Will Huff, Gerald Gergely. Effects PAs: J.J. Homel and Kevin McTurk. Assistant Cameramen: Mike Latino and John "Buzz" Moyer. Location Manager: Judy Mathews. Cat Wrangler: Chris Powoechik. Auditor: Luciano Tartaglia. First Assistant Director: Nick Mastandrea. Second Assistant Directors: Maria Melograne and Fred Donatelli. Assistant Editor: Ray Boniker. Prop Master: Marty Garrigan. Props: Norman Beck and Francine Byrne. Second Projectionist: John Bick. Script Supervisor: Joanne Small. Second Unit Director: Luigi Cozzi. Dialogue Coaches: Kenneth Gargado, Burton White. Casting: Elissa Myers

With: Adrienne Barbeau (Jessica Valdemar), Ramy Zada (Dr. Robert Hoffman), E.G. Marshall (Pike), Christine Forrest (Nurse), Bingo O'Malley (Ernest Valdemar) [The Facts in the Case of M. Valdemar]; Harvey Keitel (Rod Usher), Madeleine Potter (Annabel), John Amos (Legrand), Martin Balsam (Mr. Pym), Kim Hunter (Mrs. Pym), Sally Kirkland (Bartender) [The Black Cat].

Also With: Chuck Aber, Jonathan Adams, Tom Atkins, Mitchell Baseman, Julie Benz, Barbara Bryne, Mario Caputo, Lanene Charters, Bill Dalzell III, Anthony Dilieo Jr., Christina Forrest, J.R. Hall, Scott House, James G. MacDonald, Charles McPherson, Larry John Meyers, Jeff Monahan, Fred Moore, Christina Romero, Peggy Sanders, Ben Tatar, Lou Valenzi, Jeffrey Wild, Ted Worsley. Stuntmen: Norman Douglass, Andy Duppin, David Lomax, Phil Neilson, Mike O'Rourke, Mike Russo, Tom Savini.

Technicolor/Panavision/Dolby Sound/ 115 mins

OTHER CREDITS:

La porta sul buio *(1972): Argento supervised and presented four*

short telefilms for Italian TV - Testimone oculare *("Eyewitness"),*
Il Tram *("The Tram"),* Il vicino di casa *("Neighbour") and* La
bambola *("The Doll") - in 1972, under the compendium title* La
porta sul buio *("The Door into Darkness"). He directed two
himself:* Testimone oculare *and* Il tram, *using the pseudonyms
Roberto Pariente and Sirio Bernadotte, respectively. Luigi Cozzi
directed* Il vicino di casa.

*Luigi Cozzi describes the programme: "It was very successful
and helped establish Dario as a star. It was like the* Alfred
Hitchcock Presents *series; he appeared at the beginning of each
segment and talked to the audience. Everybody recognized him
after that... The four hour-long TV programmes were going to be
released theatrically as two features, but never were."*
Dawn of the Dead *(1978): Music by the Goblins, with Dario
Argento. Script Consultant: Dario Argento. Executive Produced
by Claudio Argento and Alfred Cuomo. Written and Directed by
George Romero.*

Dario Argento's World of Horror *(1985): Written and Directed
by Michele Soavi. This documentary features interviews with
Argento, behind the scenes footage of the making of* Suspiria,
Tenebrae, Creepers *and* Demons, *and clips from* The Bird With
the Crystal Plumage, The Cat O'Nine Tails, Four Flies on Grey
Velvet, Deep Red, Suspiria, Inferno, Tenebrae, Creepers, Demons
and Dawn of the Dead.

Demons *(1985): Produced by Dario Argento. Directed by Lamberto
Bava.*

Demons 2 *(1986): Produced by Dario Argento. Directed by
Lamberto Bava.*

Fiat Croma *(1987): Directed by Dario Argento. A television car
commercial, for the Fiat Croma.*

Trussardi Action *(1988): Fashion show for Trussardi, directed
by Dario Argento.*

Filmography

The Church *(1988): Produced by Mario & Vittorio Cecchi Gori and Dario Argento. Screenplay by Dario Argento, Franco Ferrini and Michele Soavi. Directed by Michele Soavi.*

Giallo *(1988): Produced by Dario Argento. A horror/fantasy series of hour-long programmes for Italian tv.*

The Sect *(1990): Produced by Dario Argento. Directed by Michele Soavi.*

Trauma *(1993)* (*Originally* Dario Argento's Trauma*)*

An ADC srl Production

Director: Dario Argento. Producer: Dario Argento. Executive Producer: Andrea Tinnirello. Screenplay: Dario Argento, Franco Ferrini, Giovanni Romoli and T.E.D. Klein, based on an original story by Argento, Ferrini and Romoli. Additional Dialogue: Ruth Jessup. Cinematography: Raffaele Mertes. Editor: Bennett Goldberg. Assistant Editor: Bennett I. Goldberg. Production Designer: Billy Jett. Art Directors: Nance Derby and Jack D.L. Ballance. Costume Designer: Leesa Evans. Set Decorator: Jacqueline Jacobson. Line Producer: Chris Beckman. Production Manager: Andrew Sands. Assistant Director: Rod Smith. Second Assistant Directors: Phil Elins and Daniel Carrey. Sound Recordist: Paul Coogan. Location Manager: Jon Bergholz. Production Coordinator: Abigail Scheiner. Hair and Makeup: Desne Holland. Hair Stylist: Lori Guidroz. Special Makeup Effects: Tom Savini. Special Makeup Supervisor: Greg Funk. Special Makeup Effects Assistants: Will Huff, Christopher Martin and Toni Savini. Dialogue Coach: Paul Drapper. Romanian Dialogue Coach: Michael Lupu. Stunt Coordinator: Ky Michaelson. Casting Director: Ira Belgrade.

Cast: Christopher Rydell (David Parson), Asia Argento (Aura Petrescu), Laura Johnson (Grace), James Russo (Captain Travis), Brad Dourif (Dr. Lloyd), Frederic Forrest (Dr. Judd), Piper Laurie (Adriana Petrescu).

Technicolor/Panavision/MPAA R

SELECT BIBLIOGRAPHY

The following bibliography isn't complete, but it should direct anyone interested in reading more on Argento - or certain general theoretical approaches utilized in this analysis of his works - to the appropriate sources. All books and articles mentioned in the text are given full citations here. Important entries are marked with an asterisk (*); in this context, important indicates a feature about (or largely about) Argento, critical or historical overviews of his work, or pieces about individual films that include interviews with Argento.

I've included as many citations as possible for reviews, interviews and features, both in English and in foreign languages, since there are few studies of any length devoted to Argento's work. I've also included references to articles in fanzines, though because there are many fanzines I don't see and they're tough to research, I'm sure there are many, many more pieces that have escaped my notice.

My research materials also included various press kits, first-hand interviews with Argento and his collaborators, and extensive discussions with other enthusiasts of Argento's work. I extend my special thanks to Alan Jones for his help.

Argento and His Films

Accialini, F. and Colucelli, L. *"Opera," Ciak* (September 1987)

Aubry, Jean-Paul. "Daria Nicolodi, Actrice," *Cine 2000* (Undated)

*--------. "Dario Argento Special," *Cine 2000* (September 1977)

--------. *"Phenomena," Mad Movies* 33 (November 1984)

Aubry, Jean-Paul and Simon, Isabelle, *"Phenomena," Cine Choc* 6 (June 1984)

*Balbo, Lucas, **Dario Argento: Le Montreur d'Ombres** (Cahors: Gérard Noël fanéditions, Collection Horror Pictures, in association with Fantaco Enterprises, Inc. [USA] and Titan Distributors, Ltd [England], 1988)

*--------, **Dario Argento: Portfolio** (Cahors: Gérard Noël fanéditions, Collection Horror Pictures, in association with Fantaco Enterprises, Inc. [USA] and Titan Distributors, Ltd [England], 1988)

* Balun, Chas., "Dario Argento, Face to Face", **Deep Red** Number 7 (Special Edition, 1991)

--------, "On Your Knees in The Church", **Deep Red** Number 7 (Special Edition, 1991)

Bartholomew, David. *"Dawn of the Dead," **Cinefantastique*** Volume 8, Number 1 (Winter 1979)

Beauman, Sally. *"Four Flies On Grey Velvet," **New York***, August 21, 1972

*Bény, Pierre. "Dario Argento: Le Rital Infernal," **Vendredi 13**, Summer 1988 (special issue)

Bettelli, Fabrizio - see Nicolini, Angelo

Bettelli, F. "Conversazione con Dario Argento," **Filmcritica**, Volume 35, Numbers 343/344 (April/May 1984)

Bettelli, F.; Grimaldi, A.; Nicolini, A. "Conversazione con Dario Argento," **Filmcritica**, Volume 34, Number 332 (February/March 1983)

Billiottet, Oliver. *"Inferno," **Rhesus Zero*** (Winter 1980)

Campbell, Ramsey. *"Opera," **Eyeball** 2*, (Summer 1990)

Canby, Vincent. "'*Deep Red*' Is A Bucket of Ax-Murder Cliches," **The New York Times**, June 10, 1976

Caron-Lowins, Evelyne. *"Ténèbres," **Cinéma*** (Paris) 494 (June 1983)

*--------. "Blanc, Pourpre et Or," **La Revue du Cinéma** 414 (March 1986)

*Carrano, Patrizia. "Dario Argento," **Max** (February 1985)

Carroll, Kathleen. "'*Bird*' Fails to Take Wing," (New York) **Daily News**, July 23, 1970

--------. "Real Horror Hoot" [review of *Suspiria*], (New York) **Daily News**, August 13, 1977

Chase, Donald. "The Cult Movie Comes of Age: An Interview

with George A. Romero and Richard P. Rubinstein," *Millimeter*, Volume 7, Number 10 (October, 1979)

Cohen, Richard. "'The Bird With the Crystal Plumage'," *Women's Wear Daily*, July 22, 1970

Combs, Richard. "*Il gatto a nove code*," *Monthly Film Bulletin*, Volume 38, Number 449 (June 1971)

Costa, Francesco. "Umori Maligni," [*Two Evil Eyes*] *Nosferatu* (August 1990)

Coxhead, Martin. "*Suspiria*," *Starburst* 44 (_____ 1981)

*--------. "Europe's Master of Horror," *Fangoria* 34 (March 1984)

*--------. "The Italian Hitchcock," *Fangoria* 35 (April, 1984)

*Cozzi, Luigi, "Argento: Some Personal Reflections on the Director," *Photon* 24 (July, 1975)

*--------. "Dario Argento by Luigi Cozzi," *Cine-Zine-Zine* 8 (Autumn 1981)

*————, editor. *Dario Argento*, Profondo Rosso Publications (December 1990).

*————, editor. *Dario Argento presenta Profondo Rosso* (December 1990).

*This monthly comic book features Argento himself in a series of bloody adventures, as well as other EC-style horror stories, Argento-related features, **fumetti** versions of Hammer horror films (including **The Mummy, Horror of Dracula, Curse of the Werewolf** and **The Gorgon**) and a wealth of in-jokes and references to Argento's films. At the time of this writing, Number 6 had just been published; individual issues are listed below:*

Nello Tulli. "La Piccola Bottega degli Orrori," Edizioni Scorpio Srl (December 1990)

————. "La Terza Madre," Edizioni Scorpio Srl (January 1991)

————. "La Villa del Bambino Urlante," Edizioni Scorpio Srl (February 1991)

————. "I Delitti di Edgar Allan Poe," Edizioni Eden Srl (March 1991)

Davide Longoni. "Nella Nebbia," Edizioni Eden Srl (March 1991)

Select Bibliography

Crist, Judith. *"The Bird With the Crystal Plumage," New York*, September 28, 1970

--------. *"The Cat O'Nine Tails," New York*, June 7, 1971

Darnton, Nina. "Film: *'Inferno,'* Mythic Horror Tale," *The New York Times*, August 15, 1986

Dellavalle,R., Maccarone, Bruno and Nadjar, Patrick. *"Two Evil Eyes," Toxic* (Paris) 5 (December 1989)

Duvoli, John R. *"The Bird With the Crystal Plumage," Cinefantastique*, Volume 1, Number 1 (Fall 1970)

Edelstein, David. "On a Wing and a Prayer," *The Village Voice*, September 17, 1985

Edwards, Phil. *"Inferno," Starburst* 29 (_____ 1980)

Farina, Alberto. *"The Church," Mad Movies* 63 (January 1990)

--------. *"Opera*: entretien avec Daria Nicolodi," *Mad Movies* 51 (January 1988)

Feay, Suzi. "Terror at the Opera," *Time Out*, 1074 (1991)

*French, Todd. "Dario Argento: Myth & Murder," *The Deep Red Horror Handbook*, edited by Chas. Balun (Albany: Fantaco Enterprises, Inc., 1989)

*Gans, Christophe. "Dario Argento: *Tenebrae," Starfix* 1 (January 1983)

--------. *"Ténèbres," Starfix* 5 (June 1983)

*--------. *"Phenomena," Starfix* 4 H.S. (July 1984)

Garris, Mick. *"Suspiria," Cinefantastique*, Volume 4, Number 3 (Winter 1977)

Ghezzi, E.; Giusti, M. "La paura la musica il cinema," *Filmcritica* Volume 32, Number 312 (February 1981)

Gilliatt, Penelope. *"The Bird With the Crystal Plumage," The New Yorker*, August 1, 1970

*Giovannini, Fabio. *Dario Argento: il brivido, il sangue, il thrilling* (Bari: Edizioni Dedalo spa, 1986)

Gires, Pierre. *"Suspiria," L'Écran Fantastique* 1 (Summer 1977)

Greenspun, Roger. "Argento's *'Bird With the Crystal Plumage',*" *The New York Times*, July 23, 1970

Gressard, Gilles. *"Inferno," L'Écran Fantastique* 13 (1980)

Grimaldi, Antonello - see Nicolini, Angelo

271

Guarino, Ann. "Hell bent, with leather" [review of *Deep Red*], (New York) ***Daily News***, June 10, 1976

--------. *"Deep Red,"* ***Filmfacts***, Volume 20, Number 6 (1977)

Hale, Wanda. *"Blood, Sex Murderama"* [review of *The Cat O'Nine Tails*], (New York) ***Daily News***, May 27, 1971

--------. "Murder Film Just Awful," [review of *Four Flies on Grey Velvet*] ***The Daily News*** (New York), August 5, 1972

Herridge, Frances. "Murder Mystery in Showcase Bow" [review of *The Cat O'Nine Tails*], ***New York Post***, May 27, 1971

*Hockley, Mark. "Argento: The Song of Death," ***Blood and Black Lace***, Issue 1 (Spring 1989)

Hutchinson, Tom. *"Suspiria,"* (London) ***Sunday Telegraph***, October 9, 1977

Jones, Alan. *"Inferno,"* ***Cinefantastique***, Volume 11, Number 2 (Fall 1981)

--------. "Romero," ***Starburst*** 48 (August 1982)

*--------. "Dario Argento Profile," ***Cinema*** 5 (September 1982)

--------. *"Tenebrae,"* ***Starburst*** 57 (May 1983)

*--------. "Dario Argento," ***Starburst*** 61 (September 1983)

*--------. "Argento," ***Cinefantastique***, Volume 13, Number 8/Volume 14, Number 1 (December 1983/January 1984)

--------. "The A-Z of Italian Fantasy," ***Starburst*** 72 (August 1984)

--------. "The A-Z of Italian Fantasy, Part 2" ***Starburst*** 73 (September 1984)

--------. *"Phenomena"* ***Starburst*** 83 (July 1985)

--------. *"Demons"* ***Starburst*** 90 (February 1986)

*--------. "Dario Argento's *'Demons,'*" ***Cinefantastique***, Volume 16, Number 1 (March 1986)

*--------. *"Demons,"* ***Cinefantastique*** Volume 16, Number 2 (May 1986)

--------. *"Stagefright* and Michele Soavi," ***Starburst*** Number 106 (June 1987)

--------. *"Demons 2,"* ***Starburst*** 110 (October 1987)

--------. "Des trus en plumes," ***Starfix FX Special*** (January 1988)

*--------. *"Opera,"* ***Cinefantastique***, Volume 18, Numbers 2/3 (March 1988)

--------. *"Opera," Starburst* 114 (March 1988)

--------. "Coming Soon: *Edgar Allan Poe/The Church*," *Starburst* 129 (May 1989)

--------. "Soavi," *Starburst* 130 (June 1989)

--------. *"The Church," Cinefantastique*, Volume 20, Numbers 1/2 (November 1989)

--------. "George Romero Speaks Out," *Starburst* 139, (March 1990)

--------. "Preview/*Two Evil Eyes*," *Starburst* 140 (April 1990)

--------. "Two Evil Argentos," *Starburst* 146 (October 1990)

--------. "The Eyes Have It," [*Two Evil Eyes*] *The Dark Side* (October 1990)

--------. "Gianni Romoli's *The Sect*/Edgar Allan Poe's *The Black Cat*," *Starburst* 148 (December 1990)

*--------. "The Cat That Got the Scream" [on Luigi Cozzi's *Black Cat*], *The Dark Side* (December 1990)

*--------. *"Two Evil Eyes," Cinefantastique*, Volume 21, 3 (December 1990)

--------. *"The Sect," The Dark Side* (January 1991)

--------. *"The Sect," Cinefantastique*, Volume 22, 1 (June 1991)

*Jones, Stephen. "The Technique of Terror," *Halls of Horror* 27, Volume 3, Number 3

Kermode, Mark. "Short Films About Killing," [*Two Evil Eyes*] *Fear* 23 (November 1990)

Kissell, Howard. *"Four Flies on Grey Velvet," Women's Wear Daily*, August 7, 1972

Lane, John Francis. *"Two Evil Eyes," Screen International*, January 27-February 2, 1990

LeFanu, Mark. *"Tenebrae," Films and Filming* 348 (September, 1983)

Lucas, Tim. "Terror Pioneer,"[Mario Bava, Part 1] *Fangoria* 42 (February 1985)

--------. "Bava's Terrors, Part 2," *Fangoria* 43 (March 1985)

*--------. "The Butchering of Argento," *Fangoria* 66 (August 1987)

Martinez Torres, A. "Dario Argento: dal 'thriller' al surrealismo," *Casablanca* 46 (December 1984)

M.D.G. *"Opera," **Ciak***, (December 1987)

*McDonagh, Maitland. "Broken Mirrors/Broken Minds: The Dark Dreams of Dario Argento," **Film Quarterly** (Winter 1987-88)

*--------. "Retrospective: Dario Argento," **Horror Fan**, Volume 1, Number 4 (Winter 1989)

--------. "Ed Poe's Back in Town," *Interview*, February 1990

--------. *"Deux Regards Diabolique," **L'Écran Fantastique*** 112 (February 1990)

--------. "Luigi Cozzi," **Psychotronic** 6 (Summer 1990)*--------. "The Evil Eye of Dario Argento," **Gorezone** 14 (July 1990)

*--------. "Pittsburgh and the Pendulum," **Fangoria** 95 (August 1990)

McKegney, Michael. "Film: *Crystal Plumage*," **The Village Voice**, September 10, 1970

Maccarone, Bruno - see Dellavalle, R.

Maccarone, Bruno and Nadjar, Patrick. "Interview de Michele Soavi," **L'Écran Fantastique** 111 (January 1990)

Martin, John. "Phenomenal," **Samhain** 1 (November/December 1986)

*--------. "Magic All Around Us: A New Approach to the Films of Dario Argento, Part 1," **Samhain** 6 (November/December 1987)

*--------. "Magic All Around Us: A New Approach to the Films of Dario Argento, Part 2," **Samhain** 7 (January/February 1988)

*--------. "Magic All Around Us: A New Approach to the Films of Dario Argento, Part 3," **Samhain** 8 (March/April 1988)

--------. *"Dario Argento's World of Horror,"* [review of Soavi documentary] **Samhain** 7 (January/February 1988)

--------. *"Opera," **Deep Red*** 6 (March 1989)

Martinet, Pascal. ***Mario Bava***, (Paris: Filmo, 1984)

Maslin, Janet. "'*Suspiria*,' a Specialty Movie, Drips With Gore," **The New York Times**, August 13, 1977

Mayerson, Donald J. *"Cat O'Nine Tails," **Cue***, May 29, 1971

--------. *"Four Flies on Grey Velvet," **Cue***, August 12, 1972

Meek, Scott. *"Suspiria," **Monthly Film Bulletin***, Volume 44, Number 525 (October 1977)

--------. *"Suspiria," Time Out,* 392 (October 7, 1977)

--------. *"Inferno," Time Out,* 544 (September 19, 1980)

*Menello, Riccardo. "Dark Universe: The World of Dario Argento," *Photon,* 24 (July, 1975)

Michel, Jean-Claude. *Mario Bava: L'Onirism Crépusculaire* (Cahors: Gérard Noël fanéditions, Collection Horror Pictures, 1989)

Morsiani, Alberto. "Rosso italiano 1977/87," *Sequenze* 7 (March/April 1988)

Mottus, Allan. *"Cat O'Nine Tails," Women's Wear Daily,* May 26, 1971

Nadjar, Patrick - see Dellavalle, R.

Nadjar, Patrick - see Maccarone, Bruno

Nadjar, Patrick. *"The Church," L'Écran Fantastique* 111 (January 1990)

*--------. *"Two Evil Eyes," L'Écran Fantastique* 113 (March 1990)

Newman, Kim. *"Profondo Rosso," Monthly Film Bulletin,* Volume 51, Number 610 (November 1984)

--------. "Thirty Years in Another Town: The History of Italian Exploitation III," *Monthly Film Bulletin,* Volume 53, Number 626 (March 1986)

--------. *"Phenomena," Monthly Film Bulletin,* Volume 53, number 626 (March 1986)

--------. *Nightmare Movies* (London: Bloomsbury Publishing Ltd., 1988)

*Nicolini, Angelo and Grimaldi, Antonello. "Dario Argento, ou le regard sur l'indicible," *Mad Movies* 24 (September 1982)

*Nicolini, Angelo; Bettelli, Fabrizio; Grimaldi, Antonello. "Dario Argento," *Mad Movies* 25 (January 1983)

Nuara, Ettore. *"Demoni 2," Ciak* (August 1986)

*Nutman, Philip. "Argento on *Demons," Fangoria* 53 (April 1986)

L'Officier, Jean Marc. *"Suspiria," House of Hammer* 14 (November 1977)

--------. *"Deep Red," House of Hammer* 18 (March 1978)

*Ostria, Vincent. "De l'influence des insectes sur les pubertes difficiles," *Starfix* 20 (November, 1984)

P.G. *"Suspiria,"* **L'Écran Fantastique** 1 (Summer 1977)

Padnick, Glenn. "Tales of tails," **Boston After Dark**, June 8, 1971

Piazza, Carlo. "Entretien avec Lamberto Bava," **Mad Movies** 30 (May 1984)

Pugliese, Roberto. "Lo sguardo va in scena," **Segnocinema** (January 1988)

Reed, Rex. *"Four Flies on Grey Velvet,"* (New York) **Daily News**, August 9, 1972

Rick. *"The Bird With the Crystal Plumage,"* **Variety**, July 29, 1970,

Robe. *"Cat O'Nine Tails,"* **Variety**, June 2, 1971

--------. *"Deep Red,"* **Variety**, June 23, 1976

RTJ. *"Suspiria,"* **Movietone News** 56 (1977)

Salza, Giuseppe. "L'"*Opera*" de Dario Argento," **L'Écran Fantastique** 85 (October 1987)

Scasso, Claude - see Vié, Caroline

*Schlockoff, Robert. *"Ténèbres,"* **L'Écran Fantastique** 34 (May 1983)

*--------. "Dario Argento: Les frissons de la terreur," **L'Écran Fantastique** 40 (December 1983)

Simon, John. *"Suspiria,"* **New York**, September 12, 1977

Simon, Isabelle - see Aubry, Jean-Paul

*Soren, David. "More Flies on Grey Velvet: A Further Look at the Cinema of Dario Argento," **Photon** 27 (February, 1975)

Spinaci, Alessandro. *"Opera,"* **Italian TV Guide** (January 1988)

Stein, Elliott. "Give Me More Blood," **The Village Voice**, October 17, 1989

Sterritt, David. "'*Plumage*'-- a director's whodunit," **Christian Science Monitor**, September 5, 1970

Strick, Philip. "Sotto gli occhi dell'assassino" [review of *Tenebrae*], **Monthly Film Bulletin**, Volume 50, 592 (May 1983)

Sweeney, Louise. *"Cat O'Nine Tails,"* **Christian Science Monitor**, June 2, 1971

--------. "X Factor," [review of *The Cat O'Nine Tails*] **Christian Science Monitor**, June 11, 1971

Szebin, Frederick C. *"Two Evil Eyes," Cinefantastique*, Volume 21, Number 3 (December 1990)

Taubin, Amy. "Made for the Hacking" [review of *Suspiria*], *Soho Weekly News*, August 18, 1977

Thompson, Howard. *"'4 Flies on Grey Velvet'* Suspense Film," *The New York Times*, August 5, 1972Toullec, Marc. *"Démons 2," Mad Movies* 46 (January 1987)

--------. *"Bloody Bird," Mad Movies* 46 (January 1987)

Trehin, Denis. *"Phenomena," Mad Movies* 36 (May 1984)

--------. *"Inferno," Cine Star Video* 8 (March 1984)

Vargani, Guido. "Trussardi," *La Republica* (September 1986)

Vaughn, Susan Beach. *"The bird with the crystal plumage," Take One*, Volume 2, Number 9 (January/February 1970)

Verschooten, Gilbert. "Before the Dawn," [*Dawn of the Dead*] *Halls of Horror* 23 (August 1978)

Vié, Caroline. *"Ténèbres," Star Cine Video* 1 (July 1983)

*Vié, Caroline and Scasso, Claude. "Dario Argento," *Cine Choc* 1 (March 1983)

*--------. *"Phenomena," Cine Choc* 5 (March 1984)

*--------. *"Phenomena," L'Écran Fantastique* 49 (October 1984)

*--------. "Dossier: *Phenomena," L'Écran Fantastique* 57 (June, 1985)

Weiler, A.H. *"'Cat O'Nine Tails'," The New York Times*, May 27, 1971

Werb. *"Suspiria," Variety*, March 9, 1977

Winsten, Archer. *"'Four Flies on Grey Velvet'* Opens at the Criterion," *New York Post*, August 5, 1972

--------. *"Deep Red," New York Post*, June 10, 1976

--------. "Argento's *'Suspiria'* is a fright," *New York Post*, August 13, 1977

Wolf, William. *"Suspiria," Cue*, September 3-16, 1977

Yung. *"Inferno," Variety*, April 2, 1980

--------. *"Opera," Variety*, January 6, 1988

--------. *"Due occhi Diabolici," Variety*, March 7, 1990

--------. "'Bird With Plumage'," *New York Post*, July 23, 1970

--------. *"'The Bird With the Crystal Plumage',"* (New York)

Morning Telegraph, July 24, 1970

____. *"The Bird With the Crystal Plumage,"* **MD**, October 1970

____. *"L'uccello dalle piume di cristallo,"* **Monthly Film Bulletin**, Volume 37, Number 442 (November 1970)

____. *"Four Flies on Grey Velvet,"* **Film Information**, September 1972

____. *"Inferno,"* **L'Écran Fantastique** 45 (May 1984)

*____. "Dario Argento: Retrospective 3," **L'Écran Fantastique** 41 (January 1984)

____. *"Opera,"* **Cineforum** 271 (January/February 1988)

____. *"Due occhi diabolici,"* **Segnocinema** 42 (March 1990)

*____. "Dario Argento Interview," **The Dark Side** (December 1990)

General Texts

Barthes, Roland. *S/Z* (New York: Hill and Wang, 1974)

--------. "The Third Meaning," *Image/Music/Text* (New York: Hill and Wang, 1977)

Benstock, Bernard. *Art in Crime Writing: Essays on Detective Fiction* (New York: St. Martin's Press, 1983)

Britton, Andrew; Lippe, Richard; Williams, Tony; Wood, Robin. *The American Nightmare: Essays on the Horror Film* (Toronto: Festival of Festivals, 1979)

Brown, Fredric. *Four Novels by Fredric Brown* [including *The Screaming Mimi*] (London: Zomba Books, 1983)

Carter, Angela. *The Bloody Chamber and Other Adult Tales* (New York: Harper and Row, 1979)

Chesterton, G.K. "The Dagger With Wings," *The Father Brown Omnibus* (New York: Dodd, Mead and Company, 1982)

Conan Doyle, Sir Arthur. *The Annotated Sherlock Holmes* (New York: Clarkson N. Potter, Inc., 1973)

De Quincey, Thomas. "Levana and Our Ladies of Sorrow," *Confessions of an English Opium Eater and Other Writings* (New York and Scarborough, Ontario: New American

Library, 1966)

Frayling, Christopher. *Spaghetti Westerns* (London, Boston and Henley: Routledge & Keegan Paul, 1981)

Grossvogel, David I. "Death Deferred: The Long Life, Splendid Afterlife and Mysterious Workings of Agatha Christie," Art in Crime *Writing: Essays on Detective Fiction* (New York: St. Martin's Press, 1983)

Heath, Stephen. "Film and System:Terms of Analysis" (Part 1), *Screen* Volume 16, Number 1 (Spring 1975)

Hoffman, Paul. "Rome: Italian Movies Have Become Increasingly Inward Looking," *The New York Times*, February 7, 1974

Irwin, John T. *Doubling and Incest/Repetition and Revenge* (Baltimore and London: Johns Hopkins University Press, 1975)

Lemon, Lee T. and Reis, Marion J. *Russian Formalist Criticism: Four Essays* (Lincoln and London: University of Nebraska Press, 1965)

Lippe, Richard - see Britton, Andrew

Pirie, David. *A Heritage of Horror: The English Gothic Cinema 1946-1972* (New York: Avon Books, 1974)

Propp, Vladimir. *The Morphology of the Folk Tale* (Austin and London: University of Texas Press, 1968)

Rank, Otto. *The Double* (Chapel Hill: The University of North Carolina Press, 1971)

Reis, Marion J. - see Lemon, Lee T.

Schoell, William. *Stay Out of the Shower: 25 Years of Shocker Films Beginning with 'Psycho'* (New York: Dembner Books, 1985)

Shklovsky, Victor. *Russian Formalist Criticism* (Lincoln, London: University of Nebraska Press, 1981)

Silver, Alain and Ward, Elizabeth. *Film Noir: An Encyclopedic Reference to the American Style* (Woodstock: The Overlook Press, 1979)

Stevens, D. "Tenebrae," *The New Catholic Encyclopedia*, compiled by the Editorial Staff of the Catholic University of America (New York [etc.]: McGraw-Hill, 1967)

Stevenson, Robert Louis. *Dr. Jekyll and Mr. Hyde* (New

York, Pocket Books, 1982)

Telotte, J.P. "Faith and Idolatry in the Horror Film," *Literature/Film Quarterly* Volume 8, Number 3 (July 1980) pp.143-155

Todorov, Tzvetan. "The Typology of Detective Fiction," *The Poetics of Prose* (Oxford: Blackwell, 1977)

Truffaut, François. *Hitchcock* (New York: Simon and Schuster, 1967)

Ward, Elizabeth - see Silver, Alain

Williams, Tony - see Britton, Andrew

Wollen, Peter. *Signs and Meaning in the Cinema* (Bloomington and London: Indiana University Press, 1972)

Wood, Robin - see Britton, Andrew

INDEX

Mauri, Glauco, *122*, 250
Menello, Riccardo, 67, 92
Meril, Macha, 99, *117*, *122*, 250
Metti, una sera a cena, 59
'Metzengerstein', 218
Meyer, Nicholas, 60
Miller, George, 214
Millimeter, 157
Miracle, Irene, *24*, 145, *152*, 252
Mishima, Yukio, 227
Mitchell, Cameron, *26*
Monkey Shines, 220
'Morella', 216
Morphology of the Folklore, 131-32
Morricone, Ennio, 31, 32, 69, 81, 93, 94, 146n, 158, 246, 247, 248
Motorhead, 189, 254
Murder of Roger Ackroyd, The, 49
'Murders in the Rue Morgue, The', 221, 241
Murnau, F.W., 235
Musante, Tony, *17*, 40, *41*, *57*, 59, 78, 246

Nabokov, Vladimir, 116
Narcejac, Thomas, 60, 234
Narrative of Arthur Gordon Pym, The, 222
Near Dark, 229
Neill, Roy William, 168
New Catholic Encyclopedia, The, 163
New Criterion, The, 128
New York, 69, 145
New York Times, 55, 95, 97, 107, 157
Nicolai, Bruno, 93, 246, 247, 248
Nicolau, Ted, 54
Nicolini, Angelo, 227
Nicolodi, Daria, 11n, *52*, 99, 135n, 137, 145, 167, 174, 181n, *186*, 188, 195, 204, 250, 252, 253, 255, 256
Night Gallery, 214
Night of the Living Dead (Romero), 154-55, 160, 161, 218
Night of the Living Dead (Savini), 160-61
Night of the Seagulls, 197n
Nightmare on Elm Street, A, 218
North by Northwest, 56

Index

Born and raised in New York City, Maitland McDonagh received her undergraduate education at Hunter College, City University of New York, and earned her MFA in Film History/Theory/Criticism from Columbia University. McDonagh published her first critical essay, *The Ambiguities of Seeing and Knowing in Michael Powell's 'Peeping Tom'*, while still an undergraduate, and co-founded and edited *Columbia Film Review*, a journal of film writing, as a graduate student. She has written extensively on the cinema for magazines in the United States and Europe, including *The Dark Side, Entertainment Weekly, L'Ecran Fantastique, Film / Psychology Review, Mad Movies, Premiere, Interview, Film Quarterly, Fangoria, Persistence of Vision, Gorezone* and *Film Comment. Broken Mirrors / Broken Minds*, which is adapted from McDonagh's master's thesis, is her first book.